European Integration: A Theme

European Integration: A Theme

Jaap Hage

eleven
international publishing

Published, sold and distributed by Eleven International Publishing
P.O. Box 85576
2508 CG The Hague
The Netherlands
Tel.: +31 70 33 070 33
Fax: +31 70 33 070 30
email: sales@elevenpub.nl
www.elevenpub.com

Sold and distributed in USA and Canada
Independent Publishers Group
814 N. Franklin Street
Chicago, IL 60610, USA
Order Placement: +1 800 888 4741
Fax: +1 312 337 5985
orders@ipgbook.com
www.ipgbook.com

Eleven International Publishing is an imprint of Boom uitgevers Den Haag.

ISBN 978-94-6236-981-8
ISBN 978-94-6094-430-7 (e-book)

© 2020 Jaap Hage | Eleven International Publishing

This publication is protected by international copyright law.
All rights reserved. No part of this publication may be reproduced, stored in a retrieval system, or transmitted in any form or by any means, electronic, mechanical, photocopying, recording or otherwise, without the prior permission of the publisher.

Printed in The Netherlands

Table of Contents

Preface — xi

1 Pre-History — 1
  1.1 The Western Roman Empire — 1
  1.2 The Byzantine Empire — 3
  1.3 The Franks — 4
  1.4 Religion Matters — 6
  1.5 Liberalism — 8
    1.5.1 Four Factors that Caused the Rise of Liberalism — 9
    1.5.2 Thomas Hobbes and the Pursuit of Self-Interest — 11
    1.5.3 Characteristics of Liberalism — 12
    1.5.4 John Locke and the Preservation of Natural Rights — 13
    1.5.5 Cosmopolitism — 15
    1.5.6 Free Trade — 16
  1.6 The French Revolution and Its Aftermath — 16
    1.6.1 Conservatism — 17
    1.6.2 Napoleon Bonaparte — 18
  1.7 The Rise of Socialism — 19
  1.8 The 20th Century — 22

2 The History of the European Union, in Four Phases — 23
  2.1 Introduction — 23
  2.2 The Treaties — 23
  2.3 The Communities and Their Organs — 25
  2.4 Economic Integration — 27
  2.5 Enlargement — 29
  2.6 The European Coal and Steel Community — 31
    2.6.1 Cold War — 32
    2.6.2 Relations between France and Germany — 33
    2.6.3 The Schuman Declaration — 34
    2.6.4 The European Coal and Steel Community — 34
    2.6.5 Technocracy and National Interests — 35
    2.6.6 Conclusion on the ECSC — 37
  2.7 The Empty Chair Crisis — 38
  2.8 Towards the European Union — 40

	2.9	The EU in Crisis	43
	2.10	From Spillover to Spillback	46

3 Theories of European Integration — 47

	3.1	Federalism	47
		3.1.1 The Ventotene Manifesto	47
		3.1.2 The Legal Perspective	49
		3.1.3 The Political Science Perspective: Federal Unions	50
	3.2	Functionalism	51
	3.3	Neo-functionalism	53
	3.4	Intergovernmentalism	57
	3.5	Some Defining Distinctions	58
	3.6	Evaluation	59
		3.6.1 Functionalism and Legal Federalism	59
		3.6.2 Sociological Federalism	60
		3.6.3 Neo-functionalism and Intergovernmentalism	61

4 Explanation and Understanding — 63

	4.1	The Relationship between Explanation and Understanding	63
	4.2	The Nomological-Deductive Model of Explanation	66
		4.2.1 Explanation as Logical Derivation	66
		4.2.2 What is a Law?	67
		4.2.3 Legal Explanation	68
	4.3	The Scientific (Empirical) Cycle	70
		4.3.1 A Priori and Empirical	71
		4.3.2 Steps in the Empirical Cycle	71
		4.3.3 Observation	73
		4.3.4 Law Formulation and Induction	74
		4.3.5 Deduction and Prediction	74
		4.3.6 Observation and Testing	75
		4.3.7 Evaluation	75
		4.3.8 Non-empirical Science	77
		4.3.9 Application to Integration Theories	78
	4.4	What Makes a Theory 'Scientific'?	81
	4.5	Teleological Explanation	84
		4.5.1 Limitations of the ND Model in Connection with Human Behaviour	84
		4.5.2 Goal-Based Explanation	86
	4.6	Application to the Integration Theories	89

4.7	Conclusion	90

5 The Economics of Trade: Basic Concepts — 91

5.1	The Economic Style of Thinking		91
5.2	Some Concepts		93
5.3	Transaction Costs		97
	5.3.1	Internal Costs and Benefits	97
	5.3.2	Definition of Transaction Costs	97
	5.3.3	Taxation	98
	5.3.4	Summary on Transaction Costs	100
5.4	Externalities		101
	5.4.1	Introduction	101
	5.4.2	Costs, Benefits and Decisions	102
5.5	Social Dilemmas		103
	5.5.1	Definition	103
	5.5.2	Internalizing Externalities	105
	5.5.3	Externalities and Free Trade	106

6 The Economics of International Trade — 109

6.1	Mercantilism and Free Trade		109
	6.1.1	Mercantilist Policies	109
	6.1.2	Is there a Fixed Amount of Wealth?	111
6.2	Absolute and Comparative Advantages		112
	6.2.1	Absolute Advantage	112
	6.2.2	Comparative Advantage	113
	6.2.3	Conclusion on Absolute and Relative Advantages	115
6.3	The (Dis)Advantages of Free International Trade		116
	6.3.1	Consumer and Producer Surplus	116
	6.3.2	Allowing Free International Trade in a Small Country	119
	6.3.3	Allowing Free International Trade in a Big Country	122
	6.3.4	Tariffs	123
6.4	Conclusion		124

7 Money — 127

7.1	What Is Money?		127
	7.1.1	Coincidence of Wants	127
	7.1.2	Overview	128
	7.1.3	The Functions of Money	128
	7.1.4	The Forms of Money	130

7.2		The Creation of Money	130
	7.2.1	Money Creation by Banks	131
	7.2.2	The Role of the Central Bank	132
7.3		The Value of Money	134
	7.3.1	Inflation	134
	7.3.2	Deflation	135
	7.3.3	Interest Rates	135
	7.3.4	Exchange Rates	136
7.4		Indirect Taxation	137
	7.4.1	Inflation Tax	137
	7.4.2	Interest Tax	138
	7.4.3	Exchange Rates	138
7.5		Trade Equilibria	139
7.6		The Impossible Trinity	140
	7.6.1	If There Were No Full Capital Mobility	141
	7.6.2	Exchange Rates, Interest Levels and the Free Flow of Capital	143
	7.6.3	Why the Trinity Is Impossible	143
7.7		Conclusion	144

8 Monetary Integration — 147

8.1		Attempts at Fixed Exchange Rates	147
8.2		The Road towards the European Monetary Union	148
	8.2.1	Drawbacks of Flexible Exchange Rates	148
	8.2.2	The Snake in the Tunnel and Other Failed Attempts	149
	8.2.3	The Euro	150
	8.2.4	The Stability and Growth Pact	151
8.3		Exchange Rates and Asymmetric Shocks	153
8.4		Optimum Currency Areas	156
8.5		Conclusion	158

9 Sovereignty — 159

9.1		Introduction	159
9.2		Two Crises	160
	9.2.1	The Migration Crisis	160
	9.2.2	The Financial Crises	163
9.3		Introducing Sovereignty	166
9.4		Social Reality: Basics	168
	9.4.1	Three Kinds of Facts	168

	9.4.2	The Existence of Social Facts	169
9.5	Social Reality: Rules and Rule-Based Facts		171
	9.5.1	The Main Function of Rules	171
	9.5.2	How Rules Exist	172
	9.5.3	Rule-Based Facts and Rules	174
	9.5.4	Popular Sovereignty	175
9.6	Legal Consequences		177
9.7	Legal Status		179
9.8	External Sovereignty as Legal Status		181
9.9	Internal Sovereignty Is No Legal Status		184
9.10	Conclusion		186

10 Euroscepticism — 187

10.1	Introduction	187
10.2	Anywheres and Somewheres	190
10.3	Reason and Passion	191
10.4	The Genetic Basis of Altruism	192
10.5	Dual System Decision-Making	195
10.6	Nature and Nurture in Morality	197
10.7	People Hate to Reconsider	198
10.8	Conclusion	199

Postscript — 201

References — 203

Preface

Theme and topic The European Union (EU) and its direct predecessors have existed for almost 70 years. After a modest beginning, followed by decades of flourishing and expansion, the last decennium has seen serious signs of decay. The recent history of the EU has been defined by the Eurozone crisis, the refugee crisis and secession (Brexit). Political parties with a sceptical attitude towards the Union as one of the main items on their agendas are flourishing in several Member States and are sometimes even part of national governments. This is not the first crisis the Union has seen – the empty chair crisis of the 1960s is an example of an early crisis – and until now the Union has only come out stronger. However, as the saying goes: past performance is no guarantee of future results.

The connecting *theme* of this book is the development of the EU. However, it is not merely a historical study, neither does it deal with the EU exclusively. History, including legal history, is an important tool to understand the integration and disintegration of Europe. However, history alone does not suffice for a full understanding of the integration of Europe. We will therefore use perspectives from several disciplines. The economic perspective plays an important role, but there will also be input from political science, biology, psychology and (legal) philosophy. This combined input of seemingly disconnected disciplines to deal with European integration is the *topic* of the book.

Mission Apart from the fact that the use of 'auxiliary' disciplines contributes to a better understanding of European integration, there is a more fundamental reason for addressing economy, political science, biology, psychology and philosophy in this text. Scientists often think in terms of different disciplines. We have law, political science, history, physics, chemistry, biology, economy, philosophy, and so on … All these disciplines have their own 'methods', and becoming a scientist involves the collection of much knowledge that belongs to some particular discipline – law, for instance – and some knowledge about the method of that discipline. This goes so far that it might even be said that universities do not educate scientists anymore, but only physicists, historians, linguists, lawyers or philosophers. This is somehow understandable, because we need specialist knowledge, but in the end it is also fundamentally wrong. All the different disciplines contribute to our total body of knowledge, and this body must be coherent. This means that all the different disciplines must somehow fit together.

Scientific disciplines as they are often taught at universities do not contribute to such a coherent body of beliefs. On the contrary, specialization often leads to fragmentation of knowledge. An academic physicist does not need to know about law, just as an academic lawyer does not need to know about history. In this book we try to achieve precisely the opposite. The book uses European integration as its connecting theme, but it is about all the other disciplines that are used in the argument. It is sometimes good to forget about the traditional boundaries between scientific disciplines and to realize that in the end all disciplines should contribute to a coherent body of knowledge that expands and develops over time. It is the mission of universities to introduce their students to this body of knowledge and the culture of science that goes with it.

Overview *Chapter 1* of this book provides historical background for the development of the European communities and the EU. Integration is not just a matter of unifying stretches of land under a common government. For that reason, the chapter will pay attention to the territorial integration and disintegration in Europe *and* to the influence of cultural phenomena, such as religion and political ideologies and – of course – law.

After the groundwork has been laid in the first chapter, the historical part of the book continues in *Chapter 2* with a brief history of the European communities and the EU. This history first sketches four major developments and then focuses on key events that worked as driving forces for the processes of integration or disintegration, to wit, the foundation of the European Coal and Steel Community (ECSC), the empty chair crisis, the creation of the EU and the aftermath of the Maastricht Treaty.

The same theme recurs in *Chapter 3*, but here the historical perspective is replaced by a theoretical one. The development of the European communities was preceded and accompanied by integration theories, which argue why European integration should take place and which try to explain why it actually takes place and why it took its actual shape. Some of the most prominent theories are discussed in this chapter.

It is possible to question the explanatory value of the integration theories. *Chapter 4* is devoted to a discussion of scientific explanation. Do the integration theories really have explanatory value? Here the emphasis shifts from the history of European integration to the philosophy of science and the psychology of explanation and understanding.

It is sometimes said that the recent European integration is based on the *Monnet method*: the integration starts with the introduction of free trade and spills over into more robust economic integration and is followed by other forms of integration: monetary, social, fiscal, ecological, security, foreign policy and perhaps even defence. On any account, economy plays a crucial part in the integration story. Therefore, Chapters 5 to 8 cover some economic aspects of European integration.

Chapter 5 deals with some basic concepts of economic analysis, including the concepts of consumer and producer surplus, efficiency, transaction costs, externalities and social dilemmas.

Chapter 6 continues with the economics of free trade and, in particular, the trade between different countries. First, it discusses absolute and comparative advantages. Then it will argue that free trade is beneficial if certain conditions are met. The chapter argues, however, that the conditions are not always met and that the benefits of free trade do not accrue to everybody.

Chapter 7 focuses on the role of money in general. First it deals with, among others, the functions and the value of money and the way money can be created by (central) banks. Then it pays attention to the role of money in international trade, exchange rates and the impossibility for States to conduct autonomous monetary policies if there is free international flow of money and if there are fixed exchange rates (the 'impossible trinity').

Chapter 8 addresses the monetary integration in the EU, both from a historical perspective and from the perspective of the question of whether the EU constitutes an 'optimum currency area'.

The limitation of the liberties and powers of the EU Member States that is constituted, not only by monetary integration, but also by other forms of European integration, is often described as a transfer of 'sovereignty' from the Member States to the EU. By using the 'S word', the discussion about the desirability of a limitation of liberties and powers of Member States receives an emotional load that is likely to be one of the causes of the now-popular Euroscepticism. Therefore, it is important to investigate what precisely is meant by the alleged 'transfer of sovereignty'. The investigation is in part politico-philosophical, where it deals with the philosophical origins of the notion of sovereignty. It is also legal-theoretical, where it addresses the foundation of legal systems in social reality and the relationship between sovereignty and the will of the people. The central claim of *Chapter 9* is that the idea that States transfer sovereignty to the EU is misguided.

Chapter 10 addresses Brexit and Euroscepticism and raises the question of how Euroscepticism is possible, given the generally favourable evaluation of the EU by European citizens. In this connection, the perspective is shifted from the traditional economic one to a biological and psychological approach.

Acknowledgements The author thanks, in alphabetical order, Elena Baum, Nick Frijns, Sascha Hardt, Lucas Miotto, Manuela Mühl, Janwillem Oosterhuis, Neofytos Sakellaridis and Antonia Waltermann for their useful comments on (parts of) the text, which made many improvements possible. Liza Ovsyanko assisted with the preparation of the literature references, and the people of Eleven International Publishing took care of language editing and transformed the manuscript into this book. Of course, the responsibility for remaining errors lies with the author.

Comments The present text is in its second version. It is quite likely that many improvements are still possible. Therefore, comments are welcome; they can be sent to jaap.hage@maastrichtuniversity.nl.

1   Pre-History

The foundations of the EU were laid during the years immediately following World War II, but the ground was made ready in the two-and-a-half millennia that came before. Therefore, a proper understanding of the recent developments is possible only against the backdrop of the events and the theories of many preceding years. This chapter contains a brief and eclectic history of Europe. The times and themes that are included herein have been selected with a view to understanding the integration, but also the disintegration, of Europe. The history starts with the Roman Empire and ends with Hitler's *Third Reich*. The developments after World War II are the topic of the next chapter.

When discussing European integration, it is important to focus not only on the territorial aspects of integration – how many 'countries' there are and how they are legally related – but also on the cultural aspects, such as religion, ideologies and law. Therefore, this chapter has three themes, which are mingled in the argument. The first is territorial integration, the second deals with four important ideologies that had an influence on Europe: Christianity, Liberalism, Conservatism and Socialism,[1] and the third deals with law.

1.1   The Western Roman Empire

Territory There is some disagreement about the year of Rome's founding, but an often-adopted date is 21 April, 753 BC.[2] First a kingdom, later a republic, and still later an empire, Rome grew from a small settlement on the borders of the river Tiber to a 'world power'. The territory of the Roman Empire included all the land that bordered on the Mediterranean, but also the Iberian Peninsula, present-day France and Belgium, and parts of Germany, England, Romania and Hungary. About 100 AD, the size of the territory was

---

1   A plea for treating religion and political ideologies together under the heading of 'ideology' can be found in Harari 2016, Chapter 5. Obviously, there is a major difference between, on the one hand, religions, such as Judaism, Christianity and Islam, and, on the other hand, secular doctrines, such as Liberalism and Socialism, namely that the former include a metaphysical element that is lacking in the latter. However, as Harari pointed out, these doctrines share the common characteristic of providing overarching pictures of mankind, human societies and the social world they live in. This shared characteristic justifies the common denominator of 'ideology'.

2   For dating purposes, the Western European tradition is adopted to take the alleged birth year of Christ as the year zero. The time before that year is rendered as 'BC' (before Christ), while the time afterwards has no special indication at all (e.g. 1648, for the year of the Westphalian peace treaties), or – if confusion is possible – as 'AD' (*Anno Domini*: in the year of the Lord).

4.5 million square kilometres, and most likely there were more than 70 million inhabitants.[3] The Romans adopted much of the already existing Greek (Hellenistic) culture, eventually creating a second 'capital', Constantinople, on the site of an old Greek colonial city Byzantium.

Conquest or contract? The immense territory of the Roman Empire was the result of conquest. Much later, in the 17th century, the English philosopher Thomas Hobbes raised the question of whether it makes a difference for the authority of a sovereign if the unity of his domain was the result of agreement or of conquest.[4] According to Hobbes, there is no difference; the only important thing is whether the sovereign can keep the peace and enforce the law. From this perspective, the European integration that the Romans brought about by conquest was just as valid as the present integration of Europe brought about through consent between States (treaties). Perhaps it was even more stable, because a phenomenon like Brexit would not have been possible – at least not in a peaceful way – under the Roman Empire.

Ius Civile* and *Ius Gentium The law of the Romans reflected the development of the Roman kingdom into an empire. Beginning as the customary law of a small tribe, Roman law developed into a legal system that had to account for economic and personal relations with neighbouring peoples, and later for the organizational structure of a vast empire. The Roman domination of the conquered territories (provinces) did not mean that the Roman Empire became a unitary State as we presently understand nation-states. The different provinces were allowed to maintain their own law, and Roman law was applicable only to persons who had acquired Roman citizenship.[5] The Roman *ius civile* had a personal scope – it applied to a particular kind of persons: those with Roman citizenship. It did not have a territorial scope in the sense that it applied to cases only within the Roman territory. This is comparable to modern Jewish law, which applies to persons with the Jewish religion, and not necessarily to all people who live in Israel.

In this connection, the distinction between *ius civile* and *ius gentium* was important. The *ius civile* consisted of positive Roman law, both customary law and law created by legislation in a broad sense. This law was applicable only to Roman citizens. If a person who lacked Roman citizenship was involved in a legal case, a different kind of law applied, the *ius*

---

3   *See* www.princeton.edu/~pswpc/pdfs/scheidel/040604.pdf (last visited on 5 August 2019).
4   Hobbes 1651, Chapter 20.
5   A famous example is St. Paul the apostle, who was a Roman citizen and could therefore ask for a trial in Rome, even though he was accused of violating Jewish laws. *See* in the Bible: Acts 25.

gentium. This *ius gentium* was assumed to be based on reason, and consequently it was to be accepted by all peoples.⁶

The distinction between the two kinds of *ius* is emphasized here, because it expresses a tension that is inherent in any process of integration. On the one hand, we have rules, or other cultural phenomena, that are alleged to be common to all humans for the reason that they are based on reason. In the setting of Roman law, this would be the *ius gentium*. On the other hand, we have phenomena, again including rules, which are tied to a particular community, family, tribe or nation. In the setting of Roman law, this is the *ius civile*. People make a natural distinction between what belongs to their group and what is common to all, and we will see later that this distinction has a biological basis. In favour of what is common and universal, European integration must overcome a tendency to stick to what is local and familiar.

1.2 THE BYZANTINE EMPIRE

Around 300 AD the Roman Empire was – not officially, but as a matter of fact – divided into a western and an eastern part. Rome remained the capital of the western part, while Constantinople became the de facto capital of the eastern part. The Eastern Roman Empire has become known as the Byzantine Empire, and it continued to exist until 1453, when Constantinople fell under the siege of Sultan Mehmed II.

Corpus Iuris Civilis A major event during the more than thousand years that the Byzantine Empire existed was the codification of Roman law by Emperor Justinian I. The *Corpus Iuris Civilis* was promulgated in 534 and became the conceptual basis of most continental European law. 'Conceptual basis' means that the law of the *Corpus Iuris Civilis* provided the basic concepts of private law, such as possession, ownership, obligation, sale and rent. This is comparable to the bricks that are used to build houses. Different cultures may build different houses, but they can use the same kind of bricks to do so. It may be argued that the Justinian codification has become a major source of European integration because it provided the kind of bricks used to erect the buildings of continental European law. Even though the precise rules of different continental jurisdictions differ, the concepts that they use are largely the same, and this can be traced back to the *Corpus Iuris Civilis*.

The rise of Christianity Constantine I (272-337) was not only the founder of Constantinople, but also the first Christian Roman Emperor. Christianity is an offspring of Judaism –

---

6   Digest 1.1.9.

it shares a large part of its Holy Scripture with that of Judaism. The Old Testament, or *Tanakh*, reached Rome not long after its incipience during the 1st century AD. At first, the Christians formed a minority, and even in 303, Emperor Diocletian ordered that all Christian churches be destroyed and all bibles burnt. However, the religion attracted many adherents, and by 380 Emperor Theodosius I made Christianity the official religion of the Roman Empire. Later, the bishop of Rome became the head of the special Sees that governed the Catholic Church, which was still unified. In 1054 the Catholic Church split up into an eastern part, the Eastern or Orthodox Church, and a western part, the Roman Catholic Church.

1.3   THE FRANKS

Migration Events seldom have one single cause, and the fall of the western part of the Roman Empire is no exception. One of its purported causes was migration.[7] During the 3rd and 4th centuries AD, peoples from Asia, famously including the Huns, moved from Asia into the eastern part of Europe, pushing westward the peoples who already resided in Eastern Europe. Many of these latter peoples were later called 'Germans'. They included Goths (Ostrogoths and Visigoths), Burgundians, Bavarians, Franks, Frisians, Alamans, Jutes, Angles, Lombards and Vandals. Roman culture in Western Europe was already in decline, and finally it collapsed under the pressure of these 'barbaric' peoples' migration into the Western European territories.

The political organization of the German peoples was mostly local, on the level of villages. After the fall of Rome, the contacts between the western and eastern parts of Europe became very limited, and the influx of Hellenistic civilization from the east ended. From about 500 AD onwards, Europe fell into what was later called the Dark Ages. The European integration, which was brought about by the Romans, had ended and was subsequently replaced by multiple, smaller accumulations of people.

Running ahead of the argument to follow: two centuries later, a second immigration wave flooded Europe. This time the migrants were predominantly from the Arabic countries. United under newly founded Islam, the Arabs conquered Syria, Egypt and the rest of Northern Africa and reached Spain in 711.

---

7   According to Davies (1996, p. 214), there were four main processes that led to the decline of the Roman Empire: (1) The westward drive of people from Asia into Europe, (2) The growing rift of the division between the western and the eastern part of the Roman Empire, (3) The steady export of Christianity to pagan peoples and (4) the rise of Islam.

The Church Even in the dark, some light may remain, and during the Dark Ages the Roman Catholic Church provided this glimpse of light. Christianity did not fall along with the Western Roman Empire. On the contrary, the Christian faith continuously expanded from the Roman world to many pagan tribes. Clovis (*circa* 466-511) was the first king of the Franks who succeeded in uniting all Frankish tribes under one ruler. He was also the first of the Merovingian dynasty that ruled the Frankish kingdom for two centuries and the first king of the Franks who became a Christian. The conversion of Clovis led not only to the adoption of Christianity by many Franks, but also to the religious unification of the territories presently known as France, Germany and Belgium.

As Christianity spread over Western Europe, so too did the organizational structure of the Roman Catholic Church. This structure included bishoprics under the ultimate leadership of the bishop of Rome, who became the 'Pope'. There were also monasteries in which remains of the old Roman culture were preserved, side by side with the developing Christian culture. This helped homogenize to a certain extent the peoples of Europe.

The Frankish kings tended to cooperate with the Pope, who needed their support to safeguard himself from barbarian depredations and from the claims of the Byzantine Empire. In return, the Pope provided the kings with a legitimation for their reign. The result was a pragmatic alliance between the worldly and the religious rulers in Western Europe.

Charlemagne As a result of the migration waves, Western Europe was originally divided, but gradually stronger kings succeeded in reuniting some territories. The most prominent example was Charlemagne (742-814), ruler of the Frankish Empire. In 800, he was crowned by Pope Leo III in Rome as Emperor of the West.[8] From Aachen, Charlemagne controlled a territory that included present-day France and Belgium, parts of the German territories, Italy and Spain. Presently known as the 'Carolingian Empire', older names include *Romanum imperium* (the empire of the Romans) and *Imperium Christianum* (the Christian empire). These older names better reflect that contemporaries saw this empire as a renewal of the Roman Empire, or as a new Christian empire, the two conceptions not necessarily conflicting with each other.

Indicatively, to show the importance of Charlemagne for the history of European integration, the city of Aachen has, since 1950, annually awarded somebody for his or her work for the unification of Europe. This Charlemagne prize, or – in German – the *Karlspreis*,

---

8   It was important for the Pope to do this, as it signified – in the eyes of many – the hierarchical relationship between religion and secular affairs and the supremacy of the Pope over the Emperor.

was awarded in 1953 to Jean Monnet, in 1969 to the European Commission and in 2002 to the euro!

The Holy Roman Empire Charlemagne was succeeded by his son, Louis the Pious. When Louis died, his sons fought over the right of succession. The resulting civil war was concluded in 843 by the Treaty of Verdun. This treaty divided the Carolingian Empire into three parts, corresponding by and large to present-day France, Germany and a stroke in the middle that stretched from the Netherlands to Northern Italy. Ultimately, the 'German' part absorbed this stretch of land and became the 'Holy Roman Empire'.[9] This name is the result of combining the ideas that the original Carolingian Empire was the successor to the old Roman Empire and that it was also a Christian empire. The name 'Holy Roman Empire' lasted until 1806,[10] which means that the empire existed, at least in name, for a millennium, around the same length of time as the Western Roman Empire. However, the death of Emperor Frederic II in 1250 marked the end of real power for the emperors. This real power was in the Late Middle Ages taken over by local rulers, such as kings, princes and dukes.

1.4 RELIGION MATTERS

The Holy Roman Empire illustrated a characteristic tradition of Western Europe. The secular and the spiritual leaders were, legally speaking, independent of each other, but they often depended on each other for support. However, with the arrival of the Reformation in the 16th century, things changed considerably. Northern Europe became mainly protestant, Southern Europe remained mainly catholic, and in Central Europe it was no longer obvious that populations shared the same faith. Religious wars broke out between Catholics and Protestants, for instance in France.[11] Many wars between smaller territorial units, as in Germany, as well as a war of independence in the Netherlands, must be understood in the context of these sectarian conflicts.

The peace treaties of Westphalia The first half of the 17th century was characterized by many wars, lumped together under the name of the Thirty Years' War. This war was ended by the peace treaties of Westphalia in 1648. From the perspective of European integration

---

9   There is some disagreement on the issue concerning the year in which the name 'Holy Roman Empire' became applicable. Some consider the unification under Charlemagne as the beginning (about 800); others prefer a later date.
10 See www.britannica.com/place/Holy-Roman-Empire (last visited on 5 August 2019).
11 A well-known example of the ferocity of the time is the St. Bartholomew's Day Massacre (23 August 1572) in the French Wars of Religion, with accounts ranging from 5,000 to 30,000 victims.

– or, perhaps better, disintegration – these treaties were particularly important as they established the division of Western and Central Europe into a number of independent sovereign States.

The area of Germany remained divided into about 300 minor States, which now all received sovereign rights. The Holy Roman Empire, which theoretically encompassed all these States, could not make laws, raise taxes, recruit soldiers or start wars any more without the consent of the individual States. This meant the dissolution as a matter of fact (although not in name) of the Holy Roman Empire, as the consent of so many States is practically impossible. The decision-making problems in the present EU seem minor in comparison with the problems faced by the Holy Roman Empire after the Westphalian treaties.

Although the Westphalian peace treaties may have been good for peace in Central Europe, they constituted a low point from the perspective of European integration, as they emphasized the autonomy (sovereignty) of national States, each with their own official religion.

Islam in Southern Europe Briefly after the establishment of the Islamic faith in the 7th century AD, Arabs conquered substantial parts of the Middle East and Northern Africa. In 711 the 'Moors', inhabitants of the Maghreb, the region of North Africa that presently consists by and large of the countries Algeria, Morocco, Tunisia, Libya and Mauritania, crossed the Mediterranean and set foot on the Iberian Peninsula (present-day Spain and Portugal). After conquering the peninsula, the Moor troops crossed the Pyrenees and also conquered the southern part of present-day France. The northward march was stopped by the battle of Tours (Poitiers), south of Paris, where a Frankish army, under Martel, defeated the Arabian troops in 732.

Although the Arab conquests in Southern Europe were stopped by this battle, the Moors still remained on the Iberian Peninsula, as is evidenced by, among other things, architectural marvels such as the Alhambra in Granada and the Mezquita in Cordoba. It took more than 700 years, until 1492, before the *reconquista*, the lengthy battle to recapture the Iberian Peninsula, completely ended Islamic rule.

The Ottoman Empire Apart from the Moors, a second Islamic influence on the development of Europe was brought about by the Ottoman Empire. This empire existed more than 600 years, from about 1300 until briefly after World War I. It started in Anatolia (in present-day Turkey) and at its high point, at the beginning of the 16th century, its territory included what is now Turkey, Iraq, Israel, Syria, Lebanon, Egypt, parts of Saudi Arabia, the northern shore of Africa, Bulgaria, Romania, Hungary, part of the Ukraine and the

Balkan countries. In 1529 and 1683, Vienna was besieged by Ottoman forces, and both times the siege failed. However, the Ottoman reign has been a major influence in South-Eastern Europe, particularly from the 16th until the 19th century. For example, the Ottoman army made a first concession to an independent Greece in 1832, left the principality of Serbia in 1867, and Bulgaria became autonomous only in 1878.[12]

It is sometimes thought that the Ottomans were made up of Turks who were predominantly Muslim. That makes it possible to interpret the Ottoman presence in South-Eastern Europe as occupation by the Turks or the Muslims. In reality, the Ottomans included people with heterogeneous ethnic backgrounds, and not even all of them were Muslim.

Christianity, Islam and the European identity Both the Moorish and the Ottoman conquests and clashes with Europe had implications for the continent and its integration. For instance, it was Aristotle who strongly influenced the work of Thomas Aquinas, the 13th century theologian and philosopher, whose work was to become the core of the Roman Catholic philosophical doctrine.[13] This Aristotelian influence reached Western Europe through Eastern philosophers, including the Persian physician/philosopher Ibn Sina (Avicenna; 970-1037)[14] and the Spanish Berberian lawyer/philosopher Ibn Rushd (Averroes; 1126-1198).[15]

This is in addition to the fact that after the presence of the Moors on the Iberian Peninsula for about 700 years, there was also a substantial presence of Muslims in South-Eastern Europe for around 400 years. This presence might be interpreted as evidence that the European identity – if there is such a single identity – was to a large extent also shaped by Islam and not by Christianity alone. It may also be interpreted as a sign that this European identity was shaped in a freedom-battle of Christian countries against Islamic intruders. The choice between these two interpretations may depend on a modern political agenda.

1.5 Liberalism

Liberalism arose in the Late Middle Ages, when trade developed in Western Europe and became more international. During the Early Middle Ages, economies in Western Europe

---

12   Russia negotiated with the Ottomans the existence of an autonomous Bulgarian principality. *See* https://en.wikipedia.org/wiki/Bulgaria#Third_Bulgarian_state (last visited on 5 August 2019).
13   This was confirmed in the encyclical *Aeterni Patris*, issued in 1879 by Pope Leo XIII. *See* www.newadvent.org/cathen/01177a.htm (last visited on 5 August 2019).
14   *See* Gutas 2016.
15   *See* Montada 2018.

were mainly local; villages were small, and there was relatively little trade between them. Farmers in the countryside produced for the neighbouring villages. The land was held by the Church or the nobility and was worked by serfs who were not allowed to leave the land to which they belonged. Artisans in villages produced mainly for the local market. The chain of production would be in one 'hand', meaning that a manufacturer of wooden furniture would collect the necessary materials himself, transform the trees into wood to be processed, turn this wood into the desired furniture and sell the furniture to the person or organization (e.g. the Church) that ordered it. There was no division of labour.

Status and fixed roles The social status of persons (are you a duke, a serf or a carpenter?) was determined by birth, and social mobility was very limited. The normative framework within which people lived was determined by Christianity. Life on earth was not a goal in itself but merely a preliminary to the eternal afterlife. From this perspective, earning money was not a means to becoming rich but a necessary element of an economic cycle aimed at maintaining a status quo of fixed societal relations. Everybody had to perform their own role, and if done well, society as a whole would function harmoniously and provide people with a means to be united with God in the afterlife.

1.5.1 Four Factors that Caused the Rise of Liberalism

Starting from the Late Middle Ages,[16] this changed gradually, and the interplay of at least four factors had an important role: economic development, the upcoming sciences, territorial discoveries and the Reformation.

Economic development The first factor was economic development. The isolation of local communities decreased and trade increased.[17] This made division of labour possible. A merchant might buy trees from a landowner, hire a carpenter to transform the trees into wood that could be handled by an artisan, hire the artisan to turn the wood into furniture, and have the furniture transported to the place where it would bring the biggest proceeds and profit.[18] Those performing the individual tasks would lose their independent role in

---

16 The Late Middle Ages cannot be pinpointed to a particular stretch of time, as they are defined by the described change. Because this change did not start everywhere at the same time, the transition to the Late Middle Ages took place at different times in different places. Early starters were the cities in Northern Italy and in West Flanders, where the transformation started in the 12th century. It may be argued that the transformation finished in the Russian countryside as late as the 20th century.

17 This is illustrated by the rise of the 'Hanseatic-league', a trade organization that united traders from cities from London in the west to Novograd in the east, which flourished from the 13th to the 15th century. See www.hanse.org/en/ (last visited on 5 August 2019).

18 This example was inspired by Palmer *et al.* 2002, pp. 108-109.

the economic cycle, and the merchant who provided the money (capital) to make production possible became the entrepreneur who made the profit off the enterprise, or bore the loss if it did not work out. Capitalism was born.

Upcoming sciences The second factor was the origin of modern science. During the Early Middle Ages, the pursuit of knowledge in Europe was conducted mainly within the confines of monasteries, and later the emerging universities. The 'scientific' method was scholastic. This means that authoritative texts of church fathers and philosophers were studied and discussed according to specific procedures, more or less like lawyers today still discuss authoritative texts (legislation, treaties, case law, doctrinal literature) and interpret them according to the traditional canons of legal reasoning.

This changed in the 16th century. Scientific knowledge came to be based, not on authority, but on logical reasoning (*a priori* sciences; Descartes, Hobbes) and on observation and experimentation (empirical, or *a posteriori* sciences; Bacon, Galilei, Harvey). The result was a spectacular increase in the amount of scientific knowledge and in the speed with which more knowledge was acquired. This increased speed of knowledge production has continued to the present day. It is no longer possible for an expert to keep track of all the publications even within her own field of knowledge.

Discoveries The increase in scientific knowledge went hand in hand with territorial discoveries. In 1492, Columbus 'discovered' America.[19] In 1498, Vasco da Gama sailed around Africa to reach India, and in 1520, Ferdinand Magellan managed to reach the Pacific from the Atlantic Ocean by crossing the Strait named after him, south of what is now Chile. By doing so, he would sail around the world.

The newly discovered countries turned out be sources of wealth, in the form of gold and silver (mining in the Americas), and trade and plantations (South-East Asia).

Renaissance and Reformation In the Late Middle Ages, the Roman Catholic Church was plagued by upheavals. These problems found their pinnacle in the Protestant Reformation of the 16th century, in which Protestant churches split off from their Roman Catholic mother church. On the European continent, Luther and Calvin created the foundations for new churches. In England, King Henry VIII (the one with the six wives) had a conflict with the Pope, who refused to divorce him from Catherine of Aragon. Catherine happened to be the aunt of Emperor Charles V of the Holy Roman Empire, and perhaps the Pope did not want to displease the Emperor. Nevertheless, in 1534 the English Parliament passed

---

19   America was already populated and was therefore obviously discovered before.

the Act of Supremacy, which declared the King of England to be the head of the Church of England. The time in which the Roman Catholic Church was the natural companion of the secular rulers had ended. We have already seen that this led to religious wars in Europe.

As a factor that contributed to the transition from the medieval society of fixed social classes to a new era in which individualism, liberties and social mobility played a paramount role, the Reformation was supported by a movement that accompanied it: the Renaissance. The Renaissance (Rebirth) represents a return – to some extent at least – to the Hellenistic-Roman culture that preceded the Middle Ages. A renewed study of this culture allowed the intellectuals of the Late Middle Ages to relativize the fixed medieval structures.

In this connection, the central role of the individual was crucial. During the Middle Ages, people were seen as representatives of larger structures such as families, villages and social classes. The roles of these structures did not change considerably from one generation to another. The Renaissance made it possible to separate (liberals would say 'free'; conservatives would say 'isolate') individual human beings from the structures that were assumed to define them.

1.5.2   Thomas Hobbes and the Pursuit of Self-Interest

During a period of civil war in England, Thomas Hobbes (1588-1679) wrote an apology for an absolutist State. The absolute State power that Hobbes propagated had little to do with liberalism, but the image of mankind that led Hobbes to promote this conception of power was nonetheless deeply intertwined with the liberal world view.

According to Hobbes, every human being has interests, not all of which can be satisfied at once. The result is a battle of everybody against everybody else, and – this is the important point – in the absence of a State there are no duties on anybody to respect the interests of others. A duty exists only if, and to the extent that, it is in the interest of the duty-holder to respect the duty.[20] This means that there are no normative limitations on what a person is allowed to do; the only boundaries are those of self-interest. Note that this is an important deviation from the Christian tradition, according to which people have the duty to live a moral life as defined by Christianity.

---

20   Notice that this notion of a 'duty' differs strongly from the moral or the legal notion.

If everybody pursues his own interests at the cost of the interests of others, the result is a war of everybody against everybody else, which makes it impossible for individuals to pursue a decent life. Therefore, it is in one's self-interest to end the hostilities. However, this can work only if everybody else does the same. To guarantee that you are not the only one so imprudent as to lay down arms, it is necessary to have an organization powerful enough to maintain peace. This organization is the State. The State creates laws and – more importantly – enforces them. Because the State enforces the duties it has imposed, it is in the interest of individuals to comply with these duties to avoid retribution. This means that the State duties are also duties for the citizens of the State, as it is in their interest to comply with them.

This creates a framework in which everybody can live in peace, produce goods and trade them, and eventually this leads to prosperity. It should be noted that even if a State exists, everybody can still pursue his own interests. Given the peace that the State maintains, it is in everybody's interest to respect the rules of the State and to support the State if it needs to enforce its rules. In other words, the State creates a framework in which the self-interest of individuals is compatible with the interests of everybody else. There is still morality, but it is no longer a Christian morality of a God-given fixed societal structure. It is rather the morality of a free market, which is constrained mainly by the rules that make this market possible. It is a liberal morality of enlightened egoism.

1.5.3 Characteristics of Liberalism

Liberalism as ideology of the middle classes Liberalism is the ideology of the 'middle classes'. During the Late Middle Ages and in the time of the Renaissance, these classes gained importance through trade and the wealth that it brought. Liberalism was the ideology that justified their importance.

The close relationship between liberalism and the interests of the middle classes was confirmed by liberal political philosophers such as Friedrich Hayek (1899-1992), who argued that liberalism was the best road towards the prosperity of the middle classes and indirectly to the rest of society as well. The relationship between the middle classes and liberalism was also emphasized by Karl Marx (1818-1883), who claimed that the dominant ideology of a time reflects that time's economic structure. When royals, landed nobility and the Catholic Church were in power, the dominant structure would be feudalism, Christianity and the fixed social relations of the Middle Ages. To the extent that the middle classes gained influence, the dominant ideology changed from a Christian fixed order to the social mobility and the freedom of religion and of trade that liberalism allows.

Characteristics A description of an ideology in terms of characteristic views and values is hazardous, because it is never fully correct, but, at the same time, it may be illuminating. Following Heywood,[21] we can say that liberalism is characterized by:

The primacy of the individual. Human beings are seen as individual persons, with their own preferences and values, and not as exponents of their role in the fixed structure of society. Implications of this view are the emphasis on freedom, the increased possibility of social mobility, replacement of fixed rules (*ius gentium*; natural law) by rules based on individual preferences, and methodological individualism in the social sciences.[22]

Importance of individual freedom. Individual persons are, in principle, autonomous. They are allowed to do what they want, as long as they do not harm others or violate the rights of other individuals. This is reflected in:
- tolerance for the opinions, religious beliefs and customs of others;
- emphasis on human rights; and
- curtailment of State power through legal rules (rule of law).

Faith in reason and progress. Liberalism has become part of the Enlightenment project in which faith in revealed (religious) truths and customary beliefs were replaced by faith in reason and in science. Given the rapid increase in scientific knowledge, this faith in reason was readily complemented by a faith in progress. The more knowledge we have, about physical nature, but also about human nature and about society, the better we can and will make our society.

In the following subsections, we will briefly look into further characteristics of the liberal ideology, which are particularly relevant for European integration.

1.5.4 John Locke and the Preservation of Natural Rights

According to Hobbes, the function of the State is purely instrumental: the State exists to maintain peace and to enforce the rules that it has created itself. In this way everybody can prosper by pursuing their own interests. In 1689, another English philosopher also saw a purely instrumental role for the State, but seemingly a completely different one. According to John Locke (1632-1704), human beings have rights, and the duty towards each other

---

21 Heywood 2012, p. 26.
22 This methodological individualism holds that social phenomena are to be explained from individual behaviour, rather than the other way around. We can see an example of this in the teleological explanation of human behaviour.

to respect these rights. These rights would exist in the 'state of nature', by which Locke meant a human society in which no State exists. So, contrary to Hobbes, Locke assumed that there were also real rights and duties in the absence of a State. However, the protection of these rights would be quite difficult in the absence of an organization that can enforce them. Therefore, it is in everybody's interest that a State is created that can enforce these independently existing rights. Enforcement of pre-existing rights is the essential task of the State; that is what it must do and nothing else.[23]

Three things must be noted here. First and foremost is that Locke seeks the justification of a State in the interests of individuals. Here is where Hobbes and Locke agree. The State is an instrument to safeguard the interests of its citizens. Its role is instrumental. The State is not an element of a fixed social order, as medieval theorists would have it,[24] but a tool in the hands of individuals to promote their interests.

Second, the role of the State is to protect the rights of its citizens. These rights include Life, Liberty and Property, or – in other words – physical integrity, freedoms and ownership. In particular, the first two of these are typical liberal values.

And third, because the State must protect the pre-existing rights, it does not have the competence or permission to infringe upon them, except with the agreement of the right-holders. This is the basis for the fundamental rights that are enshrined in many modern constitutions. Locke's theory provides a theoretical basis for constitutionalism, the view that the powers of a State are inherently limited.

Here Locke's view differs from that of Hobbes. According to Hobbes, there should be no limitations on the power of the State, because real limitations can exist only if they can be enforced by another entity. It is not to be expected that a State enforces limitations against itself, so there must be another organization that is powerful enough to safeguard the limitations of the State power. According to Hobbes, such an organization should not exist, because it might wage a war against the State and thereby reinstate a war of all against all.

Modern experience proves both Locke and Hobbes right. The division of powers (*Trias Politica*) in modern liberal democracies shows that one part of the State, the judiciary, can

---

23   Locke 1689.
24   One of these medieval theoreticians was the theologian/philosopher Thomas Aquinas (1225-1274), who argued that a prince (the State impersonated) fulfilled an important role in a fixed societal structure aimed at the afterlife.

check whether another part of the State, the administration, remains within the limits created by the principle of legality. So Locke's theory works. However, the civil wars in many countries such as Rwanda, the Sudan, Afghanistan and Syria illustrate that if there are two or more serious powers in a single territory, the most terrible things may happen.

The EU illustrates both views. On the one hand, the Union (or rather its predecessors) was founded to create the (Hobbesian) unity that makes war impossible. On the other hand, the EU has a separation of powers that is strongly inspired by the ideas that Locke propagated.

1.5.5 Cosmopolitism

Liberalism focuses on individual human beings and not on the social structures in which they participate, or from which, according to conservatives and socialists, they derive their identity. The role of these larger structures is, in the eyes of liberals, merely instrumental: useful only as a means for humans to conduct their own lives. Moreover, if these social structures are not useful, they lose their right of existence.

As Hobbes had pointed out, if several powers exist simultaneously, they will compete. This holds true not only for individual human beings, but also for larger social entities such as States. If the Hobbesian argument is followed to its logical end, this means that there cannot be peace in the world as long as there are several powers next to each other without a more significant power to keep order. Still following this logic, this means that there are two reasons why human beings should ultimately not be attached to social structures smaller than a world-encompassing State. The first reason is that only an all-encompassing State can bring the security that humans long for. The second reason – which depends on the first – is that human beings have no natural attachment to any social structure, and therefore neither to their national States. If only a World-State can bring them the peace and security they need, only this World-State is worthy of support. This is the logic that leads from liberal premises to a cosmopolitan conclusion: the only State that is worthwhile is a World-State. The world (*kosmos*) is one big political community (*polis*).

Liberal roots of the EU It is this logic, which leads from individualism to cosmopolitism, that – on a smaller scale – inspired the creation of the European communities after World War II. The European Economic Community (EEC) started from the ideals of free movement of goods, persons, services and capital. The EU added human rights to these four freedoms, and these rights are to a large extent meant to create a space of freedom for citizens against their governments. The notion of freedom plays a central role in present-day

Europe, and in this sense the political ideology of Liberalism, which emphasizes the freedom of individual persons, may be said to have been a major influence on European integration.

1.5.6 Free Trade

The last characteristic of liberalism that will be discussed here is that it promotes free trade. Theoretically, trade benefits all the involved parties. If Jane owns a book, which she values at €10, while Carl would like to have the book and is willing to pay €15 for it, Jane can sell the book to Carl for any price in between €10 and €15 and both will benefit. Jane benefits, because she receives more money for the book than the book is worth to her; Carl benefits, because he can buy the book for less money than it is worth to him. Let us assume – and this is not an obvious assumption – that people trade voluntarily only if the transaction benefits them. Then every voluntary trade transaction benefits both parties. Let us assume moreover – and, again, this is not an obvious assumption – that only the trade partners have an interest in the trade transaction. In this case, every voluntary trade transaction improves the situation of the trade partners and has no effect on others: the world has become better.

Given these two assumptions, trade is good for society. Interference in free trade, for example by prohibiting some transactions (e.g. drug trade, or limitations on imports or exports of goods), or by taxing transactions (e.g. value-added tax), is therefore prima facie disadvantageous to society, and, in particular, to the potential trade partners. This is why liberals tend to promote free trade.

1.6 THE FRENCH REVOLUTION AND ITS AFTERMATH

The French Revolution of 1789 was in a sense the culmination of the development from medieval societies towards liberalism. Feudalism was officially abolished, and the power of the Catholic Church was severely limited. Moreover, a bill of rights was adopted – the *Déclaration des Droits de l'Homme et du Citoyen* – which started with the claim that all men are born and remain free and equal in rights. Gone were the class societies of the Middle Ages and the possibilities of slavery and serfdom. The rights to which everybody would be entitled were primarily rights that benefit the property holding class, including the rights to freedom and property.

1.6.1 Conservatism

Ideologically speaking, the French Revolution had to be answered. Already a member of the English Parliament in 1790, Edmund Burke, published the book *Reflections on the Revolution in France*, which made him into the philosophical founder of modern Conservatism. Typical elements of this modern conservative view are that society is like an organism, that human beings are not perfect and that hierarchy and authority are important for upholding a good society.[25]

Where liberalism assumes that society is the result of the interactions of individual human beings, each pursuing their own interests, Conservatism sees society as a kind of organism that consists of several parts that must cooperate in order to keep itself alive. The parts of the societal organism must fulfil different functions, just as the parts of a human body must fulfil different functions. All parts and all roles are important, because if one of them fails, the organism cannot survive. However, as the different parts must fulfil different functions, they cannot be equal.[26] A society needs governors that take policy decisions, public servants that assist the governors in executing their decisions, workers that provide the necessary goods, such as food and housing, and people (read: women) who stay at home to take care of the household and of raising children. Inequality is not only the unavoidable outcome of different talents and skills people possess, as some liberals assume, but is a fundamental aspect of human societies that need the fulfilment of different tasks.

The organic structure of society is the product of an evolutionary development, a long selection process that did not always take place consciously. The result is a complex organic structure that nobody can oversee completely, but that hangs together in a way that was historically selected for survival value. Interference in this product of ages of evolution is more likely to do harm than to constitute an improvement.

The human beings who fulfil the respective functions of society are imperfect. They are often psychologically limited and fear isolation and instability. As a result, they are drawn towards the familiar, preferring stability over change; they seek the security of their own place in society. A good society takes these limitations into account, for instance by preventing sudden and big changes and by allowing people to continue the life to which they are accustomed. It does not take much imagination to see how the reactions of many

---

25 Heywood 2012, pp. 70-77.
26 This metaphor can already be found in the writings of St. Paul (1 Corinthians 12: 12-27). There is an obvious link between the conservative ideology and the medieval Christian doctrine that society has a fixed functional structure.

people to the sudden large-scale influx of immigrants into Europe fit into the conservative view of mankind.

Plato Given human imperfection, not everybody is equally suited to determine the guiding lines of his or her own life. Some people are more suitable to lead than others. The Greek philosopher Plato used a famous metaphor in this connection: if a ship is to transport people overseas to another land, the captain and the navigator should determine the course of the ship, not the passengers. It is to everybody's advantage that guidance is left to suitable rulers, where suitability refers to both the cognitive and managerial capacities of the rulers and to their willingness to use these capacities for the common interests rather than for their private advantage. This view leads to the acceptance of inequality in society and to the recognition of the need for authority.

1.6.2   Napoleon Bonaparte

After the initial turmoil of the French Revolution, the political situation in France stabilized when Napoleon Bonaparte rose to power. He became first the consul and then, in 1804, the Emperor of France; and he became (in)famous through his wars in which he conquered Egypt and large parts of Europe. He was ultimately defeated in the Battle of Waterloo (1815) and died in exile on the island St. Helena.

The reason why Napoleon is mentioned here is not his short-lived attempt to integrate Europe under French reign, but the longer lasting influence of the reforms he brought to Europe. Through Napoleon, many achievements of the French Revolution and other forms of modernization were passed to the rest of Europe. They include:
- the overthrow of feudalism as a system of land ownership;
- the introduction of meritocracy: the societal position of people is determined by what they - can do, rather than by birth;
- equality before the law;
- the protection of property rights;
- religious toleration;
- modern secular education;
- the introduction of the metric system: based on the metre as a measure of length and a kilogram as a measure of weight; and last but not least
- the Napoleonic Codes as modern standards for legislation and codification.

All of these are a more lasting cultural contribution to the integration of Europe than the brief territorial integration that was brought about by the Napoleonic conquests.[27]

1.7 The Rise of Socialism

Labour as commodity We have seen that in the Late Middle Ages, capitalism began its development. Originally, an entrepreneur was responsible for the production chain of a good, from the beginning to the end. Earlier, we used the example of a manufacturer of wooden furniture. In the example, there was no division of labour, and it was clear that the producer of the furniture would receive the proceeds of his labour. Later, a merchant might buy trees from a landowner, hire a carpenter to transform the trees into wood that could be handled by an artisan, hire the artisan to turn the wood into furniture, and have the furniture transported to the place where it would bring the biggest proceeds and profit. The provider of the capital would run the business, and the labour necessary to produce the goods had become a commodity, just like the raw materials from which the product was ultimately manufactured.

More in general, an enterprise consists of three elements (production factors): labour, management and capital. Under capitalism, capital is used to buy everything needed for the enterprise, such as production facilities and raw materials, but also management and labour. In turn, the providers of the capital bear the losses or take advantage of the profits of the enterprise. Management and – in particular – labour have become mere production factors, controlled by the providers of capital (e.g. shareholders).[28] Labour can be bought; just like basic materials it has become a commodity.

Wage slaves After the French Revolution, serfdom and a fortiori slavery were formally abolished in almost all of Europe.[29] However, many labourers could provide only for their own subsistence and that of their families by selling large parts of their lives to entrepreneurs who hired them to perform labour. The conditions of these labourers had always been difficult, both in industrial production and in agriculture, but after the industrial revolution

---

27 *See* Roberts 2015.
28 Capitalism does not exclude the possibility that the production factors capital, management and labour are all united in the same person, as in a one-person enterprise. The separation between the three factors can be seen clearest in limited companies, in which the shareholders appoint the managers and (through them) hire the workers.
29 In Russia, serfdom was abolished in the emancipation reform of 1861.

in the 18th and 19th century, working conditions became particularly harsh.[30] It requires only a little metaphor to call these labourers 'wage slaves'.

Marxism The harsh labour conditions in industrialized Europe provided fertile soil for communist and socialist ideas. These ideas had already existed for many centuries, but in the 19th century there were two factors that increased their impact. One factor was the effects, already mentioned, of industrialization; the other factor was the creation of a 'scientific' version of socialism in the form of Marxism.

Although Karl Marx (1818-1883) did not consider himself to be necessarily a Marxist,[31] his philosophical and economic ideas were the foundation of Marxist ideology. For the history of European integration, several of these ideas are relevant, including the supervenience of culture on economic relations (historical materialism), class struggle and the international organization of labour.

Historical materialism A central idea in Marxist theory is that economic relations determine the structure of society. In other words, the structure of society at large supervenes on its underlying economic relations. These economic relations develop spontaneously, driven by progress in science and technology. For example, increasing knowledge about the building of ships and about geography makes overseas trade possible, including the colonial exploitation of mines elsewhere in the world and the use of plantations in areas with a different climate. The new economic relations are, in turn, reflected in cultural phenomena such as the law (protection of property and of free trade) and political theories (e.g. the rise of liberalism). The relationship between the economic base and the cultural superstructure is, according to Marx, one-way: economic organization determines the culture, and not the other way around. This is called 'historical materialism'; historical, because it is a theory about the development of society over time; materialism, because the basis consists of the material economic relations.

Within Marxist theory, law is part of the superstructure that reflects the underlying economic relations. This means that law will, almost by definition, protect the interests of the ruling class, the owners of the means of production, against the conflicting interests of those who can only sell their labour. We can see this, for instance, in the protection of property rights, which is to the advantage of those who own property. It is not obvious that some goods belong to particular persons who can exclude others from their use. Nevertheless, criminal law makes theft punishable and thereby enforces this exclusivity.

---

30   *See* https://en.wikipedia.org/wiki/Industrial_Revolution#Labor_conditions (last visited on 5 August 2019).
31   *See* https://en.wikipedia.org/wiki/Marxism#Etymology (last visited on 5 August 2019).

Property law allows an owner to vindicate the object of his ownership, and this possibility further enforces the exclusive use of goods by some at the cost of others.

This reflection of economic relations can also be seen in such concepts as the freedom of contract, because this freedom allows capitalists to hire workers on one-sided conditions. The State, as an organization that enforces law, is then automatically an instrument in the hands of the ruling class to maintain the legal status quo.

Class struggle A corollary of historical materialism is the idea of class struggle. According to Marxist theory, the historical development of societies consists of different phases, determined by production (economic) relations. However, each phase has owners of means of production and non-owners, or proletarians, who depend on the owners to hire their labour. In the age of feudalism, the owners were the landowners, and the proletarians were the serfs who had to work the land for a living. After the industrial revolution, the owners were the industrialists (providers of capital) who hired workers (proletarians) to work in their plants. Every economic phase has its own class opposition, and in each phase there is an opposition of interests between the haves and the have-nots. This opposition is the *class struggle*. The existence of class struggle is, according to Marxist theory, a continuous phenomenon. It may take different guises in different periods, but it can only end if there is no separation any more between the owners of the means of production and the workers who create value from these means.

International organization of labour This separation would, according to Marxists, end after the final, communist revolution, in which the workers would confiscate all means of production. This final revolution would be inevitable, as societies with their built-in tension between social classes are unstable. However, to promote this inevitable revolution and to make it successful for the proletariat, workers in the different (industrialized) countries should unite.[32] They should cooperate in order to improve their situation as long as the final revolution has not yet occurred and to promote the occurrence of this communist revolution. This plea for a union of European workers was, as we will see when we look at the ideas of Spinelli, one of the ideas that inspired the EU.

---

32 The *Communist Manifesto* (Marx and Engels 1848) ends with the call to all proletarians to unite: *Proletarier aller Lände, vereinigt euch!*

1.8 The 20th Century

As is well known, the Russian revolutions of 1917 were not the revolutions that Marx had in mind, and the final communist revolution did not take place (yet). Nevertheless, Marxist ideas have influenced the course of history in large parts of the world, and perhaps this has been an influence in improving the conditions of the working class (a Marxist term) in Europe.

However, from 1914 to 1918, the world, including Europe, suffered under World War I, and from 1939 to 1945, Hitler tried to reinstate a third version of the (Holy) Roman Empire, in the form of his Third Reich, which led to World War II.

The devastations brought about by the two successive World Wars were so monumental that strong calls were heard to avoid another round of war by uniting the countries of Europe. These calls succeeded to some extent, and in 1951 six European countries formally established the European Coal and Steel Community. This step leads us from the pre-history to the history of the EU, a history that will be outlined in the next chapter.

2 The History of the European Union, in Four Phases

2.1 Introduction

Following the sketch in the previous chapter of almost two-and-a-half millennia of history that preceded the creation of the EU, this chapter will outline the development of the EU itself. Although less epigrammatic than the 'big' history of what went before, this 'little' history of the EU itself will be limited as well. It is confined to four key periods:
- the creation of the European Coal and Steel Community (ECSC) in the 1940s and 1950s;
- the so-called 'empty chair crisis' in the 1960s;
- the period of revival that started at the end of the 1970s and resulted in the creation of the EU and the introduction of the euro as common currency; and
- the period of Euroscepticism in the 21st century.

These four periods were chosen to illustrate the fundamental tension in the process of European integration. This tension exists between, on the one hand, the aspiration for an integration that results in unity, and, on the other hand, close cooperation in the promotion of national interests. We will meet these two approaches to European integration in the next chapter on a theoretical level as supranationalism and intergovernmentalism. In this chapter, our focus will be on the actual events that became the basis of the theoretical accounts.

Before going into some of the details, we will first look at the development of the EU from the legal, institutional, economic and geographical perspectives.

2.2 The Treaties

Not only is the EU a legal phenomenon, but it also has economic, geographical and political dimensions. However, for lawyers it is tempting to see the EU first and foremost as something legal. In their eyes it is an organization that was created by means of legal sources (treaties) and that was developed through secondary EU law (law created by EU organs) such as regulations, directives, decisions and – last but not least – judgments of the European

Court of Justice. In this section, we will adopt the legal perspective on the EU and look at the development of the Union at the hands of its treaties.

The EU may be seen as a fusion of three pre-existing Communities: the ECSC, the EEC and Euratom. These three communities were founded by treaties, and their fusion into the EU was also brought about by a treaty. Moreover, the Communities and the Union were also reformed by means of treaties. Table 2.1 contains an overview of the main treaties and the main changes they brought about.

Technically speaking, most of these treaties were modifications of already existing treaties (the ECSC, EEC, Euratom treaties, and later the EU treaty).

Table 2.1   The treaties

Name	Signed On	Entered into Force	Comments
Treaty establishing the ECSC (Paris)	18 April 1951	23 July 1952	This treaty created the ECSC for a period of 50 years.
Treaty establishing the EDC	27 May 1952	Never, as it was never ratified	This treaty illustrates the failed attempt during the 1950s to achieve military integration by creating a European Defence Community
Treaty establishing the EPC	Never, as it became useless with the failure of the EDC		This treaty was meant to combine the ECSC and the EDC, but failed together with the EDC treaty.
Treaty establishing the EEC (Rome)	25 March 1957	1 January 1958	This treaty created the EEC.
Treaty establishing Euratom (Rome)	25 March 1957	1 January 1958	This treaty created the European Atomic Energy Community.
Merger Treaty (Brussels)	8 April 1965	1 July 1967	This treaty provided that the Commission of the EEC and the Council of the EEC should fuse with the Commission and Council of Euratom and the High Authority and Council of the ECSC. The EEC became the European Community (EC).
Single European Act (Luxembourg, The Hague)	17 and 28 February 1986	1 July 1987	This treaty: – identified the completion of the internal market in 1992 as a specific goal, – codified European Political Cooperation, and – officially recognized the European Council as an institution of the EU.

Name	Signed On	Entered into Force	Comments
Treaty on European Union (Maastricht)	7 February 1992	1 November 1993	This treaty: – merged the ECSC, the EC and Euratom into the first 'pillar' of the EU, – identified a Common Foreign Policy (CFP) and Cooperation in the spheres of Justice and Home Affairs (CJHA) as separate 'pillars' of the EU, and – defined the main features of Economic and Monetary Union (EMU)
Treaty of Amsterdam	2 October 1997	1 May 1999	This treaty increased the power of the European Parliament and expanded the use of Qualified Majority Voting in the Council of Ministers. The CFP was strengthened by, among others, creating the function of High Representative for EU Foreign Policy. The Schengen convention was brought under the EU umbrella.
Treaty of Nice	25 February 2001	1 February 2003	The treaty contained a number of provisions dealing with the institutional effects of European enlargement.
Constitutional Treaty	29 October 2004	Never, as it was never ratified by all undersigning Member States	This treaty was a (failed) attempt to give the EU its own Constitution.
Treaty of Lisbon	13 December 2007	1 December 2009	This treaty is seen mainly as an alternative to the Constitutional Treaty, which did not succeed. It contains a Fundamental Rights Charter.

2.3 The Communities and Their Organs

The ECSC The ECSC was the first community that was created on the trajectory towards the EU. It was an organization of six European countries, set up after World War II to regulate their industrial production under a centralized authority.

The ECSC was formally established in 1951 by the Treaty of Paris, signed by France, West Germany, Italy, Belgium, the Netherlands and Luxembourg. Its central organ was the High Authority, a supranational body that was to govern the ECSC. However, an intergovernmental body was added: the Council of Ministers. The point of this Council was to limit the power of the supranational High Authority and the influence of France and Germany in that organ.

There was also a kind of Parliament, the Parliamentary Assembly, which was to oversee the High Authority, and a court, the Court of Justice.

In 1958, when the EEC and Euratom entered into existence, the Parliamentary Assembly became a common institution of the three communities. The name of the Parliament changed to 'European Parliamentary Assembly'. The Court of Justice also became a common institution.

In 1967, when the Merger Treaty entered into force, the High Authority and the Commission of the EEC were joined, just as the ECSC Council of Ministers and the EEC Council of Europe. The Parliament changed its name again, and became the 'European Parliament'.

In 1993, when the Treaty on European Union (Maastricht) entered into force, the ECSC became a part of the EU.

In 2002, 50 years after its foundation, the ECSC stopped existing as a separate community. The remaining relevant parts of its functions were moved to the EC part of the EU.

Euratom The European Atomic Energy Community (Euratom) is an international organization, established by the Euratom Treaty on 25 March 1957, with the purpose of developing peaceful uses of atomic energy in Europe.

From the moment Euratom came into existence, it shared its Parliament and court with the ECSC and the EEC. The Merger Treaty also merged its Commission and Council with the ECSC and the EEC. The role of the European Parliament in Euratom has remained small.

The EEC The EEC was a regional organization that aimed to bring about economic integration among its Member States. It was created by the Treaty of Rome of 1957 and entered into existence in 1958. It inherited two of its main institutions, the European Parliamentary Assembly and the Court of Justice, from the ECSC and shared these institutions also with Euratom.

The Commission of the EEC was the executive arm of the Community, initiating Community law, dealing with the day-to-day running of the Community and upholding the treaties. It was designed to be independent from the EEC Member States, representing the Community interest first and foremost.

The Council of Ministers was a body holding legislative and executive powers and was thus the main decision-making body of the Community. It consisted of a representation of ministers from the Member States with a variable composition that depended on the topic at issue. For example, if agriculture was being discussed, the Council would be composed of the national ministers for agriculture. The ministers represented their governments and were accountable to their national political systems. Votes were taken either by majority – with votes allocated according to the size of a Member State's population – or unanimity.

Since the 1960s the Council also began to meet informally at the level of national leaders. These meetings were called 'European summits', or 'Eurosummits'.

The Court of Justice of the European Communities was the highest court on matters of community law. Its role was to ensure that Community law was applied in the same way across all Member States and to settle legal disputes between institutions or states. It became a powerful institution, as Community law overrides national law.

The EU The EU is an umbrella organization. Originally, it consisted of three 'pillars'. The first pillar was the supranational part of the EU and held the three communities that existed at the moment that the EU entered into existence. The two other pillars covered two additional fields of policy: 'Justice and Home Affairs' and the 'Common Foreign and Security Policy'. These fields fell outside the communities and were areas of intergovernmental cooperation.

The EU was created by the Treaty of Maastricht, which entered into force in 1993. In 2009, when the Treaty of Lisbon entered into force, 'Justice and Home Affairs' was renamed the 'Area of Freedom, Security and Justice' and moved from the intergovernmental to the supranational part of the EU. By then, the ECSC had already ceased to exist.

The main institutions of the EU are the Commission, the European Council, the Council of Ministers, the European Parliament and the Court of Justice of the European Union. The European Central Bank has acquired an important role because of the financial crises of the 21st century.

2.4 Economic Integration

When the ECSC and the EEC began the trajectory towards the EU, the main objective was safeguarding the peace, and the main instrument to achieve this was economic integration.

Following an analysis by Balassa,[1] the literature of economic integration distinguishes between four or five degrees – or 'stages' – of economic integration. We discuss these degrees in terms of Member States that participate in the economic integration.

Free trade area In a free trade area, the Member States remove all barriers on trade between themselves. However, they retain the freedom to implement different commercial policies towards third countries. For example, there would be no trade barriers between France and Germany, but France and Germany may use different commercial policies towards former French colonies. This means that the members of a free trade area are not obligated to use a common tariff on imports from countries outside the area.

An example of a free trade area is the EFTA (European Free Trade Area), which was created in 1960 by the UK, Norway, Sweden, Finland, Portugal and Switzerland when these countries were not (yet) members of the EEC. Members of the former Soviet Union are also a free trade area, formed in 1994, namely the CISFTA (Commonwealth of Independent States Free Trade Area). There are also free trade areas in North America (NAFTA), between Asia, Australia and New Zealand, and many others.

Customs union A customs union may be characterized as a free trade area with a common external commercial policy. An example of such a common policy might be a common tariff on imports. Examples of such customs unions are the EEC (from 1968) and the customs union between the EU and Turkey (from 1995; most agricultural products excluded).

Common market We speak of a common market if a customs union allows for free 'factor' mobility. The factors are goods, services, labour and capital. The 'four freedoms' of the EEC and later the EU illustrate this free factor mobility. As soon as these four freedoms had been realized to a sufficient degree, the EEC changed from a customs union into a common market.

Economic and monetary union An economic and monetary union (EMU) goes beyond a mere common market. Ideally, it includes, next to a common market, coordination or even central control of monetary and fiscal policies, a common currency – or at least fixed exchange rates between national currencies – and a common central bank. As we will see, the trajectory towards an EMU has proved particularly troublesome for the EU Member States.

---

1   *See* Balassa 1961.

Political integration Political integration lacks a precise definition. Arguably, it includes the existence of a central authority with supranational powers. Strictly speaking, political integration is not considered a form of economic integration. However, political integration may be a necessary complement to an EMU, given that such a union requires coordination or central control of monetary and fiscal policies.

The EEC and the EU When the EEC was designed and created, at the end of the 1950s, the plan was that it would develop into a customs union within 12 years. To the extent that this involved the abolition of tariffs on internal trade and the introduction of a common external commercial policy, the plan succeeded well. However, getting rid of other trade impediments turned out to be more difficult. For this reason, there was an initiative during the 1980s to revive the process leading towards economic integration: the EEC area would endeavour to become a common market, or even an EMU. This revival was supported by the Single European Act in 1986/7 and the Treaty on European Union in 1992/3.

2.5 Enlargement

The EEC and the EU did not develop autonomously or independently of what was happening in the rest of the world. The rising tensions between the eastern and the western part of Europe and the war in Korea, during the 1950s, were major inspirations for the creation of the ECSC, the forerunner of the EEC. The ending of dictatorships in countries bordering the EEC (Spain, Portugal, Greece) made these countries eligible for participation in the community. When the Soviet Union, and with it the Eastern Bloc in Europe, collapsed, many East-European countries wanted to become EU members as well. One way in which these external influences on European integration became visible was through the enlargement of the EEC and the EU.

The six founders When the ECSC, the EEC and Euratom were founded, only six countries participated: France, West Germany, Italy, Belgium, the Netherlands and Luxembourg. No East-European countries were involved, and neither was the United Kingdom. The non-participation of East-European countries can be explained by the fact that the creation of the ECSC was as much a step in the polarization between East- and West Europe as it was a means to maintain peace in Western Europe. The absence of the UK may have had to do with the fact that the UK – one of the victors of World War II – did not feel the need to participate in a project that was meant to avoid another war in Europe. Moreover, and perhaps more importantly, for its trade and foreign relations, the UK was more focused on transatlantic ties – the US and the Commonwealth countries – than on the European continent.

The first enlargement: Denmark, Ireland and the UK The first round of enlargements took place in 1973, after the EEC had existed for 15 years. Accession of the new Member States was motivated mainly by the availability of easier access to the European market. The UK had already twice attempted, but failed, to accede to the EEC. The main explanation for this failure was the role of the French President Charles de Gaulle, who resisted accession because he feared a decreasing influence for France. In 1969, De Gaulle was succeeded by President Pompidou, who had no principal objections against the participation of the UK, and then accession became possible. In 1973, not only the UK, but also Denmark and Ireland acceded.

The southern enlargements: Greece, Spain and Portugal After World War II, Spain and Portugal remained under the right-wing dictatorships of Franco and Salazar respectively. Greece was, after a coup in 1967, under a military dictatorship: the 'Regime of the Colonels'. These dictatorships disqualified the three southern countries from EEC membership. However, as soon as the dictators died (Spain and Portugal) and the military junta had been replaced by a democratic government (Greece), it became possible, in principle, for these countries to become members of the EEC. After negotiations of the details, the three countries acceded in 1981 (Greece) and 1986 (Spain and Portugal).

The 1995 enlargement: Austria, Finland and Sweden For some countries, the Cold War between the Soviet bloc and the Western world was a reason *not* to accede to the EEC. Austria, Finland and Sweden wanted to remain neutral in this 'war'. They did not want to become members of an organization that strived for a common foreign policy, as this would put them in the Western camp. However, as soon as the Cold War had ended, this desire for neutrality lost weight, and another desire – to have easier access to the common market that was developing – prevailed. Meanwhile, former East Germany reunited with West Germany in 1990, and the West German membership expanded into the united German membership of the EEC. Austria, Sweden and Finland started accession negotiations around 1990, and the three countries joined the EU in 1995.

The 'Eastern enlargements' The fall of the Iron Curtain that separated the Soviet bloc from the western part of Europe created a long list of potential new EU members. Many countries of the former Eastern bloc wanted to accede, but there were substantial differences between these former communist countries and the existing EU members, in terms of both prosperity and political culture. There were also substantial differences between the former Eastern bloc countries themselves, which meant that they could not all accede at the same time.

In 2004, eight countries acceded: The Czech Republic, Estonia, Hungary, Latvia, Lithuania, Poland and Slovakia.

In the same year, Slovenia and the Mediterranean countries Malta and Cyprus also joined the EU.

In 2007 there was a second round of 'Eastern' accession, when Bulgaria and Romania joined.

Croatia followed in 2013.

Pending negotiations Although more enlargements are not expected in the short term, negotiations concerning accession are still ongoing with several countries. These countries include Turkey, Macedonia, Montenegro, Albania, Serbia and Bosnia and Herzegovina.

Brexit Although, strictly speaking, Brexit does not belong to a section on enlargement, the UK's leaving the EU is an important event that requires mentioning. At the moment of writing, the political process in the UK concerning Brexit is still ongoing, and, provided nothing spectacular happens, the UK is expected to leave the EU ultimately on 31 January 2020.

2.6 The European Coal and Steel Community

Causes and effects Writing history would be easier if the causes of events came neatly labelled as such. In practice, the job is more difficult, at least if one does not wish to describe history as an unending set of unrelated events (and then…, and then…). Rather, if the relationships between certain occurrences and their outcomes are important, it becomes mandatory to choose and select specific causes and their effects from the endless chain of events that succeed each other. The following contains such a selection, and, unavoidably, it is to some extent subjective and open to disagreement.

The post-war years Immediately after World War II, much of Europe was in ruin. Millions of people became refugees or were left homeless because their houses and livelihoods were destroyed. Industry was either decimated or one-sidedly devoted to war, and infrastructure such as roads and bridges was also a casualty of war. The consensus was that something like this should never happen again – a feeling that had been experienced more often throughout the history of mankind. Accordingly, some had begun planning how a better Europe could be built after the war had ended.

Economic cooperation played a central role in many of these plans, but some plans went further and proposed the creation of a large federal State in Europe, which would include at least Germany and France, and preferably many other countries. Churchill, who had been the United Kingdom's Prime Minister during the war years, gave a famous speech in 1946 in which he pleaded for 'a kind of United States of Europe'. Characteristically, however, there was no mention of the UK being a member of these United States. In 1948 a large conference was held in The Hague to address the future of Europe, but despite its many important attendees, the conference did not lead to anything substantial. Apparently, Europe was still divided.

Nevertheless, a combination of several factors led towards integration, the most important among them being the upcoming Cold War.

2.6.1 Cold War

Germany had been defeated in World War II by an alliance, of which the Soviet Union (USSR), the United States (US), the UK and France had been important members. Although there had been severe tensions between the Western countries and the Soviet Union before the war, the countries had been united for a while in their battle against a common enemy. In February 1945, when it had already become clear that the allies would win the war, the USSR, the US and the UK (but not France, which was not invited) held a conference in Yalta, at which they made plans for Europe after the war. Part of these plans was that Germany, after being conquered, would be split into four territories, occupied by the Soviet Union, the US, the UK and France. Already at an earlier meeting in October 1944 in Moscow, Churchill and Stalin, the Prime Ministers of the UK and the Soviet Union, respectively, had decided that after the war, Europe would be divided into two spheres of influence, a Western sphere and a Soviet sphere.

These divisions were a foundation for the splitting of Europe into a Western and an Eastern bloc and the hostile relations between the two blocs that were characteristic of the so-called Cold War. The Cold War was a war between, on the one hand, the US and its allies, and, on the other hand, the USSR and its satellites and allies, which lasted from approximately 1947 to 1989. The war was called 'cold' as it did not lead to direct military interactions between the US and the USSR. However, the war divided the world and reduced the Security Council to a lame body, as the USSR would veto any Western proposal, and vice versa. Moreover, it fuelled many proxy wars, such as the Korean war and the Vietnam war, as the Cold War parties supported different sides in these local conflicts.

From the beginning of the Cold War, in the 1940s, the USSR tried to expand and consolidate its zone of influence in Europe, while the US attempted to halt this development. One element of this attempt was the promotion of a rehabilitated and rearmed Germany, which might prove useful in resisting the expansion of the USSR into the West.

2.6.2 Relations between France and Germany

A second important factor with regard to European integration were the relations between France and Germany. Traditionally, this relationship had been one of rivalry. At the beginning of the 19th century, Napoleon had conquered large parts of Germany. In 1870 there had been a war between the French Republic and the North German Confederation, led by Prussia.

During World War I, France belonged to the coalition that defeated Germany. As a result, France could enforce territorial and monetary compensation for the war against Germany, which in turn led to resentment in Germany. In World War II, Germany had occupied France. After World War II, France was afraid of a renewed rise in the influence of Germany and initially resisted the rehabilitation and – even more – the rearmament of Germany.

International Ruhr Authority The Ruhr area played an important role in this connection. This is the area encompassing the cities Dortmund, Bochum, Recklinghausen, Essen and Duisburg. The area had an important function in the German production of weaponry for World War II. This was particularly the case because the area contained coal mines, and coal was essential for the production of steel. France did not have such mines, which made it more difficult to develop a decent French steel industry. After World War I, the Ruhr area had for a while been occupied by French and Belgian troops, and after World War II, the area was occupied by American and British troops.

The US pressure to reunite at least the Western-occupied zones of Germany as a means of resistance to the expansion of the USSR ignited serious doubts in France; it feared a revival of the German arms industry. Part of the solution was to place the Ruhr area, including its coal mines and heavy industry, under the control of the International Ruhr Authority. This Authority would oversee the production and distribution of coal, adding an element of control, but also making it possible for France to use coal from the Ruhr area for its own industries. This International Ruhr Authority can be seen as a predecessor of the ECSC. The foundation of West Germany and the creation of the International Ruhr Authority were accomplished by the London Agreements of 1949.

2.6.3 The Schuman Declaration

France was under pressure from the US to consent to the reunion, rehabilitation and rearmament of West Germany. Not wanting to relive the horror of two World Wars, France looked for a way to accommodate international pressure, while simultaneously restricting the possibilities for Germany to become a threat once again. A high-ranking French public servant, Jean Monnet, found a way to combine these two objectives, and he convinced the French Minister of Foreign affairs, Robert Schuman, to adopt his plan.

The plan was to place French and German production of coal and steel under one common High Authority. Other Western European countries could also participate in the project. This plan had at least three advantages. First, by combining the coal and steel production of Germany and France and placing it under supranational control, no single country could use the available means to create arms to threaten another country. This would be a safeguard for peace in Western Europe. Second, the plan would allow Germany to re-industrialize and to rearm, which would protect Western Europe against Soviet expansion. And third, the pooling of the production capacity for coal and steel might function as a first step to further economic integration and to any of the benefits that this might have. This is the famous idea of 'spillover': integration in one important field would necessitate integration in other fields too. Such integration would be desirable not only for rebuilding the West European economy, but also for safeguarding peace between European countries in general.

On 9 May 1950, Schuman gave a press conference in which he presented the plan, with emphasis on both the solution for the Ruhr issue and the implications for the European integration. This 'Schuman declaration' became the basis on which the ECSC would be built.

2.6.4 The European Coal and Steel Community

The Schuman declaration was received with sufficient enthusiasm to make the creation of the ECSC possible. The negotiations between representatives of France, Germany, Italy and the Benelux countries started in June 1950. Although the Schuman proposal was also open to Britain, the UK did not want to participate, fearing it would weaken its relations with the US and the Commonwealth (the former British colonies).

The spirit of the negotiations was positive, in general, with attention to the value of European integration, supranationalism and sacrifice of national interests to the common interest. However, when it came down to practical issues such as the localities of the institutions of the ECSC, it became difficult to overcome the clash between national interests.

Subject to debate was the precise nature and role of the institutions. An agreement was reached that the ECSC would be led by a supranational High Authority. There was also agreement about the limited involvement of a Common Assembly, consisting of 78 members of national parliaments, as well as about a Court of Justice to safeguard the observation of ECSC law, and the interpretation and application of the upcoming treaty. The Schuman proposal did not mention a role for national governments of the Member States, but on the insistence of the Dutch, who feared German and French dominance in the High Authority, room was made for a Council of Ministers, where the Ministers would represent the national governments and the interests of the Member States.

2.6.5 Technocracy and National Interests

The inclusion of the Council of Ministers to the institutions of the ECSC was not a mere technical detail but signified a fundamental position on the nature of governance. On a superficial level, it seems that the Council's role was to protect the national interests of the Member States against the influence of potentially dominant French and German interests in the High Authority. However, this is not all. There was also the question of what the function of governance was.

Plato's metaphor about the ship can help clarify the point. Plato raised the question about what should determine the course of a ship that is to transport people overseas to another land. Should the passengers whose interests are at stake determine the course, or the captain and the navigator? According to Plato, it is to everybody's advantage that guidance is left to suitable rulers, where suitability refers to both the cognitive and managerial capacities of the rulers and to their willingness to use these capacities in the common interest. This means that the captain and the navigator should determine the course of the ship, and not the passengers, even though it is the interests of the passengers that are to be advanced. This approach is 'technocratic': the power (*kratos*) should lie with those who possess the relevant capacities (*technè*) and not with those whose interests are at stake.

In science, this technocratic approach is widely accepted. There has been no vote on whether $E = mc^2$,[2] even though the truth or falsity of Einstein's formula has far-reaching practical implications, such as the possibility to use nuclear energy. The truth or falsity of the formula is, as always in scientific debate, provisionally determined in an approach where nobody has the status of final arbiter.

In politics, technocracy is less widely accepted. The general view is that governance should be done by politicians who are democratically responsible. In other words, in modern politics, broad support exists – in terms of Plato's metaphor – for having the passengers decide the course of the ship.

Why is technocracy less accepted in matters of governance? Several possible reasons present themselves:
1. Perhaps expertise on good governance is not possible because there is no objective good or bad, but only subjective preferences. If knowledge of good and bad is fundamentally impossible, there can be no expertise on the topic, and it does not make sense to have a government of 'experts'.
2. A related alternative is that perhaps there is such a thing as the objective good or bad, but it is impossible for us, humans with limited cognitive capacities, to discover what it is. If that holds, a government of 'experts' makes no sense either, because the experts lack expertise.
3. A more positive reason for letting people decide for themselves is that what is objectively good or bad depends in the last instance on the subjective interests of humans. In this view, people are the best judges of what is in their own interest.
4. An in-between position is that people tend to be quite good judges of their own interests but that they sometimes make mistakes. That would plead for letting people choose representatives who are more knowledgeable than 'ordinary' people. Such a 'representative democracy' combines aspects of technocracy and of democracy.

The choice of a technocratic High Authority as executive for the ECSC indicates that the negotiating States did not accept possibilities 1 and 2. If knowledge of good or bad policy is fundamentally impossible, it makes no sense to have a technocratic institution at all. The most benevolent explanation for a combination of a technocratic High Authority and a political Council of Ministers is that the States accepted that good policy in the area of coal and steel can be the object of knowledge and that such knowledge is accessible to experts, but that political control is necessary to avoid biases in expert decision-making

---

2   This formula, which captures one result from Einstein's general theory of relativity, means, by and large, that the energy of something with mass m equals m, multiplied by the squared velocity of light.

and to safeguard the common interest. A less benevolent explanation is that the participating States wanted the possibility to protect their national interests, even if that would mean a sacrifice of the common interest. The difference between these two interpretations reflects the difference between European integration as a reflection of aspirations for unity and as a tool for promoting national interests.

2.6.6 Conclusion on the ECSC

Achievements and failures of the ECSC The Treaty of Paris, by means of which the ECSC was established, was signed on 18 April 1951. The Treaty entered into force on 23 July 1952 for a period of 50 years. This means that the ECSC expired on 23 July 2002. At that date it had already been incorporated in the EU.

According to its mission, the ECSC was to contribute to the expansion of the economy, but it is doubtful whether the organization had a substantial impact on Europe's economic growth.[3] However, the ECSC succeeded in solving the Ruhr problem and in overcoming the difficult relationship between France and Germany. Moreover, it has been a forerunner of later organizations, such as the EEC and the EU. In this way, it fulfilled a valuable function by being an important trial and a trailblazer in supranational regulation.

EDC and EPC In approximately the same period in which the ECSC was created, there were also attempts to create organizations that aimed at further integration in other sectors: the European Defence Community (EDC) and the European Political Community (EPC). The EDC would provide for a supranational European army, with – controversially – a German contribution. The same States that participated in the ECSC would also participate in this defence community. On 27 May 1952 the six participating States signed the Treaty establishing the EDC, but the treaty was not ratified by France, and, as a consequence, never entered into force. In 1955, West Germany became a member of the NATO, which took the urgency of an EDC away.

The EPC was meant to serve as a combination of the ECSC and the EDC. With the failure of the EDC, the fate of the EPC was also sealed in 1954.

One year later, European leaders would meet in Messina and take the first steps on the road to the EEC.

---

3   Dinan 2004, p. 55.

The first years; an evaluation The initial years of the developments leading to the EU already showed which factors both drove the integration of Europe and also contained the seeds of disintegration. The desire to avoid future wars in Europe was certainly a driving force, and it was still present in the 1940s and the 1950s, briefly after World War II. This factor was supported by the desire to build a flourishing economy and regain the prosperity that was lost during the war years. And then, there was also the fear for the spread of communism and – hand in hand with that – the westward expansion of the Soviet Union. The United States supported these factors by putting pressure on France and England to participate in the integration. At the same time, the future Member States of the EU were driven not only by collective motives, but also – and perhaps even primarily – by the desire to promote their national economic interests. As long as integration promoted these interests, there was no tension between the idealistic and the pragmatic approaches to integration. However, as soon as the national interests of a State are at stake, it is not obvious any more that the process of integration will continue.

2.7 The Empty Chair Crisis

In July 1965, the French President, Charles de Gaulle, caused a serious crisis in the EEC by suspending France's participation in the Council of Ministers. The French chair remained empty, which explains the name 'empty chair crisis'. To understand what happened and why this event was so significant, it is necessary to go back in time for some years, to the beginning of the EEC.

The creation of the EEC Even though the EDC and the EPC failed in 1954, the idea still existed that a closer cooperation between the Western European States (Eastern Europe having already dropped out of the picture) would be beneficial. France strongly favoured cooperation in the field of energy, and, in particular, atomic energy, as this was in those years a promising new development towards a seemingly unlimited production of energy. Other European countries were less enthusiastic, as they feared that the desired cooperation was mainly a façade to hide the French desire to acquire the relevant technology cheaply. West Germany would have liked to eliminate trade barriers by means of a common market, as its industry had started to flourish again and needed a broader market. This idea initially had less support from France, as French industry was not sufficiently developed to compete with the German industry.[4]

---

[4] If this gives the reader the impression that the developments were guided mainly by attempts to compromise German and French interests, that impression is correct. It must be admitted that in those years, other States also played some role in developing European integration; for example, the role of the Belgian Foreign

After a year of preparation and negotiations, two treaties emerged, one concerning atomic energy, leading to Euratom, and the other regarding the customs union, leading to the EEC. Both France and Germany could be satisfied. The two treaties were signed in Rome on 25 March 1957 by France, Germany, Italy and the Benelux countries and entered into force on 1 January 1958. In retrospect, it turned out that the EEC Treaty was all-important, while the Euratom Treaty remained essentially a dead letter.

Although the starting point in thinking about a customs union was to facilitate the trade of industrial products, agricultural policy soon entered the picture. This topic was, in particular, pushed by France, as it had a large agricultural sector. There would be a customs union for agricultural products as well, and the national subsidies for the agricultural sector would be replaced by community protection for the farmers.

The customs union, in the form of the abolishment of tariffs and quotas on internal trade, would be introduced gradually, over a period of 12 years. That meant that the customs union would be completed by 1970. In practice, the development went much quicker, and it was possible to have a full customs union on 1 July 1967.

The funding of the EEC The institutions of the EEC were quite similar to those of the ECSC. There was a Council of Ministers of the Member States that would represent the Member States and their interests, a Commission – the counterpart of the High Authority – that would safeguard the community interests, a Parliament (Assembly) and a court. As we will see, the tension between the two approaches to European integration, the aspiration for unity as opposed to promotion of national interests through cooperation, has its counterpart in a tension between the Commission and the Council, respectively.

Originally, the Common Agricultural Policy (CAP) was paid out of contributions of the Member States to the EEC. However, the plan was that this arrangement would end as soon as the customs union was in full effect. The 'rebates' that the EEC would raise on foodstuffs imported into the EEC and the tariffs raised on all other imports would provide the money to pay the EEC. This would give the Commission and the Assembly more financial elbow room and would make it possible to grow. In other words, the implementation of the customs union would indirectly also mean a shift in the balance of powers from the Council to the Commission. The Commission would gain, and the Council would lose. This, in combination with the fact that starting from 1 January 1966 qualified

---

Minister, Paul-Henry Spaak, was crucially important. However, it was still predominantly France and Germany, and their competing interests, that determined the course of events.

majority voting (QMV) would apply in the Council, implied that the influence of individual Member States on the course of the EEC would shrink.

The crisis Charles de Gaulle did not see the EEC as a means to unify the West European States but as a means for the States to cooperate to each other's advantage. From this perspective, the States should retain their power to take their own decisions and not lose this power to supranational bodies such as the Commission. The developments in the EEC in the 1960s threatened this approach to integration, and the resulting frustration came to a head in the negotiations in the Council about the way to finance the CAP. The negotiations were still ongoing when the deadline arrived, but that was not unusual for EEC negotiations. The standard policy was to 'stop the clocks', and pretend that the deadline had not arrived yet. However, this time the French foreign minister, who presided over the session, refused to do so. France withdrew its representation from the Council, meaning that the relevant French ministers did not show up in council meetings any more. The French chair remained empty.

In September 1965, De Gaulle gave a press conference in which he explained that he would not agree with the upcoming QMV in the Council. There were two reasons, one fundamental, the other pragmatic. The fundamental reason was that De Gaulle did not want QMV because it would be another step in the direction of supranationalism. The pragmatic reason, perhaps more important, was that he feared that QMV would have detrimental effects on French agricultural and trade interests.

In the end, the crisis was solved by means of the 'Luxembourg compromise': when very important interests were at stake, the Council would not use QMV. It was not defined what very important interests were, and as a matter of fact the compromise gave Member States a veto if they did not want QMV to apply. With this compromise in place, the immediate crisis was solved. However, the solution meant a serious delay on the path to European integration. Moreover, it was an indication that in the 'war' between the supranationalists and the intergovernmentalists, the latter had won an important battle.

2.8 Towards the European Union

Eurosclerosis There is no simple causal link between, on the one hand, the empty chair crisis and its 'solution' and, on the other hand, the 'Eurosclerosis' that followed in the 1970s. However, the crisis cast a shadow on the process of European integration, which was only deepened by other events.

In the EEC Treaty of 1960, it was agreed that the following objectives were to be pursued during a 12-year transition period from 1958 until 1970:[5]
- the abolition of tariffs and of quantitative and qualitative restrictions in intra-EC trade;
- the creation of a common external trade policy and a common external tariff;
- the elimination of obstacles to the free movement of people, capital, goods and services (the 'four freedoms');
- a common agricultural policy;
- a common transport policy;
- the introduction of means to ensure fair competition;
- the coordination of the economic policies of the Member States to avoid balance-of-payment disequilibria;
- the creation of a European Social Fund to improve employment opportunities and raise living standards for workers;
- the creation of a European Investment Bank to help reduce regional disparities;
- special trade and development arrangements for colonies and former colonies.

The first two of these items had largely been realized in 1968. However, the removal of non-tariff barriers to trade and to free movement of people, capital, goods and services had made little progress. The years to follow would not change this very much, as financial troubles – an oil crisis in 1973 and the economic recession that it caused – plagued the world, including the EEC members. Rather than pursuing more integration, Member States tended to focus more on their own interests. Even the abdication of De Gaulle as President of France in 1969 did not prevent this development.

However, at the end of the 1970s, the wheels began turning again. In 1985, there was a 'watershed year'[6] that marked the transition from a difficult period for European integration to a period of new progress.

Institutional reforms In 1974, the French President, Giscard d'Estaing, proposed that there should be regular meetings of the Heads of States of the Member States. This proposal was accepted, and the 'European Council' came into existence as a matter of fact. The European Council is a typical intergovernmental body whose existence was only officially recognized in the Single European Act of 1987. To balance the intergovernmental and the supranational forces in the Community, it was also decided to increase the power of the European Parliament, by having this body elected directly and no longer through the national parliaments of the Member States. The first direct elections were held in 1979.

---

5 Nello 2012, p. 23.
6 Bache *et al.* 2015, p. 372.

In 1984, a meeting of the European Council decided to introduce QMV in the Council of Ministers, thereby undoing the effects of the empty chair crisis.

The internal market In a meeting in 1985, the European Council asked the Commission to make a timetable for the completion of the internal market. In that same year, the Commissioner for Trade and Industry produced a White Paper with a list of what still needed to be done and a timetable for completion that specified 1992 as the deadline. The to-do list included the harmonization of technical standards, opening up of public procurement to competition within the Community, free movement of capital, removal of barriers to free trade in services, harmonization of the rates of indirect taxation and the removal of physical frontier controls between Member States.[7] In the same year, a (new) Eurosummit adopted the White Paper, including its timetable. Moreover, it was decided to set up an intergovernmental conference to discuss the necessary changes. The conference made a plan that materialized in a draft for the Single European Act. Moreover, in December 1985 – still the same year – the European Council adopted this draft, which was consequently ratified by the national parliaments and entered into effect in July 1987.

Monetary union In 1969, during the The Hague Summit, the Community announced its intention to proceed to an EMU. A study group produced the 'Werner report', which proposed a three-stage procedure, leading to full integration in 1980. There would be fixed exchange rates between the European currencies, and ultimately a common currency might be adopted. Because of international financial turbulences, not much came out of this plan in the short term, but in 1978 the German and French heads of state proposed a revival of the old plans in the new shape of the European Monetary System (EMS). This system included the fixation of currency exchange rates within a relatively wide bandwidth, and – arguably more important – the creation of a new European currency unit, the ECU.

Late in the 1980s the more ambitious project of the EMU was revived, inspired mainly by the desire to reduce the transaction costs attached to exchange rate uncertainty. In this connection, different States had different priorities. The Germans were afraid that the stable monetary policies that are necessary for fixed exchange rates would not be realized by all participant Member States. To avoid this, they insisted on stringent fiscal criteria and independent (that is, technocratic) institutions to guard the project. France wanted fixed dates for the introduction of the monetary union, afraid that Germany would drop out, after all. Ireland, Portugal and Greece wanted support for weaker regions and countries, to allow them to meet the strict monetary demands that would be connected to fixed

---

7   Bache *et al.* 2015, p. 372.

exchange rates, or even a single currency.⁸ The final step towards EMU was made in the Treaty of Maastricht in 1992.

The Treaty of Maastricht Legally speaking, the Treaty on European Union (TEU; Treaty of Maastricht) represented a landmark in the progress of European integration. It contained the results of a long development, from the tentative creation of three communities during the 1950s and the early 1960s, the doldrums of the later 1960s and most of the 1970s, and the revival of the integration process in the 1970s and the 1980s. Although it did not officially put an end to the three communities, as a matter of fact it united them in the EU.

Moreover, it added two areas in which European integration had already taken place to some extent but had not yet been consolidated in the treaties. One of them was foreign relations and security policy, 'including the eventual framing of a common defence policy, which might in the end lead to a common defence'. The other one was cooperation in the spheres of justice and home affairs. This would include, among others, asylum and immigration policy, internal and external border controls and the combat of crime. On the institutional level, the TEU shifted legislative power to the European Parliament by adapting legislative procedures. Moreover, the scope of QMV in the Council of Ministers was expanded. On the economic and monetary front, the main features of EMU were defined, as well as a timetable for establishing it. The EMU included the introduction of the euro as a common currency and the establishment of a European Central Bank. And last but not least, the treaty introduced the concept of European citizenship.

All in all, an impressive list, and the worthy outcome of an optimistic period in post-World War II integration of Europe. However, it might seem that it was the last optimistic period.

2.9 THE EU IN CRISIS

It is now fashionable to state that the EU is in crisis.⁹ The crises that are often mentioned in this connection are the Eurozone crisis, the refugee crisis and Brexit. However, there is much to be said for the claim that these three are merely symptoms and that the 'real' crisis goes deeper. Until the Treaty of Maastricht and perhaps a few years following it, the EEC and the EU were growing, both in size (enlargement) and in the topics that they dealt with (deepening). There have been ups (the 1960s and the 1980s) and downs (the 1970s), but from an overall perspective, the integration of Europe went prosperously. Although it is

---

8   Nello 2012, p. 224.
9   *Cf.* the title of Desmond Dinan *et al.* 2017.

notoriously difficult to interpret recent history, it seems that somewhere during the 1990s this prosperous development came to a halt. The three aforementioned crises illustrate this reversal but do not constitute it: there is more than the three crises alone.

(Lack of) institutional reform The institutions of the EEC and the EU have a built-in tension between supranationalism and intergovernmentalism. The Commission, the European Parliament and – to some extent – the Court of Justice can be seen as supranationalist institutions; the Council of Ministers and the European Council represent the intergovernmentalist aspect of the EEC and the EU. The development of the EU has undeniably been towards less supranationalism and more intergovernmentalism and can, among other factors, be seen in the lack of institutional reform, even though such reform had become necessary.

A major reason why the institutions of the EU call for reform is the enlargement of the EU. The ECSC and the EEC started with six members, and even if all members had *de facto* veto power in the Council of Ministers – remember the empty chair crisis – this power would not stop necessary developments, because with only six Member States the opportunities for negotiating unanimity were manifold. However, after the Eastern enlargements, in which the number of EU Member States had increased to 28, the potential for reaching unanimity through negotiations had become much smaller. To some extent, this problem was addressed by introducing QMV in the Council of Ministers for still more topics. However, some crucial areas were still immune to collective decision-making, or even outside the competences of the EU altogether. This became clearly visible during the financial and the refugee crisis, when it turned out to be difficult to make the far-reaching decisions that were necessitated by the crises.

A smaller problem resulting from the enlargement, which is nevertheless illustrative for the underlying issue, has to do with the size of the Commission. Traditionally, there was a commissioner for each Member State, and two commissioners for Germany, France and Italy because these three countries had more inhabitants than the Benelux countries. The policy to let bigger Member States have two commissioners rather than one became counterproductive when the number of Member States increased. There are only mandates for a fixed number of commissioners, and as the EU grows, there will ultimately be superfluous commissioners. For this reason, it was decided at a Eurosummit in 2000 that from 2005 on each Member State could send only one member to the Commission. Moreover, from 2014 on, the size of the Commission would be reduced to two-thirds of the number of Member States. This last idea, pragmatic as it may seem, did not make it into the Lisbon Treaty. The one member-one commissioner rule was kept in the Treaty in order to facilitate an Irish approval in a referendum on the Treaty of Lisbon.[10] This illustrates that, in the end, many people and many countries see the EU as a tool to promote the national interests of their countries. European integration is a means to realize national ambitions rather than a goal worth pursuing for its own sake.

The 'transfer' of sovereignty Another illustration of this same point – that for most, if not all, Member States the EU is a means towards national goals, rather than a goal in itself – is the lack of willingness of Member States to give up a measure of their power and to empower the EU to formulate and execute the relevant policies. Mistakenly, this phenomenon is often described as the unwillingness of Member States to transfer more of their sovereignty to the EU.

There are several manifestations of this unwillingness. One of them is the reluctance of, in particular the bigger, Member States to give up control over their foreign policy and a fortiori over their armed forces. This is certainly not a new phenomenon. We have already seen that the initiative for a EDC failed in 1952 and dragged the EPC down in its wake. A common foreign and defence policy has officially been part of the EU policies only since the Treaty of Maastricht, but even then it turned out to be difficult for the EU members to follow a common policy during the civil war in the Balkans during the 1990s, the 'Arab Spring' and the civil wars that followed it, and when Russia invaded Crimea in 2014.

Another manifestation is that Member States have safeguarded their fiscal autonomy, even if and when they adopted the euro as a common currency. Monetary integration without corresponding economic integration, fiscal policy included, is not feasible. The financial crisis of 2007/8 might have been much milder if the EU had had a common fiscal policy.

A similar story can be told about the refugee crisis. For diverse reasons, millions of people sought refuge in the EU during the last decade.[11] Different EU Member States employed different policies when deciding whether and which refugees could find protection within their territories. Not all Member States were willing to comply with the policies that were formulated in EU circles. A result of this unwillingness to 'transfer' sovereignty is that the free movement of people between the Schengen countries was sometimes suspended.

---

10   Nugent 2010, p. 105.
11   *See* www.europarl.europa.eu/news/en/headlines/society/20170629STO78630/eu-migrant-crisis-facts-and-figures (last visited on 6 August 2019).

Unhappiness about the transfer of powers to the EU was most likely also one of the driving factors behind the result of the referendum in the UK on the basis of which it was decided that the UK would leave the EU (Brexit).

2.10 From Spillover to Spillback[12]

Spillover An important idea in the history of the EU is that the development of the European institutions would be guided by a phenomenon called 'spillover'. In general, spillover means that the full realization of one concern requires the realization of other, related matters. The general idea is well illustrated by a pyramid of glasses. There is a continuous stream of water into the glass at the top, and once this glass is full, the water flows over into the glasses on the second level, until the glasses in this layer are full and the water flows over into the glasses on the third level, and so on. When applied to the EU, spillover means that the realization of full cooperation in one field requires other forms of cooperation. For instance, in order to have a fully functional internal market, the impediment of different monetary currencies and continually changing exchange rates should be set aside. The main function of the introduction of the euro was to accomplish precisely this. However, a shared currency is possible only if there is a common economic policy, including social security and fiscal policy. This means that, strictly speaking, a common market requires economic integration.

Spillback European cooperation started on a relatively small scale, but was compelled by the intentions of some to grow through more and more cooperation into a fully fledged European economic and political community. The projected trajectory towards an ever closer union with spillover as the driving force is known as the *Monnet method* of integration, after the French public servant whose work laid the foundation for the ECSC and later the EU. However, if cooperation and integration in one field necessitate cooperation and integration in another field, and if the latter is deemed undesirable, the former will also be undesirable. The same force that drives the integration of Europe forward may also drive it back, if the final outcome is not considered acceptable. Spillover may mean that European integration is an all-or-nothing matter. And where some have hoped that it would turn out to be 'all' – a full European community - others see this as a reason to completely abandon the project of European integration. The spillover has then become spillback.

---

12   This section was adapted from Hage et al. 2017, Chapter 10, Section 9.1.

3 Theories of European Integration

Kinds of theories In this chapter some of the theories of European integration will be described and analysed. As will be seen, theorists are not always in agreement about how integration should take place (if at all) and how the integration that did take place should be explained. In this chapter we will discuss five different theories. However, we will see that these theories have different aims. Some are normative theories, which try to indicate why integration should take place. Others take the course of integration as their starting point, and try to give an explanation for the events as they actually occurred. Still other theories are interpretative, aiming to provide us with a better insight into the process of European integration by offering new interpretations of facts and events. The boundaries between the different kinds of theories are not always clear-cut. For a proper understanding and evaluation of the theories it is nevertheless important to keep in mind what their main purpose is.

3.1 Federalism

One reason to wage war, is to solve a conflict of interests. A simple way to avoid war is therefore to take the conflict away. A conflict can only exist if there are different agents: persons or States. If all the different agents were to be united into one single agent, there would not be agents with conflicting interests anymore, and therefore no cause for war.

This is the line of thought that underlies theories that seek to create peace in Europe by joining the different States into a single federation. These theories are normative: they neither *describe* what actually happened nor aim to *explain* a course of events but rather *prescribe* a particular line of action that should be taken. In this case, the line of action is to create a federation of (continental) European States. The reason why this line of action is prescribed is that this is the way to avoid another war in continental Europe.

3.1.1 The Ventotene Manifesto

One such theory was proposed in the *Ventotene Manifesto*. This document was written by Altiero Spinelli and Ernesto Rossi, when they were political prisoners in Italy during the fascist regime of Mussolini. The manifesto is named after the island on which the two were held captive and was written in June 1941; in the same year it was smuggled to the Italian mainland and published by the underground press. In 1943 Spinelli founded the European Federalist Movement, which adopted the manifesto as its programme.

The manifesto is quite optimistic – perhaps even naïve – about the role of federalism as a solution to many problems:

'The multiple problems which poison international life on the continent have proved to be insoluble: tracing boundaries through areas inhabited by mixed populations, defence of alien minorities, seaports for landlocked countries, the Balkan question, the Irish problem, and so on. All matters which would find easy solutions in the European Federation.'[1]

Part of this federalist view may be explained by Spinelli's roots in socialism, which at that time meant Marxism. The problem to be dealt with was the conflict between States, which, according to Marxist theory, promoted the interests of the ruling classes. A conflict between States is, from this perspective, a continuation on a larger scale of the competition between enterprises. Federalism as removal of the conflict of interests between States is comparable to the removal of the conflict between capitalists and proletarians by collectivizing the means of production.

This parallel between class struggle and the struggle between States would explain why Spinelli had doubts about leaving the step towards federalization to the States. States and their ruling classes would have an interest in safeguarding their own interests, and that would make them averse to rendering powers to a supranational level. The initiative to create a European federation should come from the people, who would immediately benefit from a European federation and who would have very little to lose.

If we replace the 'people' in this story with the 'proletariat', we have almost the Marxist story about the big communist revolution which would take the means of production from the capitalist class and put them into the hands of the workers. Still, the parallel between class struggle and the struggle between States is not completely correct, because the competition between enterprises is not the same as the class struggle between capitalists and proletarians. Yet, there is a connection, because if the workers would own the means of production, there would no longer be a need for competition between enterprises. Analogously, if the people would have the power, there would be no need for States anymore, and therefore no need for wars between States.

---

1 Quoted from Nelsen and Stubb 2003, p. 5.

However, it should be emphasized that Spinelli was not a revolutionary. On the one hand, he believed that States should play a role in the transition towards a European federation and that such a transition should be done within the confines of law. On the other hand, he was sceptical whether the representatives of States could be made willing to take the necessary steps, and there Spinelli saw a role for a people's movement to support the federalization of Europe.[2]

Looking back, we can see that Spinelli was correct in his view that traditional States would be reluctant to transfer powers to a supranational level. Whether a people's movement would have led to radically different results remains a matter of speculation. The rejection of a Constitution for Europe in French and Dutch referenda in 2005 does not give hope in this respect.

3.1.2 The Legal Perspective

The traditional way to look at a federation is from a legal point of view. A federal State is then defined in opposition to a unitary State. A unitary State has a central government, legislature and judiciary, which exercise authority over the whole State territory and with regard to every topic. In a federal State there is a central level – the federal level – with authority over the whole territory, but this authority is limited to a number of topics, for instance foreign relations and defence. Side by side with this federal level there are Sub-State levels where the administration, the legislature and the judiciary have authority over the territory of the Sub-State.[3] The authority of the Sub-States is typically limited to certain topics, and there must be a boundary that delineates the authority and powers of the Central State from those of the Sub-States. Whether a State is a federation (a federal State) is a legal matter, usually laid down in the Constitution of the federation. This Constitution also defines the powers of the federal level and the Sub-State level. For example, the German Constitution determines which legal powers belong to the German State (the federation) and which powers to the *Bundesländer*.

Characteristic of a federation is that the delineation of powers cannot be modified one-sidedly: the federal level and the Sub-States must all agree if the boundaries between their respective powers are to be modified. Moreover, a Sub-State cannot legally withdraw from

---

2   Pistone 2003.
3   Depending on the federation, the Sub-States go by different names, such as 'State' (USA), 'Land' (Germany), 'Kanton' (Switzerland), or 'Gewest' (Belgium).

the federation without a change in the Constitution, which typically requires the cooperation of both the federal level and the (other) Sub-States.[4]

Is the EU a federal State? The EU has many traits of a federal State, including the division between the central level and the sub-central levels and a division of the competences between the levels. However, as Article 50 of the TEU states and Brexit illustrates, Sub-States can withdraw from the EU without the cooperation of the EU and the other Sub-States.

Article 50 TEU states that:

> '1. Any Member State may decide to withdraw from the Union in accordance with its own constitutional requirements'

Moreover, the Sub-States have, via the European Council and the Council of Ministers, a decisive role in decision-making procedures on the central level. If the EU is a federal State, it is a rather exceptional one.

3.1.3 The Political Science Perspective: Federal Unions

It is also possible to look at federations from a political science perspective. From this perspective, the question whether some social entity is a federation is not primarily answered by means of legal rules, but by looking at what happens as a matter of fact. What are the relevant facts, then? In an essay entitled 'The Political Theory of Federalism: The Relevance of Classical Approaches',[5] Forsyth uses the expression 'federal union' to contrast federations in the political science sense from federations in the legal sense. He mentions three defining characteristics of federal unions:

1. A union between States means, first and foremost, that the relationships between the States exceed a certain threshold of intensity. In particular, if this intensity has as a consequence that the States of the group distinguish between 'us' (the States within the group) and 'them' (the States outside the group), the group has become a federal union.
2. The union manifests itself through a set of institutions that enable the union to act as one, both within the union and in relations with outsiders.
3. The union does not replace its members, but exists next to them.

---

4 See Heringa and Kiiver 2016, p. 63.
5 Forsyth 2003.

When measured against this standard, the EU has many traits of a federal union. Forsyth argues that this is a reason to look at the EU as if it were such a federal union, as this would increase our understanding of the Union. This makes his theory fundamentally an interpretative theory: the EU should be interpreted as (a kind of) federation. However, it is also part of Forsyth's message that if the EU 'really' is a kind of federation, it is better to treat it as a federation and to create the rules about the delineation of powers that a federation needs. To this extent, his theory is also a prescriptive one.

3.2   Functionalism

The approach that Monnet took to promote European integration – not to integrate countries, but rather a particular field of policy, the coal and steel sector to begin with – became known as the 'Monnet method'. One of the theories about European integration took this Monnet method as its starting point. The theory in question is called 'neo-functionalism' and will be discussed in the next section. As the name suggests, neo-functionalism is a more recent version of functionalism, and for a proper understanding of neo-functionalism, it is necessary to come to terms with the revolutionary ideas of functionalism and its underlying ideology: anarchism. That is the topic of this section.

Anarchism A society is the collection of all people in a particular territory who live together and interact with each other. A State is a particular kind of organization that claims the ultimate authority over a territory and the people inhabiting it. The defining characteristics of such a State are that a State is tied to a particular stretch of land, its territory, and that the State organization exercises (or claims to exercise) ultimate authority over this territory and its population. Anarchism is the view that societies are better organized without such a territorial organization and the hierarchy that it perpetuates.[6]

States tend to fulfil particular functions, such as keeping the peace, warding off foreign enemies and enforcing law. These three functions might be called the 'minimal State functions'. Frequently, States take up other tasks and responsibilities as well, such as providing infrastructure, healthcare, education and social security. Libertarians (extreme liberals) such as Robert Nozick (1938-2002) claim that a State only needs to fulfil the minimal State functions.[7] Anarchists claim that even for the minimal functions, a State – defined

---

6   Many think that there is a connection between anarchism and phenomena such as terrorist bombers, who want to overthrow the government and to create chaos. That is a misunderstanding; anarchism is a respectable political philosophy and should not be associated with terrorism.
7   Nozick 1974.

as a territorial organization – can be missed. In their view, other organizations can do the job better.[8]

Functionalism Suppose that there were a society without a State. Which organization should then fulfil the functions that are traditionally fulfilled by the State?

The question itself is misleading, because it presupposes that there must be *one* organization fulfilling all the functions that were originally attributed to the State. Why can there not be many different organizations, for many different tasks? This is the idea that underlies functionalism and that also circulated among some defenders of anarchism. A State is defined in terms of a territory, but many functions that a State fulfils are not necessarily tied to territory.

Functionalists believe that organizations should be defined in terms of the functions they fulfil rather than by the territory on which they fulfil their functions. Moreover, the territory on which organizations fulfil their functions should be determined by the nature of the function, and not by the borders that particular States happen to have. Mitrany (1888-1975), the most famous proponent of functionalism, suggests, for example, that aviation and broadcasting – the Internet would be a modern equivalent – should have a worldwide organization, while transport by train should be organized on the level of continents.[9]

Following this line of thinking, primary education, because it contains a major linguistic component, should be organized close to the people, as languages depend on the close interrelations between people who share and thereby also determine the language. The same holds – to a slightly lesser degree – if we think of expensive hospital equipment, which needs to be shared in a system of healthcare. The best level for organizing social security might depend on the degree of solidarity between people. How far can other people live and still be recognized as one's neighbour?[10]

---

8   One reason why anarchists are opposed to having States as a form of territorial organisation is derived from the Marxist idea that the State, as a law-enforcing agency, will necessarily become an instrument in the hands of the ruling class. The October Revolution in Russia (1917) was interpreted by many of its contemporaries as the long-awaited communist revolution in which the workers took possession of the means of production. After this revolution, there was a discussion between the leader of the revolution, Lenin, and some anarchists. Lenin (1917) wanted to maintain the State apparatus, as it was in the hands of the workers now. It could be used to do useful things for all the people (and not only the capitalists). The anarchists were opposed to this, because they feared that the State would merely become an instrument in the hands of the new ruling class.
9   Mitrany 2003.
10 The use of the term 'neighbour' here is no coincidence. People tend to have compassion with other people to whom they somehow feel related, and the degree in which they feel related depends, amongst others, on

The general picture that arises is that of a set of organizations with a different territorial scope that partially overlap with each other. Perhaps there must also be 'meta-organizations' that deal with the cooperation between primary organizations. For example, it would be preferable if there were some mutual alignment between the ways in which aviation and railroads were organized. The nature of those meta-organizations would depend on the nature of the organizations that they have to coordinate, and there is no guarantee that a territorial definition is appropriate for meta-organizations. In other words, States may be useful, but whether this is the case depends on the circumstances.

The role of States This picture leaves little room for States as we presently know them. For Mitrany this is an advantage. The title of one of his publications is *Towards a Working Peace System* (1966). He considered functional organization as an alternative for territorial organization. This alternative would make States superfluous. Because Mitrany saw war as a conflict between States about territory, functionalism would not only lead to a more efficient performance of tasks, but would also eliminate the main cause of war.

The nature of functionalism Functionalism does not describe how the world is actually organized: the present world is primarily organized along territorial rather than functional lines. Functionalism is a normative theory: it indicates how the world *should* be organized in order to make it work more efficiently and to avoid wars.

3.3 NEO-FUNCTIONALISM

The ECSC was an example of sectorial integration. Cooperation between people was organized on the basis of a particular economic sector – coal and steel – and not on the basis of the country the people lived in. Replace the word 'sector' in 'sectorial integration' by 'function', and sectorial integration becomes a variant of functionalism.

Where functionalism is a normative theory, neo-functionalism aims to be an explanatory theory. The original theorists whose work is labelled as 'neo-functionalist' had an explanation of the developments on the European continent as their objective. These original theorists were political scientists situated in the US. Here we will focus on the work of Haas, whose book *The Uniting of Europe* has almost become the Bible of neo-functionalism.

---

the physical distance between them. Compassion translates into solidarity and willingness to help others in need, without seeing these others as free riders.

A similar phenomenon can be found in tort law, where the question arises as to whom a person owes a duty of care. The English rule that deals with this issue is called the 'neighbour rule' for a good reason: physical proximity is one of the factors that determine the scope of the duty of care.

Not coincidentally, *The Uniting of Europe* appeared in its first edition in 1958. The ECSC had already been in existence a few years and was in full swing. The negotiations about the EDC and the EPC had taken place and had even led to comprehensive treaty texts, even though the treaties never entered into force. Finally, the treaty establishing the EEC was being negotiated while Haas' book was written. There was something spectacular going on in continental Europe: a supranational organization was created next to the States participating in this organization. This was a phenomenon without a proper precedent and therefore also a phenomenon that asked for explanation. Haas' aim was to provide such an explanation.

Integration as a process Characteristically, political integration is, in the definition of Haas, not a state of affairs, but a process:

> '[Political integration is the] process whereby nations forgo the desire and ability to conduct foreign and key domestic policies independently of each other, seeking instead to make joint decisions or to delegate the decision-making process to new central organs.'[11]

Apparently, political integration is, according to Haas, not a complete replacement of territorial organizations by functional ones. If the new central organs to which Haas refers are functionally defined – which we may assume, since Haas has the ECSC and its High Authority in mind – political integration is a process of increasing cooperation between nations (peoples, not States) and functional organizations.

Several factors would interact in this connection as causes of the integration:
1. Growing economic interdependence between the integrating nations.
2. The rise of supranational organizations that can handle disputes and build international legal regimes.
3. Supranational market rules that replace the rules of the individual nations.[12]

These three causes seem to be taken directly from the development of the ECSC. The Member States of the Coal and Steel Community all depended – among others – on steel production, for which coal was needed. They needed to cooperate to facilitate this use of coal and the production of steel. Where cooperation exists, disputes will arise. The organs of the ECSC were also meant to handle these disputes. Moreover, the ECSC issued rules

---

11   Quoted after Ilievski 2015.
12   *See* https://en.wikipedia.org/wiki/Neofunctionalism (last visited on 25 August 2018).

in connection with coal and steel production that superseded the rules of the Member States.

Spillover Spillover would play an important role in this connection. Integration in one economic sector would make integration in other sectors desirable. We have already seen the example that free trade is served by fixed exchange rates between currencies and that fixed exchange rates make common fiscal policies desirable. This means that if the seed of integration has been sewn in a particular sector (e.g. the coal and steel industry), and if this seed sprouts, there will be a source for integration that may spread to increasingly more sectors of society.

Transfer of loyalty Another factor would be a transfer of loyalty from national to transnational organizations. Neo-functionalists claim that as the process of integration gathers pace, interest groups and associations will transfer their allegiances away from national institutions and towards the supranational European institutions. They will do this, because they will come to realize that these newly formed institutions are a better conduit through which to pursue their material interests.

For example, the car industry will lobby for subsidies not only with the national government but, to an increasing extent, also in Brussels. They expect more from the European Commission than from national governments, if only because these governments are no longer allowed to subsidize national industries of their own volition.

Non-governmental agents An important aspect of the neo-functionalist theory of integration is that integration is driven not only, and perhaps not even primarily, by States and their governmental representatives. It is interest groups, both commercial and non-commercial, that interact. They promote their interests across traditional borders and, in doing so, transfer their loyalties to supranational organizations.

We have already seen the example of the car industry as a commercial interest group. An example of a non-commercial group would be the environmentalists, who need transborder cooperation to achieve an efficacious environmental policy.

This was already seen by Haas, who wrote that

> 'The "good Europeans" are not the main creators of the regional community that is growing up; the process of community formation is dominated by nationally constituted groups with specific interests and aims, willing and able

to adjust their aspirations by turning to supranational means when this course appears profitable.'[13]

Technocratic automatism As integration proceeds, the technocratic supranational bodies become more powerful and independent of the Member States. They will take the lead in promoting further integration. This idea is embodied in the prerogative of the Commission to initiate EU regulation.

Functionalism or federalism? It may seem that the neo-functionalist account of integration can easily be transferred from the ECSC to the EEC. However, this is not obvious. The ECSC was an organization that was defined in terms of the function it had to fulfil, that is to organize the coal and steel business. Perhaps the same might be said about the EEC in its primacy, when it was first and foremost aimed at economic integration. However, the EEC soon collected more tasks, and as this happened, it became increasingly difficult to see it as a functional organization. Clearly, the EEC did fulfil functions, but, just like an ordinary State, it fulfilled many different functions. Moreover, the ties to a particular territory (that of its Member States) became stronger than its ties to a particular function. Even if the EEC never became a federation in the legal sense, it arguably became a federal union in the sense of Forsyth, more than a functional organization.

Limited tenability The overall picture that arises from the neo-functionalist theory is that integration is driven both by States and by private organizations. If there are supranational functional organizations, the transfer of loyalty to them gives these organizations more power, and in turn they use this power to effect further integration. Moreover, through spillover effects, the integration spreads like an ink stain from one sector of society to others. Integration becomes an almost autonomous process.

The peak of neo-functionalism was at the end of the 1950s and the beginning of the 1960s, when the ECSC flourished and new European communities were being negotiated. The feeling existed that something new was in the making, and this attracted the attention of integration theorists. We have already seen that this optimism faded later in the 1960s, and Ernst Haas even called neo-functionalism in 1975 an 'obsolete' theory. Seemingly, neo-functionalism had only a limited tenability.

Later we will discuss the scientific tenability of theories such as neo-functionalism. However, first we will consider intergovernmentalism as a theory that seemingly better accounts for the delay in European integration that occurred in the 1970s.

---

13   Quoted after Bache *et al.* 2015, p. 12.

3.4 INTERGOVERNMENTALISM

Events in the 1960s, such as the empty chair crisis, fuelled theories that denied the autonomous development of European integration. Prominent among these alternative theories was the intergovernmentalism defended by Hoffman. Just as Haas' work on the uniting of Europe fit the events in the 1950s perfectly, the crucial papers written by Hoffman appeared in 1964 and in 1966, when De Gaulle chose to deny the automated neo-functionalist process of ever further integration.

Hoffman's views, which may be interpreted as a criticism of neo-functionalism, can be summarized in a few main points[14]:
1. European integration is not an autonomous process that can be analysed in isolation of what happens elsewhere in the world. It is an aspect of the development of the global international system, and its explanation requires reference to international politics.
2. In the explanation of European integration, national governments play a crucial role, which is more important than that of private agents. Moreover, in their control of the integration process, governments are guided by the protection of national interests. In other words: integration is not a goal in itself, but a means towards the promotion of the national interest.
3. Even if integration is a means towards national interests, this need not stop integration in sectors that are merely technical, such as trade or regional development. However, this becomes different in areas of 'high politics', such as foreign policy, national security and defence. In these sectors, States are not willing to transfer their power to supranational organizations such as the EEC. We can see this, for example, in the resistance of De Gaulle against the UK becoming a member of the EEC, as this would change the balance of power within the EEC and would give the US as an ally of the UK more influence on the European continent.

In summary According to Hoffmann's intergovernmentalism, European integration is driven by national governments that promote their national interests. Close cooperation between States can contribute to these interests, but especially in areas of 'high politics', it is in the national interest to keep the decision-making power in the hands of the States themselves. The exercise of powers by national governments is constrained by the events on the world stage. European integration is not autonomous but is part of worldwide international developments.

---

14 Inspired by Bache *et al.* 2015, pp. 13-14. Later it will be argued that intergovernmentalism is better seen as an amendment to neo-functionalism, rather than as an alternative.

3.5 Some Defining Distinctions

Kinds of theories This chapter hinges on distinctions. One major distinction is between normative, explanatory and interpretative theories of European integration. This is, in principle, a clear distinction, but the actual theories do not fall nicely into each of the three categories.

Legal versus sociological Another important distinction is between theories that focus on the legal aspects of European integration and theories that focus on the sociological aspects. This distinction is best seen in the contrast between Spinelli's and Forsyth's federalism. Spinelli's plea was for a legal organization of Europe according to the model of a federation. That would mean a distinction between a central (European) layer and a decentralized layer of States, and a corresponding division of competences and tasks. Forsyth did not, in the first place, plead for a particular model, but thought that if we look closely at the way Europe actually functions (the sociological or political science perspective), we can recognize the characteristics of what he called a 'federal union'.

Automatic versus decision-based A third distinction is between theories that emphasize the 'automatic' process of European integration and theories that claim that the development of European integration is a matter of explicit decisions. This distinction is a major point of difference between neo-functionalism, with its emphasis on automatic spillover, and intergovernmentalism, which points to the crucial role of decisions that can, but need not, be taken by States.

Political and non-political agents The distinction between automatic and decision-based processes goes hand in hand with the distinction between political and non-political agents. According to neo-functionalism, the process of European integration would – if the proper setting of competent functional agents were available – be automatic in the sense that it would be driven by non-political agents. Such agents would include commercial enterprises as well as lobbying groups for immaterial interests such as the environment. According to intergovernmentalism, the process of integration is not automatic but requires decisions that are made by political agents, with a crucial role for national governments.

Ideal types This chapter discussed two theories that aim to explain European integration: neo-functionalism and intergovernmentalism. In the next section we will take a closer look at these two theories from the perspective of the philosophy of science. In doing so, we will identify serious deficiencies in both of these theories.

However, the theories may nevertheless be illuminating if they are seen as idealized descriptions of two different ways in which European integration can take place.[15] One way is described by neo-functionalism and emphasizes the automatism of spillover and the role of non-political agents in the integration in Europe. The other way is described by intergovernmentalism and emphasizes the role of political decisions, taken by the governments of the EU Member States.

Some steps in the integration process illustrate the neo-functionalist view, while other steps illustrate the intergovernmentalist perspective. The function of the ideal types is to draw our attention to particularly relevant aspects of the events that take place. The distinctions that were mentioned in this section can help to recognize these aspects.

3.6 Evaluation

What to think of these theories about European integration?

3.6.1 Functionalism and Legal Federalism

Functionalism and legal federalism are prescriptive theories: they propose to organize society (functionalism), or Europe (legal federalism), in a particular way in order to achieve a better, and in particular a more peaceful, society. This means that a functional organization of society or a federal structure for Europe is seen as a means towards a goal. Their justification lies in the fact, if it is one, that they contribute to peace.

Conditions for goal-based justification If such a justification is to be successful, several conditions must be met:
1. *A valuable goal.* A goal can justify a means only if the goal itself is valuable or justified. Peace can justify a federal structure for Europe only if peace itself is valuable. Given the horrors of the World Wars, there will be little doubt about the value of peace.
2. *Efficacious means.* A goal can justify a means only if the means leads to, or at least promotes, the goal. If a federal structure for Europe does not prevent war, and does not even reduce the likelihood of war, the intended achievement of peace cannot justify this structure.
3. *No better means.* A goal can justify a particular means only if there is no alternative, better, way to achieve the goal. For instance, if an absolute monarchy were to be a more

---

15 This way of looking at the theories was suggested to me by Janwillem Oosterhuis in personal conversation.

efficacious means to ensure peace in Europe than having a federation, the fact that a federation would contribute to peace does not justify the introduction of a federal Europe. The reason is that an absolute monarchy works even better, and is not compatible with federalism. This condition is familiar in law as the demand of *subsidiarity*.
4. *Means not worse than missing the goal*. A means should be compared not only with alternative means, but also with the goal itself, or rather to the possibility that the goal is not achieved. Suppose – to change the example a little – that a functional organization of society is even worse than having a war in Europe. In that case such an organization cannot be justified by the fact that it would prevent war. 'Better a war than functionalism!' would then hold. This condition is familiar in law as the demand of *proportionality*.
5. *Goal more important than negative side effects*. The use of a means to achieve a goal can have negative side effects. For instance, if a functional organization of society leads to peace, but also to a much lower level of services in society, a balance must be struck between the negative side effects and the achievement of the goal. Is peace worth the lower level of services? This is a *cost-benefit trade-off*. It must be mentioned, though, that positive side effects should also be weighed in this cost-benefit trade-off.

This is not the place to use these conditions for an actual evaluation of legal federalism and functionalism as means to achieve and maintain peace in Europe. An actual evaluation of this kind would require much factual information that is presently not available. However, the conditions do provide us with clues on what kind of information we should look out for.

3.6.2   Sociological Federalism

Forsyth designated the EU as a 'federal union'. In calling the EU so, he wanted to do at least three things:
1. admit that the EU is not a federation in the strict legal sense;
2. claim that the actual EU has much in common with what the EU would have been, had it been a federation in the legal sense;
3. use this claim to support another claim: the EU should (for many purposes) be treated as if it were a legal federation.

We categorized Forsyth's sociological federalism primarily as an interpretative theory: it is, first and foremost, meant as a proposal to see the EU in a particular way, namely as a kind of federation as a matter of sociological (or political) fact. How can we evaluate such an interpretative theory?

It is difficult to evaluate an interpretation – and therefore also the interpretation of the EU as a kind of federation – independently. An interpretation is attractive, or good, if it is part of a larger theory that is attractive or good. The goodness of this larger theory is then, by way of speaking, 'inherited' by the interpretative theory that is attached to it.

Let us become more concrete. Forsyth wants to see the EU as a kind of federation (interpretation) to support the claim that the EU should also be treated as a federation (prescription). This latter view is a prescriptive theory, just like functionalism and legal federalism. However, the latter two theories were means to promote peace, and their evaluation was therefore based on the success in promoting this goal. Forsyth's proposal was meant to make the EU function better as a federation. A federation needs particular kinds of rules to function well, and legal federations normally have these rules. A 'functional union' such as the EU may lack some of the rules that a federation needs, but by interpreting the EU as a kind of federation, the claim is supported that the EU should have these rules too. The issue at stake then becomes whether the EU functions better if it is treated as a legal federation than if it is not.

Most likely, the rules that govern legal federations are in place because they make these federations function better. So from this point of view it is most likely better to treat the EU as a full-blown federation if it already has so many of its traits. However, the rules for federations assume that we already have a federation. In the case of the EU there is much resistance against a full-blown federation, the 'United States of Europe'. So perhaps it is better not to treat the EU as a legal federation. There is a trade-off between the advantages of the rules that make federations function smoothly and the resistance against a full-blown European federation. The outcome of this trade-off is highly relevant for the question of whether the EU should be interpreted as a kind of federation.

3.6.3 Neo-functionalism and Intergovernmentalism

Both neo-functionalism and intergovernmentalism aim to explain the process of (non-)-integration in Europe. Intergovernmentalism began as a criticism of neo-functionalism and may therefore be seen as an alternative to the latter. However, on closer inspection it is rather a complement. Neo-functionalism is based on the idea that if sufficiently powerful functional organizations are available, there will be an automatic transfer of loyalty by societal agents from governmental and territorial organizations to these functional – and therefore non-territorial – organizations. It will be automatic, in the sense that no State action is required to bring about the predicted transfer of loyalty. Spillover effects would even strengthen this shift of power from governmental to functional organizations.

European Integration: A Theme

Hoffman's intergovernmentalism did not claim that this theory was fundamentally wrong, but merely that neo-functionalism had to operate within a governmental and international setting. Yes, there might be an 'automatic' process in which ever more powers are moved to functional organizations, but in the end it is States that determine the extent to which this process is possible. In this connection two factors would be highly relevant. One is international relations, the field of powers in which States must operate and that strongly influences State behaviour. The other is the phenomenon of 'high politics', the area in which States want to maintain their power and will not allow these powers to slip away to functional organizations. Within these confines of international and 'high' politics, States can allow an increase in the power of functional organizations. This means that intergovernmentalism presupposes neo-functionalism: the distinction between areas in which governments are willing or not willing to give up their power is possible only against a background where the exercise of non-governmental power is possible. In other words, there must be areas in which neo-functionalism seems to hold if intergovernmentalism is the correct explanatory theory of European integration.

Is intergovernmentalism the correct explanation, and are there areas in which neo-functionalism seems to be so? These questions can be answered only if we know what explanation is and how we can distinguish 'the' correct explanation – if there is one – from incorrect explanations, or even non-explanations. In the next chapter, we will address the nature and purposes of explanation and the setting in which it fulfils its role and apply the results to neo-functionalism and intergovernmentalism.

4 Explanation and Understanding

In the previous chapter about integration theories, we encountered two theories that aim to explain the (non-)integration of the European countries and economies. We argued that these two theories, neo-functionalism and intergovernmentalism, are not real competitors, but that intergovernmentalism is best seen as an amendment to neo-functionalism. It explains why the latter theory works better in some areas (low politics) than in others (high politics) and why States and international politics remain important factors in the process of European integration.

We also raised the questions of whether the two theories provide 'good' explanations for the (non-)integration of the European countries and economies and whether they lead to a 'real' understanding of what goes on. These questions can be answered only if we know what explanation and understanding are. As a little reflection will make clear, it is not easy to tell what it is to explain or to understand something, let alone what makes for a good explanation, or for real understanding. The purpose of this chapter is to explain what explanation and understanding are and to create a better understanding of these two phenomena.

Overview The discussion of explanation and understanding starts in Section 4.1 with the question of the nature of understanding and its relation to explanation. Section 4.2 introduces the nomological-deductive (ND) model of explanation and its application, both in the physical sciences and in legal science. Section 4.3 explores how the ND model of explanation fits into the empirical cycle. At the end the findings are applied to intergovernmentalism. Section 4.4 is an intermezzo that addresses the question of how scientific theories differ from non-scientific ones. Because the ND model is less suitable for the explanation of human behaviour, Section 4.5 discusses teleological explanation as an alternative and extends this description to goal-based and functional explanation. Section 4.6 applies the findings of the chapter to the explanatory integration theories and Section 4.7 concludes the chapter.

4.1 The Relationship between Explanation and Understanding

The notions of understanding and ND explanation are closely connected, and different views on what understanding is may lead to different views on explanation, or the other way around. We will discuss two notions of understanding and two notions of explanation that match them.

Mechanistic and purposive understanding The first notion of understanding is 'mechanistic understanding'. According to this notion, understanding consists in a grasp of how different facts and events hang together and how the one kind of fact leads to the other. In the words of the methodologist of the social sciences John Elster, we look for the 'mechanism' that connects the facts and events.[1] This inspired the name 'mechanistic understanding'. Examples of this way of understanding are to grasp why a piece of metal that was heated expanded and why a person who shoplifted was liable to be fined by the police.

Connected to this notion of understanding is the model of explanation where a fact or event is explained from other facts and a 'law' that connects them. For instance, the expansion of the metal bar is explained from the fact that it was heated and the physical *law* that metals expand when heated. Or the liability to be fined was explained with reference to the fact that the punished person was caught shoplifting and the legal *rule* that shoplifting is punishable with a fine.[2]

A special case of mechanistic understanding is the understanding of human behaviour on the basis of the intentions or the purpose of the acting person. We will call it 'purposive understanding'. To illustrate this notion, we will use the examples of a lady who puts on a black dress when she attends a funeral and of John who opens the door when the bell rings.

Purposive understanding is connected to 'teleological' explanation, where actions are explained from the intentions of the agent. For example, the fact that the lady put on a black dress is explained from her intention to show respect for the deceased person and the fact that John opened the door when the bell rang is explained from his intention to let his date in.

Purposive understanding is more shallow than understanding based on a law. One of the reasons why this is the case is that purposive understanding is 'myopic'. If understanding becomes very shallow, it is little more than a certain tranquillity of mind.

---

1   *See* Elster 2007, pp. 32-51.
2   As will be discussed later, in mechanistic explanations (legal) rules play a role that is similar to the role of physical laws in the physical sciences.

Cognitive dissonance In our minds we store a multitude of beliefs about the world. Some of these beliefs are quite ordinary, such as the belief that every half hour a train leaves from Maastricht Central Station in the direction of Eindhoven. Other beliefs are highbrow, such as the scientific belief that the space component of the travel of light through the space-time-continuum is zero, the metaphysical belief that every event has a cause, or the religious belief that people can deserve a good afterlife by obeying God's commands during their 'ordinary' lives. Beliefs can exist, even if we are not constantly aware of them. For instance, most people have firm beliefs about their age, but on most days they do not even think of their age.

If we believe something, this is no guarantee that what we believe is true. Many of our beliefs will be true, but some of them will be false. We have so many beliefs that it should come as a surprise if they were all consistent. We also believe many inconsistent things, but most often we are not even aware of it. Actually, as soon as we become aware that our beliefs are inconsistent, we try to remove the inconsistency by abandoning (at least) one of the beliefs.

We also try to avoid having any inconsistencies in our beliefs. The psychologist Festinger devised a term for this phenomenon: we try to avoid 'cognitive dissonance'.[3] This sometimes even goes so far that we refuse to believe new information if that conflicts with what we already thought to be the case. For example, if Jane thinks that at every half hour a train leaves from Maastricht Central Station to Eindhoven and if her friend informs her that today there will be no train to Eindhoven at 15h30, she will be tempted not to believe her friend. This is an innocent example, but there are more serious ones. Leaders may be unwilling to change their organizations when it is pointed out to them that they do not function optimally, as this would contradict their original view on how to run the organization. Bad policies are continued by governments, because they do not want to admit that they were wrong, and so on.

Psychological understanding Having inconsistent beliefs does not have to be mentally disturbing, but being aware of inconsistencies in one's belief set leads to cognitive dissonance and the mental discomfort that goes with it. As soon as somebody discovers such an inconsistency, she realizes that somehow she lacks understanding. For example, Jane does not understand how it is possible that there will be no train to Eindhoven at 15h30, while there is a train every half hour. She is puzzled, and this feeling of puzzlement signals a lack of understanding.

---

3   *See* Festinger 1957.

A lack of understanding arises only if a person comes to realize that her beliefs are inconsistent, because then she will experience cognitive dissonance. This means that the account of (non-)understanding that is offered here is essentially a psychological account. Therefore, we will call the kind of understanding at issue here 'psychological' understanding. Psychological understanding differs from mechanistic understanding, because it is a kind of tranquillity of mind that does not require that a fact be situated in a mechanistic chain of events or other facts.

4.2 The Nomological-Deductive Model of Explanation

During the 1950s, two philosophers of science, Hempel and Oppenheim, developed an influential model of scientific explanation that was primarily meant for the physical sciences.[4] For reasons that we will soon encounter, the model was called the ND model of explanation, although other names such as the hypothetical-deductive model, or even the Hempel-Oppenheim model, are also in use.

4.2.1 Explanation as Logical Derivation

The basic idea underlying the ND model is quite simple: explanation is nothing more than a logical derivation. It is the details of the derivation that make it into an explanation or – as we will see – a prediction.

Example Let us study a simple example to get a grip on the model in question.

Metals expand when heated (*nomos*).

This is a piece of metal and it was heated (*explanans*).

This piece of metal expanded (*explanandum*).

The three foregoing sentences embody a logical argument. The first two sentences are the premises of the argument. From these two premises, the third sentence is derived as a conclusion. The argument can function as an explanation if one interprets the facts

---

4   Hempel 1966, pp. 47-69.

expressed by one of the two premises – the *explanans* – together with the law (*nomos*) mentioned in the other premise, as explanation of the fact expressed by the conclusion. The explanation then consists in relating the fact that is to be explained – the *explanandum* – to the facts that do the explaining on the basis of a physical law.

Elaboration The third sentence describes a fact: this piece of metal expanded. This is the fact that needs to be explained. The second sentence describes two facts: that this is a piece of metal and that it was heated. These two facts together explain why the piece of metal expanded. The *explanans* can only explain the *explanandum* if there is a physical law that connects the two. In this case the law reads that metals expand when heated. The Greek word for law is *nomos*.

Deduction An explanatory argument must be a deductive argument. In this context, being deductive means applying a law to initial facts in order to explain or predict new facts.[5] Let us take our example of heating a piece of metal again. The law that metals expand when heated is applied to the initial facts, that this is a piece of metal and that it is heated, to derive the new fact that this piece of metal expands. Since an explanatory argument must have this logical form – it must be deductive – the model is called 'nomological-deductive'.

4.2.2 What is a Law?

A crucial aspect of a scientific explanation is that it contains a physical law. To see why this is the case, we will look at an argument that looks a bit like an explanation but in fact is not an explanation as it does not contain a law.

All students in this class have a brown skin.

Frank is a student and he is in this class.

Frank has a brown skin.

---

5   In formal logic, being deductive is not a kind of argument, but an evaluation of an argument on the basis of the standard for deduction. So, logically speaking, an argument is not deductive, but deductively *valid*. According to this standard, an argument is (deductively) valid if and only if it is logically impossible that all the premises of the argument are true, while the argument's conclusion is false. *See*, for instance, Hodges 1977, p. 55.

This is a deductive argument, just like the argument about the expanding piece of metal. It has a conclusion: Frank has a brown skin. It also has a premise expressing two facts, and there is a general statement, combining the factual premise and the conclusion.

However, the general statement in this case does not express a law. There is no inherent connection between, on the one hand, being a student and being in this class and, on the other hand, having a brown skin. That all students in this class have a brown skin is merely a coincidence. And because it is merely a coincidence, the facts that Frank is a student and that he is in this class cannot *explain* why he has a brown skin. The conclusion follows from the two premises; that is not the issue. However, the argument is not an *explanatory* argument because the first premise is merely a description of a fact; it does not express a law that connects facts.

What, then, distinguishes a law from a mere description? The crucial difference is that a description is true or false, depending on what the facts are. The facts are there first, and the truth of the description depends on them. However, if there is a law, it *influences* the facts. That the piece of metal in the first example expanded was *caused* by the law. Laws influence the facts, while descriptive sentences merely describe the facts. This difference between influencing (causing) and merely describing means that arguments containing a law can explain, while similar arguments with a mere description cannot. The facts that Frank is a student and that he is in this class do not make his skin brown. That is why the former two facts cannot explain the latter fact.

4.2.3 Legal Explanation

The ND model was developed primarily with a causal explanation in mind. However, quite soon attempts were made to also use it for statistical explanation. (Why do many people fall ill when exposed to other people with Ebola?) and for explanation of historical and social phenomena. Moreover, the ND model can also be used for legal explanation.

Use of the ND model for legal explanation There is a big similarity between the use of the ND model for causal explanation and the use of 'legal syllogism' to explain – and also to justify – the legal consequences of a concrete case.[6] Let us consider a somewhat simplified example:

---

6   A more extensive discussion of this 'legal syllogism' can be found in Hage 2017.

Thieves are punishable (law; *nomos*)

John is a thief (initial facts; *explanans*)

John is punishable (legal consequence; *explanandum*)

This argument explains why John is punishable: he is a thief and thieves are punishable. The argument uses a law, so it is deductive. This time the law is not causal, but a legal rule. However, for the structure of the argument this difference does not matter. The law is applied to initial facts and connects these facts to the fact that needs explaining. The argument is still 'nomological', and the explanation of the fact that John is punishable is a good example of an ND explanation.

Legal prediction and justification The argument can also be used to predict legal consequences: if John commits theft, he will be punishable. And, finally, the model can be used to justify legal consequences: the judgment that John is punishable is justified by the rule that thieves are punishable and the fact that John is a thief.

Legal laws cannot be falsified empirically Although there is a big similarity between the use of the ND model in causal and in legal explanation, there is also an important difference. Because the law is legal, it cannot be falsified by the observation that John is not punishable. If John is not punishable, even though he is a thief, there must be some *legal* reason for it.

Legal rules cannot be falsified by the observation that they are not complied with, or that their legal consequences are not recognized. Nevertheless, non-compliance and non-recognition of legal consequences may be treated as signs that these laws lack popular support. In turn this may be a reason to change these laws. However, changing existing laws is not the same as showing that they are untrue.

Legal and causal consequences It is important, however, to distinguish the example of legal explanation from the following causal explanation:

Thieves are punished (law; *nomos*)

John is a thief (initial facts; *explanans*)

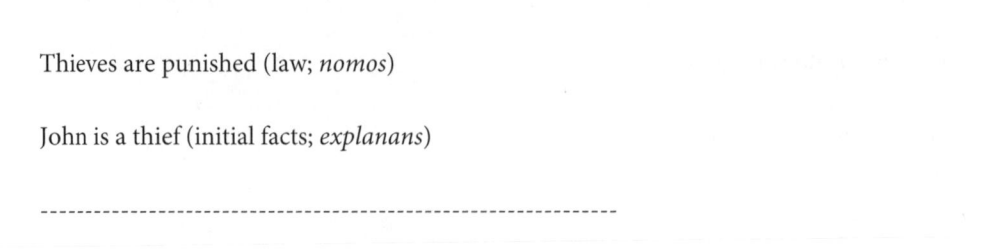

John is punished (social consequence; *explanandum*)

In this explanation, the legal law is replaced by a causal law: theft leads to punishment. This is actual punishment, not legal liability to be punished. If John is observed not to be actually punished, this would falsify the causal law.

Justificatory, explanatory and predictive use of legal rules As we can see from these examples, legal rules can be used to justify, to explain and to predict. In their explanatory and predictive role, it is important to distinguish between the explanation and the prediction of legal consequences, and the explanation and prediction of physical events. The legal rules as such are used to explain and predict legal consequences, for example that John is punishable. On the assumption that legal rules are, or will be complied with, the rules indirectly also play a role in explaining and predicting physical events, such as the event that John will actually be punished for his theft.

4.3 The Scientific (Empirical) Cycle

This section is dedicated to a simplified description of how scientific theories are developed. It deals with a generalized version of what is more generally known as the 'empirical cycle', because the ideas about this cycle were developed with the empirical sciences in mind. Knowledge of the empirical cycle is important for lawyers for at least two reasons:
1. The way in which a theory is constructed, including the use of the empirical cycle, is important for determining whether the theory is a scientific one. This theme will be developed in the next full section.
2. Empirical knowledge is relevant to lawyers, in particular when the issue at stake is whether a legal rule is good or whether it has the consequences for which the rule was created. Suppose that a State makes a rule that forbids the possession of certain substances (drugs) to protect public health. Then it is important to know whether this prohibition, which limits the freedom of the population, actually promotes public health. This knowledge is empirical, and the use of the empirical cycle is relevant to the acquisition of such knowledge.

4.3.1 A Priori and Empirical

Sciences can, very coarsely, be divided into sciences in which sensory perception plays a central role and sciences where this is not the case. The former sciences are called 'empirical'; the latter non-empirical, or *a priori*. Mathematics is the prototypical example of a non-empirical science, and the same holds for doctrinal legal science, but by far most sciences are empirical.

A priori (before) is the opposite of *a posteriori* (after). The 'before' and 'after' relate to sensory experience. An a priori science is done preceding sensory perception. An a posteriori science is done on the basis of sensory perception. The latter is also called 'empirical', with a replacement of the Latin *a posteriori* by a term based on the Greek noun *empeiria*, which stands for 'experience'.

4.3.2 Steps in the Empirical Cycle

The empirical cycle is called a cycle – spiral would have been more appropriate – because it is based on the presumption that empirical sciences consist of a cycle of observation, law formulation, deduction and prediction, testing (observation), evaluation (choice) and – perhaps – formulation of a better law (Figure 4.1). If everything works out well, the end point of such a cycle is a better theory than that from which the cycle started. However, it is still a theory, which can perhaps be improved in a new cycle. And so on …

European Integration: A Theme

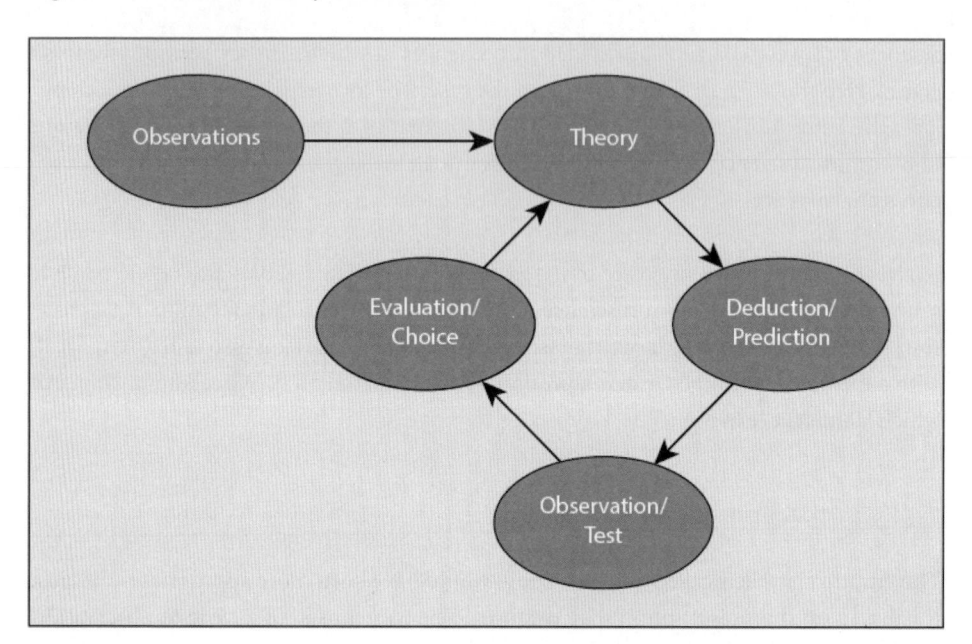

Figure 4.1 Numbers of asylum seekers

[Diagram: Observations → Theory → Deduction/Prediction → Observation/Test → Evaluation/Choice → Theory (cycle)]

Theories In ordinary parlance, the word 'theory' is often used in opposition to 'certainty'. A theory is only what somebody believes, but it might actually be false. In methodology, this opposition does not exist. A theory is a set of hypotheses that may very well be false but that may also be true. All knowledge is provisional, and that is precisely why all our knowledge is contained in 'theories'. Some theories have (provisionally) been refuted, and we now believe they are false. However, the best parts of our present-day knowledge also consist of theories. The custom to call clusters of one or more scientific laws 'theories' reflects a very basic assumption for sciences, namely that all knowledge is provisional. New research may always lead to new results. Scientific laws that were at one moment the pinnacle of scientific 'knowledge' may – and most likely will – at some later stage turn out to be a mere step in the development of a better theory.

The scientific (empirical) cycle consists of the following five steps:
1. Observation
2. Law formulation
3. Deduction and prediction
4. Observation and testing
5. Evaluation

4.3.3 Observation

Theories consist of beliefs, beliefs about what the facts are and beliefs about what the correct scientific laws are. They even include beliefs about what the facts will be, as when Charles holds the theory that it will rain in five minutes from now. Many beliefs are the product of observation, sometimes in combination with reasoning. For example, Jane believes that this iron fork is held above a (burning) Bunsen burner, because she actually sees that this is the case. She also believes that the fork is being heated, because she infers this from the fact (which she believes) that the fork is held above a Bunsen burner.

Observation is 'theory-laden' Jane cannot see that the fork is being heated, because her eyes are not suitable for the perception of heat. Perhaps this seems like nitpicking, because 'everybody' knows that you can see that something is being heated. Still, it is important to recognize the inference part in this observation, because observation in science often includes a component that involves theory and inference. When we look at a thermometer to 'see' what the temperature is, we can only see directly what the thermometer indicates, and we derive the temperature. This derivation is based on a theory that relates the indicator on the thermometer to the temperature of the environment.

Strictly speaking, even seeing what the thermometer indicates involves 'theory'. Our brains 'translate' the impulses they receive from our eyes into a 'theory' about what we see, and this translation is based on an unconsciously held 'theory' about what our sensory input represents. However, since this step is typically taken unconsciously, we work with the simplified assumption that we can at least see what the thermometer indicates.

Typically, we do not realize that there is a theory in between our sensory experience and what we believe to be observing, and most of the time we do not know the contents of this theory. Still, it is important to keep in mind that all observation is – to state it technically – 'theory-laden'.

Observation and expectation Our observations lead us to expectations. The first time that Jane grasped a fork that had been held above a Bunsen burner, she burned her fingers. Since that happened, she has become more cautious. This caution is based on the expectation, perhaps not even conscious, that forks that were held above Bunsen burners will be hot. It is even likely that Jane's expectation extends to spoons that were held above a burner, and perhaps also to terra cotta plates. The first extension would be justified: Jane might very well burn her fingers by grasping a spoon that was held above a burner. The second extension is most likely not justified: terra cotta does not become hot as easily as forks or spoons. This illustrates that induction is not infallible.

4.3.4   Law Formulation and Induction

Jane's expectation that forks and other things that were held above a burner will have become hot is based on a generalization. People generalize automatically, often without even realizing it. That is how our brains operate.

Induction If we make our generalizations explicit, we arrive at inductive arguments. In an inductive argument, we create from one, or – preferably – a combination of several facts, a 'law' that connects the facts. Of course, such a law is not a legal law, but a physical, biological or otherwise scientific law. For example, if every time we encounter a swan we notice that the animal is white, we can induce the law that all swans are white. Another example would be that observations that something was held above a Bunsen burner and became hot may make us induce the 'law' that things held above a Bunsen burner become hot.

It is quite clear that this latter 'law' is both too broad and too narrow. It is too broad because not everything that is held above a Bunsen burner becomes hot. For example, a terra cotta plate may become only lukewarm, and a newspaper will only become hot for a short while, before it goes up in flames and turns into ashes. The law is also too narrow because any way of heating will do, and not merely by using a Bunsen burner. The results of induction are fallible and may need to be adapted, and this leads us to the third step of the empirical cycle: deduction and prediction.

4.3.5   Deduction and Prediction

Jane's expectation that she might burn her fingers with a heated spoon is based on the law she adopted – perhaps only unconsciously – that items that are heated become hot.[7] To test this provisional law, she must use it to deduce predictions about what will happen if things are heated. For instance, she may deduce that the spoon she heats will become hot, and also that the terra cotta plate that Carol heats will become hot. By deducing future consequences of the law, it becomes possible to make predictions. These predictions can be tested.

---

[7]   The attentive reader may have noticed that 'being held above an operating Bunsen burner' has been generalized into 'being heated'. This is an example of generalization (from laws to more general laws) to which we will pay no more attention here.

Relevance If the hypothetical law reads that things that are heated become hot, it makes some facts relevant to the prediction and leaves other facts aside as irrelevant. For this hypothetical law it is only relevant that some item was heated. It does not matter:
- how it was heated (by a Bunsen burner, or in some other way);
- what kind of material was heated (iron or terra cotta; forks, or spoons);
- who did the heating (Jane or Carol).

We know that the way of heating is irrelevant, as is the person who did the heating, but that the kind of material (iron or terra cotta) is relevant, though not what the material is used for (fork or spoon). This knowledge can only be the result of testing the predictions that were made.

4.3.6 Observation and Testing

When a prediction is made by applying a theory, it can be checked whether the prediction is realized. In an empirical science, this check is based on sensory perception. So if Jane predicts that the spoon that was heated will also be hot, she might grasp the spoon and use her sense for heat to test the hypothesis. In the case of the spoon, the prediction will be confirmed. However, in the case of the terra cotta plate that was heated by Carol, the prediction will prove wrong: Jane can grasp the plate without burning her fingers. Obviously, the testing of the hypothesis (the law that heated things become hot) can lead to confirmative instances, and to seeming refutations. This raises the question as to which conclusions should be drawn from the tests. This question is answered in the fifth step of the empirical cycle: evaluation.

4.3.7 Evaluation

On a simple model of theory testing, a test either leads to refutation of the theory or to provisional continuation of acceptance. Take again our example of the fork that is being heated. Jane formulated the theory that things that get heated will become hot. She tests this theory on a spoon, and, yes, the spoon became hot. This does not prove the theory, but the test with the spoon at least did not refute the theory.

The theory has become somewhat stronger as it has now been tested under more diverse circumstances (not only forks, but also spoons). Now Jane also tests the theory on a terra cotta plate. Although the plate becomes warmer, it does not become really hot. On the simple model of theory testing, this means that the theory has been refuted or falsified.

Apparently, not all things that are heated become hot. This means that the theory *in general* is false, although it may still be correct for forks and spoons.

Did the test with the terra cotta plate really refute the theory that things that are being heated become hot? Yes and no. Yes, because the terra cotta plate was heated, but became only lukewarm, not hot. This is a counterexample against the theory, and therefore also a falsification. However, we should take into account that all experience is theory-laden. Very theoretically, Jane may have developed a nervous condition that disturbs her experience of heat. Very theoretically, it is possible that the terra cotta plate also became hot but that Jane just did not feel it any more. Although this is not very likely, the point must be taken seriously.

Where to place the blame? If we expect something to become hot, and we test it with a thermometer, the thermometer may be defective and indicate the wrong temperature. Then the fact that the thermometer indicates that the terra cotta plate did not become hot is not a refutation of the theory that things that are being heated become hot. It is a refutation of the implicit theory that the thermometer indicates the correct temperature.

The simple model of theory testing assumes that we can test a theory in isolation of all our other beliefs. This assumption is not always correct. If we test a theory by means of our sensory experience, we include a theory about the proper functioning of our senses and the devices that support our senses. If the test leads to an unexpected outcome, we must still make a choice of what we are going to blame for the outcome: the theory we tried to test, or the theory on which our sensory experience was based. Only if we blame the former theory can we say that this theory has been falsified by the test.

Improve or abandon? Let us ignore the possibility that if a test falsifies our expectations we should blame our senses and testing equipment. The falsification has, we assume, refuted our original theory. Suppose that this refutation happened when Jane heated the terra cotta plate and the plate became only lukewarm. After a brief test whether she could still feel heat (yes, she felt that she burned her fingers to the Bunsen burner flame), Jane decided that terra cotta plates do not become properly hot when heated. Does this mean that she should completely abandon the law that things that are heated become hot?

Not really. After all, the fork and the spoon did become hot. So apparently, the law worked for forks and spoons, even though it did not work for terra cotta plates. Perhaps the best thing to do is to improve the original law in a way that explains why the fork and the spoon became hot, while the plate did not. A better law might read that pieces of metal become hot when heated. This law does not say anything about terra cotta, and was therefore not refuted by the experiment with the heated plate. The new law has only instances that confirm it – the fork and the spoon – and has thus far not been refuted. So it provides a better theory than the original one that held for all objects being heated.

4.3.8   Non-empirical Science

Until here, our focus has been mainly on the scientific cycle as applied in empirical sciences. The empirical nature of, for example, physics, is manifested in the fourth step of the cycle, where a theory is tested against observations. In this connection we used the example that Jane tested her theory that heated things become hot by grasping a fork and a terra cotta plate with her hands. By doing so, Jane used her sense of touch to test whether the heated object was hot (Figure 4.2).

Figure 4.2   Theory testing

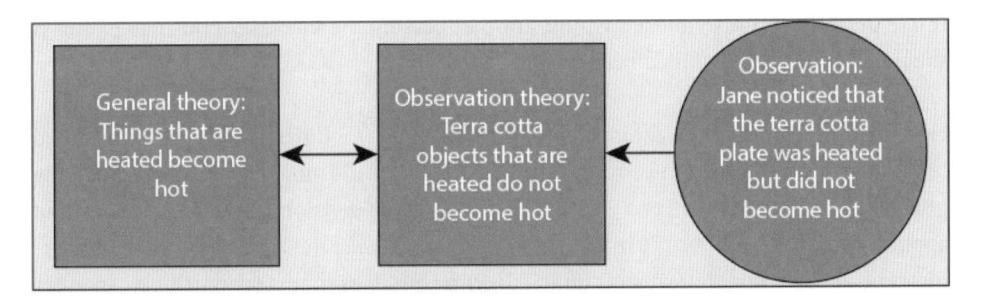

```
┌─────────────────┐    ┌─────────────────┐    ┌─────────────────┐
│ General theory: │    │Observation      │    │ Observation:    │
│ Things that are │◄──►│theory:          │◄───│ Jane noticed    │
│ heated become   │    │ Terra cotta     │    │ that the terra  │
│ hot             │    │ objects that are│    │ cotta plate was │
│                 │    │ heated do not   │    │ heated but did  │
│                 │    │ become hot      │    │ not become hot  │
└─────────────────┘    └─────────────────┘    └─────────────────┘
```

Observation theories It may seem that it is only possible to test a theory against observations, but the contrary is true. Strictly speaking we never test a theory against observations, because there are no logical relations between theories and observations. We test a theory against another theory, and in empirical sciences this other theory is the result of observation. When Jane grasps a terra cotta plate, she does not experience much heat. Therefore, she forms the theory that the plate is not hot, and – more in general – that terra cotta objects that are heated do not become hot. This is a so-called 'observation theory', and this observation theory is in turn used to test the more general theory that things that are heated become hot.

Testing against theories that are not the result of observations In empirical sciences the theories that are used to test other theories are the result of observations. However, it is also possible to test abstract theories against more concrete theories that are not based on observations. For example, it is possible to test theories about what the law should be against moral intuition.

In general, we do not want that persons apply violence against other persons, and for that reason the use of violence against human beings is punishable in most societies. The rule that makes such behaviour punishable is based on a moral theory that violence between humans is undesirable and should be punished. However, if a woman kills her rapist in self-defence, many find intuitively that the woman should not be punishable. This concrete intuition conflicts with the more abstract moral rule that violence between humans should be punished. The cognitive dissonance that results from this conflict must be resolved, and therefore one of the two theories must give in. Either the abstract rule survives and we must admit that the woman who killed her rapist in self-defence should also be punishable, or the concrete intuition survives and the abstract rule is in need of revision.

Ad hoc and fundamental revision The insight that the woman should not be punished and that the original rule needs to be revised may lead to the adoption of the following rule:

If one person commits violence against another person, the former is punishable, unless she is a woman and she killed her rapist in self-defence.

However, the introduction of this rule would be an ad hoc modification of existing criminal law, which would already need revision if the woman did not kill her rapist but only punched him in the face. Better would be a fundamental revision with a broader scope of application. That might be the introduction of a *lex specialis* stating that if somebody performs an act that would normally count as a crime but does so in a proportionate manner to ward off an impending crime, this person is not punishable. This more general exception would include the rule about killing rapists in self-defence as a special case, but is not ad hoc and includes a standard for when self-defence is justified: the behaviour must be proportionate. In many legal systems, this more general exception was introduced in legislation or in the doctrinal literature.

4.3.9 Application to Integration Theories

Integration theories as laws Both neo-functionalism and intergovernmentalism aim to explain the process of European integration. These theories follow the developments in the integration process, with more emphasis on autonomous processes if the integration accelerates (neo-functionalism) and more emphasis on external forces and political influence if the integration process slackens (intergovernmentalism).

For both neo-functionalism and intergovernmentalism it holds that if they are seen as explanatory theories in an ND fashion, they should fulfil the role of laws. They must be combined with initial facts to deduce phenomena that occurred in connection with European integration. In schema:

Integration theory (*nomos*)

Initial facts (*explanans*)

Event in the history of integration (*explanandum*)

Formulation The first step in evaluating the theories would be to give a precise formulation. That would allow the theories to be used for derivations about past and future events.

Neo-functionalism

IF there are functional organizations with supranational powers, which fulfil important functions,

THEN
1. interest groups will use these organizations, rather than States, to further their interests, and
2. new important functional organizations with supranational powers will arise.

Intergovernmentalism

IF a decision needs to be taken on a topic in which important interests of a State are involved (a topic that belongs to the field of 'high politics')

THEN the State will not allow this decision to be taken by a functional supranational organization

Intergovernmentalism as a refinement of neo-functionalism If these formulations are studied closely, it becomes clear that neo-functionalism and intergovernmentalism do not contradict each other. Neo-functionalism points to a process of development of functional supranational organizations, while intergovernmentalism claims that this development takes place only if States allow it and that the importance of the subject (high or low politics) determines whether States will allow it or not.

Interpreted in this way, intergovernmentalism functions as a refinement of neo-functionalism. There may be a spontaneous process in society that involves a transfer of loyalty and leads to a further growth of functional supranational organizations. However, this process is controlled by States that can allow it, but can also stop it. If intergovernmentalists criticize neo-functionalism, this is not because the latter theory is completely wrong, but because its scope may be taken too widely. The spontaneous process can take place only within the boundaries defined by State politics.

Falsification of neo-functionalism If intergovernmentalism is seen as a refinement of neo-functionalism, this means that if neo-functionalism is fundamentally wrong, intergovernmentalism is wrong too. Neo-functionalism predicts that in the areas allowed by States, functional supranational organizations will take over tasks that were originally handled by States. Did this actually happen? Clearly, the (EC and later the) EU took over a number of tasks from the EU Member States. It may therefore seem that neo-functionalism has at least an important kernel of truth.

However, the more tasks that were taken over by the EU, the less functional and the more territorial the EU became. The core idea of functionalism is that different kinds of tasks are handled by different functional organizations, and not by States any more. The EU took over tasks from its Member States, but in doing so, the EU became a large territorial, not a functional, organization. That does not fit into neo-functionalism, and the development of the EU may therefore be interpreted as a falsification of neo-functionalism. Interest groups do not use functional organizations to further their interests, but instead they use a different territorial organization. Moreover, there is no increase in the number of functional supranational organizations, but merely a transfer of tasks from one kind of territorial organization (States) to another (the EU).

If this analysis is correct, the development of the EU has falsified neo-functionalism and also intergovernmentalism, if the latter theory is seen as a refinement of the former.

4.4 What Makes a Theory 'Scientific'?

Historical background About a century ago, a young man had a problem with his own political views. It was briefly after World War I, and the location was Vienna. Our young man had socialist convictions, in part because the main alternative at that time and place was fascism. Socialism in those days was still strongly inspired by the 'scientific' version of communist ideas that was developed by Karl Marx.

A shooting incident in which some young socialists and communists were killed by the police did not strengthen our hero in his socialist convictions but rather made him doubt.[8] The shooting incident would fit nicely into the Marxist theory. According to this theory, such incidents were an inevitable step on the path towards the communist revolution. In this revolution, the proletariat would take possession of the means of production, and the class struggle would be put to an end, because there would not be a separation of classes any more.

Thinking about Marxist theory, the young man discovered that it was very difficult to refute it. Every seeming piece of counter-evidence could, with some ingenuity, be given a place in the theory and would only prove its strength. Marxists would happily accept this, as it would show how good Marx's views were. However, Karl Popper, who would become the most influential philosopher of science of the 20th century, did not find this acceptable. If everything fits into a theory, the theory cannot distinguish between what is right or wrong any more. That makes the theory irrefutable, but also useless.

Falsifiability as hallmark of being scientific That is why Popper decided to make falsifiability the litmus test to distinguish between science and metaphysics. Scientific theories are falsifiable; metaphysical theories are not.[9]

Notice that the distinction between scientific and non-scientific (metaphysical) is not the same as the distinction between true and false. A theory may be false, but also scientific. Think, for example, of Newton's theory of gravity. This theory was refuted by experiments in the 20th century that confirmed the predictions made by the competing theory of Einstein. This does not detract, however, from the fact that Newton's theory was a real scientific theory. The very fact that it was falsified even proves this.

---

8   Popper 1976, p. 42.
9   Popper 2002, pp. 34-44.

At first sight, this idea of falsifiability seems very attractive. Of course, it must be possible to test a scientific theory against the facts; of course, it must be clear when the facts conflict with the theory, and, of course, the theory must be given up if it conflicts with the facts. However, quite soon the issue turned out to be a bit more complicated. Let us reconsider the theory about objects that become hot when heated to see what the complications are.

Word meaning Suppose that Jane heated a fork and found it hot when she grasped it. She considers this as support for the theory that objects that are heated become hot. Jane immediately gives the heated fork to Carol, who disagrees with Jane: the fork is not hot, only a little warmer. Therefore, Carol thinks that this experiment falsified the theory and that the theory should be rejected.

Who is right, Jane or Carol? That is hard to say, as it was not sufficiently specified what counts as 'hot'. To be falsifiable, the theory must be sufficiently specific to allow all observers to reach the same verdict on whether the theory was falsified. But then, what counts as sufficiently specific? Should all observers reach the same verdict, even the unreasonable observers? And how to distinguish between reasonable and unreasonable observers? It is not easy to specify when the formulation of a theory is sufficiently precise.

Boundaries of the theory Suppose that Jane heated a terra cotta plate and found it only lukewarm when she grasped it. Should that refute the theory that objects that are heated become hot? Perhaps, but if the experiment were done with a fork in a cold storage unit, at a temperature of minus 20 degrees Celsius, and the fork would not become hot, would that also falsify the theory? One might argue that the theory was never meant for application in cold storage units and that this experiment cannot refute the theory. However, how can we know what are the boundaries of application of a theory? Which experiments shall we consider as candidates for falsifying the theory, and which experiments can be disregarded as falling outside the theory's boundaries?

Theory-laden observations Suppose that Jane and Carol solved their disagreement about the temperature of the heated fork by agreeing that they would not test the theory by grasping the fork but by holding a thermometer against it. The experiment is repeated, but with different brands of thermometers.

The one thermometer shows a temperature of 200 degrees Celsius, which both Jane and Carol consider as hot. The theory seems to be saved.

However, the second thermometer shows a temperature of 60 degrees Celsius, which both Jane and Carol consider as only lukewarm. The theory seems to be falsified.

The two thermometers are based on different physical theories about the measurement of heat. Most of the time, both theories, and therefore also both thermometers, lead to the same result. However, this is not always the case, and the latest experiment by Jane and Carol belongs to the exceptional cases. How should the outcome of this experiment be evaluated? Does the experiment refute the theory that forks that are heated become hot, or does the outcome falsify one of the two theories about heat measurement?

This example illustrates that observation is theory-laden, and that it is not possible to test a theory (about the relationship between being heated and becoming hot) in isolation from other theories.

We see that Popper's simple falsifiability test as a means to distinguish between scientific and non-scientific theories is not as simple as it might seem. However, the basic idea that a theory cannot be scientific if it is even in theory impossible to falsify it remains forceful.

Application to intergovernmentalism One reason why a theory is not scientific is that it is insufficiently precise to be falsified. Intergovernmentalism distinguishes between high and low politics to explain why some tasks are transferred from the Member States to the European level, while States cling to other tasks that they want to fulfil themselves. Is this distinction between high and low politics sufficiently clear to allow intergovernmentalism to be falsified? This theory can, according to Popper, only be classified as a scientific theory if it can be falsified in principle, and that presupposes that the distinction between high and low politics is sufficiently clear.

It is useful to see how the vagueness – if it exists – of the distinction between high politics and low politics prevents the falsification of intergovernmentalism. Suppose that intergovernmentalism seems to predict that some task will not be transferred to the European level but that the transfer nevertheless takes place. At first sight, this might be interpreted as a falsification of intergovernmentalism. However, the theory may be rescued by claiming that the transfer proved that the State in question did not consider the task to belong to high politics. The opposite may also take place; a task is not transferred although it seemed to belong to low politics. Then the fact that the transfer did not occur may be interpreted as a sign that this task belonged to high politics for the State. If the distinction between high and low politics is not defined sharply, the boundary can be shifted to save intergovernmentalism from falsification. Then the theory becomes unfalsifiable, and also unscientific. We will not decide here whether the distinction is sufficiently clear, but it is obvious that intergovernmentalism has a weak spot on this issue. Moreover, if intergovernmentalism is interpreted as a refinement of neo-functionalism, this weak spot is also a weak spot of neo-functionalism.

4.5 Teleological Explanation

It is not easy to use the ND model for the explanation of human behaviour, and there are several reasons why that is the case:
1. It is not easy to find laws by means of which reliable predictions of behaviour can be made, and we also lack the laws that we need for good explanations.
2. Human behaviour is meaningful, and to understand it, we need to know this meaning. The ND model seemingly lacks room to give the meaning of behaviour its proper place.
3. An ND explanation typically works from the past to the future: events or facts are explained from earlier events and facts. Human behaviour, on the contrary, often aims to bring about future results, and this aim should play a role in its explanation.

These drawbacks have inspired a different way of explaining human behaviour: teleological explanation.

4.5.1 Limitations of the ND Model in Connection with Human Behaviour

Lack of proper laws One attractive aspect of the ND model is that the laws used for making explanations should also be laws that can be used for reliable predictions. The law that light travels in vacuum at a speed of about 300,000 kilometres a second can be used to explain why we see the sun as it was eight minutes ago but also to predict how long it will take to send a light signal to astronauts on the moon. Only if a law is good enough to make reliable predictions, is it good enough to be used in good explanations. Regrettably, we rarely avail of laws by means of which human behaviour can reliably be predicted and that means that we also lack the laws that are required for proper ND explanations.

Human behaviour is meaningful The German sociologist Weber (1864-1920) wrote that social scientists should aim at understanding the social world (*Verstehen*) and that we understand why somebody did something if we understand what this person wanted to achieve with her action. We will return to this later. However, in Weber's account, understanding also plays a second role. People act in a meaningful world: the facts of the world and the actions humans perform have meanings. The proper explanation of human behaviour should take into account what meanings human beings assign to the facts and the events in their social environment and to the actions that they perform.

Take the following example: On the border of a town lies a piece of land, which contains only a few buildings. However, on the plot there are quite a number of big stones with inscriptions. Moreover, on a regular basis small crowds of people gather there, and then most of these people are dressed in black. How can this be explained?

If one tries to explain this phenomenon by means of physical laws, one will have a hard time. However, the explanation is much easier to give if one knows that the plot of land is a cemetery, that the stones mark graves and that the people who arrive in small crowds attend a funeral. That they are mostly dressed in black is explained from the facts that black is the colour of mourning and that these people want to express their sorrow for the loss of the person who is being buried.

A proper explanation in this case requires that one understand the social practice of burying the dead and the rites and customs that belong to this practice. The events that take place are not mere physical events; they have meanings, and these meanings play a crucial role in the explanation of what happens. Therefore, a proper explanation requires an understanding of the meaning of what happens. Therefore, the ND model of explanation, which lacks room for these meanings, is arguably not a good model to explain meaningful behaviour.

Explanation from intentions Closely connected to the point that human behaviour is meaningful and that this meaning should play a role in the proper explanation of behaviour is the point that human agents often act with the intention of bringing about a particular result and that their behaviour is best explained from this intention. Let us return to the funeral example. Understanding the meaning of what happens may be crucial for the understanding of acts that take place in a social world, but it does not suffice. Why do the attendees of a funeral wear black? To explain this, it does not suffice to point out that it is customary to wear black, because why should a particular person do what is customary? For a full explanation, more is needed, and this includes the beliefs and desires of the agents.

Let us take Louise as an example. Her good friend has died, and she wants to express her sorrow at the funeral. This is something that she desires to do. Moreover, Louise believes that the best way to express her sorrow is to wear a black dress at the funeral. This desire and this belief together explain why Louise wore a black dress to the funeral.

This example illustrates the usefulness of the *belief-desire model of motivation* for explaining behaviour. The belief-desire model is a general theory of human motivation: people desire something, believe that some action will fulfil their desires, and therefore form the intention of performing that action.[10] This intention, in turn, explains the behaviour (Figure 4.3).

Figure 4.3 The belief-desire model of motivation

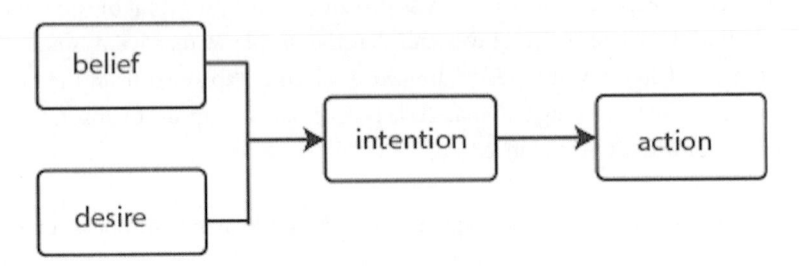

```
belief ──┐
         ├──▶ intention ──▶ action
desire ──┘
```

Because desires are future-directed, it is not easy to accommodate them in the ND model of explanation, as this model is past-oriented. We explain why a piece of metal expanded from the fact that it was heated in the near past. We explain why Louise put on a black dress from her intention to express sorrow at the funeral in the near future.

4.5.2 Goal-Based Explanation

The explanation of an action from the goal that was pursued by means of the action is called 'teleological', from the Greek word *telos*, which means 'goal'. Teleological explanation is forward looking; the action in the present is explained from the goal that will be reached in the future.

Logic of teleological explanation It is possible to make a logical model of teleological explanation that resembles the ND model of Hempel and Oppenheim. All teleological models share the same law, namely that if an agent has a goal G and believes that Action A will realize G, the agent will perform A. This law needs to be combined with two other premises, one stating the goal and the other stating the belief. The result looks as follows:

If P wants to achieve G and believes that doing A will achieve G, then P will (try to) do A (*nomos*).

---

10 The belief-desire model of human action is usually traced back to the work of David Hume (Hume 1978, Book II, Section III). It is still influential in psychology.

P wants to achieve G (*explanans*).

P believes that doing A will achieve G (*explanans*).

P will (try to) do A (*explanandum*).

The attentive reader will have noticed that this is the ND model again, but now with an explanans that consists of two parts: a belief and a goal (or desire). Apparently, it is possible to accommodate future-oriented explanations in the ND model.

Limited to actions The strength of teleological explanations is that where they are applicable – that is when actions are to be explained – they increase our understanding more than other ND explanations. If we want to understand why John walked to the door, we are better helped by the information that the bell rang and that he wanted to open the door than by the information that certain neurons in his brain fired and thereby made the muscles in his legs contract.

However, a weakness of intention-based explanation is that they can only explain actions, not other events. It is not possible to explain why this piece of metal expanded in terms of goals and beliefs.

Myopic Another weakness – for our present purposes perhaps more important – is that a teleological explanation mentions only one of the factors that may be relevant for some action. They are in that sense myopic. This becomes clear if we use this style of thinking for a future action:

> The doorbell rings, and John believes that his date is standing at the door, waiting to be let in. We predict, therefore, that John will walk to the door. However, John pretends that he did not hear anything, because – contrary to his expectations – his wife Dora did not leave for the bridge club yet.

This example illustrates that intention-based explanation can account for single motivating reasons but that it cannot handle situations in which a person's actual behaviour is the result of conflicting reasons. John's desire to let his date in, and his belief that opening the door for her would realize his desire, explains why John feels some motivation to open the door. However, this desire cannot account for John's motivation to pretend ignorance. The latter motivation can be explained from John's desire not to hurt Dora and his belief that he would hurt her if he would let his date in. John's actual behaviour – did he open the door or not – is the result of this conflict of motivations.

Teleological explanation and prediction If we only look at the past, to an action that actually took place, we can often explain it in terms of a desire and a matching belief. From the fact that the action occurred, we already know which belief and desire we need for the explanation. If John remained seated when the doorbell rang, we can perhaps explain this from John's desire not to hurt his wife Dora, and his belief that opening the door for his date would hurt Dora. So we might point to this belief and desire to explain John's actual behaviour. However, if John had opened the door, we would explain it from his desire to let his date in.

Teleological explanations often work well for behaviour that already took place, because then we can use the actual events to select the matching belief-desire pair. If we try to predict future actions, however, a single belief-desire pair only points to one reason for action and cannot say anything about other potential motivating reasons. This means that desire-based *predictions* can be unreliable, even though desire-based *explanations* create understanding.

To account for this difference between prediction and explanation, Elster introduced the notion of a 'mechanism'. A mechanism is a weaker version of a law. Where a law guarantees its consequences if its conditions are met, a mechanism is only one factor which may determine behaviour, but which may also be set aside by other factors.[11] A belief/goal combination triggers a mechanism, but may be set aside by, for example, another belief/goal combination. Only after the event, when we know what happened, can we point out which mechanism turned out to be decisive. This makes that, after the event, a mechanism can be pointed out that *explains* the event, but since this mechanism might have been set aside, it could not be used to *predict* what happened.

Functional explanation Strictly speaking, teleological explanations can be used only for actions, because only agents have goals. However, it may be useful to apply the teleological style of thinking also to facts that do not involve actions. Then we speak of 'functional explanation', because the function that something fulfils plays a crucial role in this style of explanation.

The best-known example of functional explanation is the evolution theory. According to this theory, characteristics of plants or animals are explained from the usefulness of these

---

11 Elster 2007, p. 36.

characteristics for survival of the species. For instance, the green colour of plants is explained from the usefulness of this colour for photosynthesis, which has, in turn, survival value for green plants, or for their genes. So if we want to know why plants are green, we can explain this by pointing out that plants (or their genes) 'want' to survive and that being green contributes to this survival.

Functional explanation can also be used for social institutions such as democracy. Why does democracy continue to exist? Because it provides human societies with a peaceful means to determine their futures. Why did the EEC survive? Because – let us assume – it withheld its Member States from waging war against each other.

4.6 Application to the Integration Theories

We have already seen that the predictions one would be tempted to make on the basis of neo-functionalism do not always come true. Intergovernmentalism can be seen as an explanation why this is so: the neo-functionalist predictions come true only in areas of low politics. Since neo-functionalism itself does not distinguish between low and high politics, it is a myopic theory, which explains integration when it takes place but which has no explanation when States interfere to block the integration process. Intergovernmentalism can explain such interventions, but is weak in predicting when they will take place. If integration occurs as neo-functionalism predicted, the area must have belonged to low politics, and if it does not occur because of State interference, the area must have belonged to high politics.

For Popper this would have been a sign that either neo-functionalism has been refuted, e.g. by the empty chair crisis, or that the combination of neo-functionalism and intergovernmentalism is not a scientific theory, since it cannot be falsified because of its vagueness (what counts as high politics?). For Elster this is a sign that both theories merely describe 'mechanisms' that fall short of being full-blown scientific laws. Who is right, Popper or Elster, depends on the demands one makes on explanation. If one looks for understanding based on exceptionless laws, Popper would be right, but one should be satisfied with the conclusion that there are hardly any decent explanations for social phenomena, including human action. If one is satisfied with a tranquil mind because the explanandum has been given an acceptable place in the course of events, many more explanations will be available, but the resulting understanding will be much more shallow.

4.7 Conclusion

We started this chapter from the question relating to whether the two explanatory integration theories, neo-functionalism and intergovernmentalism, do their jobs well and whether they make us understand when and why European integration (does not) take place. It was immediately pointed out that there is, at one extreme of the explanatory scala, a demanding type of explanation, which leads to a strong type of understanding, which we called 'mechanistic understanding', and which is based on scientific laws without exceptions. There is, at the other extreme, a less demanding type of understanding, which we called 'psychological understanding', that can result from relatively weak types of explanation, such as explanation based on a 'mechanism' rather than an exceptionless law, on teleological or functional explanation, or even on a 'narrative'.

It turned out that both integration theories cannot lead to mechanistic understanding, because they have either been falsified, or lack the precision that is required for scientific theories. However, it is possible to envisage these theories as mechanisms, which can retrospectively lead to the tranquillity of mind that characterizes mere psychological understanding.

Whether neo-functionalism and intergovernmentalism perform their jobs as explanatory theories for European integration well depends on the demands one makes on an explanatory theory and the kind of understanding one wants to achieve.

5 THE ECONOMICS OF TRADE: BASIC CONCEPTS

One of the driving forces behind European integration is the economic advantage of free trade. The next chapter deals with both the advantages and the disadvantages of free international trade. To facilitate this discussion, this chapter starts with an introduction to the economic way of thinking and applies this style of thinking to topics that lawyers typically approach in a very different way.

Outline The economic style of thinking is introduced and contrasted with the legal style in Section 5.1. Section 5.2 introduces a number of concepts that are characteristic of this style of thinking and that will be used in the discussion of the rest of this chapter. Three of the introduced concepts – transaction costs, externalities and social dilemmas – are elaborated in Sections 5.3, 5.4 and 5.5, respectively.

5.1 THE ECONOMIC STYLE OF THINKING

Legal perspective Both law and economics deal with human behaviour. In one prominent view, law aims to guide human behaviour by means of norms that prescribe or prohibit particular kinds of conduct. Compliance with these norms is promoted through the use of collective enforcement, including the tools of criminal law (e.g. fines and incarceration), private law (e.g. seizure) and administrative law (administrative sanctions). Although public enforcement may be a defining characteristic of law, it is not law's core business. The core business is to guide behaviour by making this behaviour legally prohibited, obligatory or permitted. This means that a legal discussion of behaviour often ends with the question of whether the behaviour was allowed or not.

Economic perspective The economic perspective on behaviour is twofold. Economics deals with the explanation and prediction of human behaviour, but traditionally does so from the perspective of rationality. A typical economic line of reasoning would be the following: Andrew wants an audio amplifier. He has seen one that costs €1,200. To Andrew, the amplifier is worth €1,500. On a cost-benefit comparison, it would be rational for Andrew to buy the amplifier if he can afford it. Under the assumption that Andrew will do the rational thing, we can predict that he will buy the amplifier, or – if he has already done so – explain why he bought the amplifier.

Cost-benefit thinking This line of reasoning contains two steps. The first deals with rationality, which is typically seen as means-ends rationality. Andrew wants the amplifier (end), and he is willing to pay money for it (means). As the price of the amplifier is less than what Andrew is willing to spend on it, the benefit of buying the amplifier is bigger than the cost of doing so. Therefore, it is rational for Andrew to buy the amplifier.

Rationality assumptions The second step makes the transition from rationality to actual behaviour. It is presupposed that people tend to act rationally. If we know that some action would be rational in the eyes of the agent, we can predict that the agent will perform this action. This second step makes two assumptions. One assumption, which was already mentioned, is that agents will do what is rational in their eyes.[1]

The other assumption, not yet mentioned, is that behaviour that is actually rational will be seen by agents as rational. In other words, this is the assumption that agents recognize rationality when they encounter it. Given these two assumptions, the economic explanation or prediction of behaviour takes two steps:
1. from what is rational to what agents see as rational;
2. from what agents see as rational to actual behaviour.

In the rest of this chapter we will join the economic theorists in making these rationality assumptions, and we will use theory about what is rational as a tool for predicting and explaining behaviour.

Two styles of thinking Legal thinking aims at establishing what is allowed, prohibited or obligatory. Although these legal categories aim at guiding behaviour, the realm of legal reasoning reaches its limits before individuals take actual decisions.[2] Economic thinking aims at establishing what is the rational thing to do, based on a cost-benefit analysis. In the end, it aims at predicting or explaining behaviour, but, not unlike legal reasoning, it typically stops before the issue arises of what people actually do.[3]

---

1 This assumption is dropped in 'behavioural economics', a branch of economic theory which focuses on the psychological aspects of behaviour. *See*, for example, Kahneman 2012.
2 Perhaps this does not do justice to legal thinking in full, which also addresses the question of what are good norms and which uses efficacy in answering that question. *See*, for example, Leeuw and Schmeets 2016. However, most legal thinking takes positive law for granted and focuses on the legal consequences of the existing norms.
3 Perhaps this does not do justice to economic thinking in full, which also addresses descriptive questions including how economic processes actually operate. However, much economic thinking takes social reality for granted and focuses on the rationality of behaviour.

Law deals with the normative status of actions, while economy deals with their rationality. Nevertheless, there is an important link, because the rationality of actions is an important determinant of which actions should be permitted, prohibited or obligatory. Take, for example, the prohibition to run red traffic lights. In combination with a threat of sanctions, this prohibition influences what kinds of behaviour are rational. In itself, running a red traffic light may be rational, especially if one can see that there is no other traffic. However, if there is a sufficiently serious risk of a large fine, the behaviour becomes irrational on a cost-benefit analysis. A prudent driver will therefore not run a red traffic light. The wish to make 'wrong' behaviour irrational can motivate the legislature to forbid this behaviour and to strengthen this prohibition by the threat of a sanction.

This means that the economic style of thinking is an important tool for evaluating actual and potential legal rules. Another example would be that if a State introduces free trade without additional measures to safeguard competition, economic theory can predict that companies will try to create monopolies in order to maximize profits. This advantages companies at the expense of consumers. This insight can be used by legislators, who know that if they want consumers to benefit from free trade too, they must also make rules that promote competition between companies.

5.2   Some Concepts

This section will introduce some concepts that are useful for the discussions in the rest of the chapter.

What is trade? Trade is exchange. Consider a simple case where one person has something that another person wants and, in return, this person has something that the first person wants. If they both value what the other has more than what they have themselves, they can exchange their possessions, and both can have what they prefer. This is the essence of trade.

Trade can consist in the exchange of material goods, but labour can also be the object of trade. If Arnie hires Bert to wash his car, Arnie gives Bert money in exchange for labour. Even doing nothing can be part of a trade deal. If Carol prefers to have room for parking before her house, she can offer Desdemona a book if the latter parks her car elsewhere.

In this chapter and the following, we will focus only on the trade of goods.

Money A frequent form of trade is the exchange of money for a good. This form of trade is so common that it has a name of its own: sale. It is perhaps tempting to assume that trade always consists of buying and selling goods, that is as exchanges in which money plays a role. However, even if we consider only sales, it is still important to realize that exchange of something for money is still exchange. Money is not completely similar to other goods, but economically speaking it is still a good.

Later, we will pay extensive attention to the role of money, but for now it is important to point out that money has instrumental value. Money is valuable only to the extent that it can be used for buying other things. Expressing the value of things in terms of money is useful and has become customary in economic theory, and we will use this practice here as well. However, the reader should be warned that money is at best an approximation of the value inherent in things that are 'really' valuable to human beings.

Although the value of money is not the same for everybody and under all circumstances,[4] the discussion of trade is much easier if we ignore this relative value of money and assume that money has the same value to everybody. This means that we will also ignore the existence of different currencies.[5]

Utility and price The basis for trade is that a good may have a different value to one person than to another. To facilitate the discussion, we will use the word 'utility' for the value a person attaches to a good and express the amount of utility by means of a number. This number may be read as the number of units of a particular currency. For example, the utility of a book for a person may be 45, and the reader may understand this as 45 euro or 45 yuan. For the examples in this chapter, the currencies are not relevant.

The reader should be careful not to confuse the utility of a good for somebody with the price for which this good is traded. The price is objectively given and is the same for everybody, while the utility depends on the person who values the good. Suppose, for instance, that Alice owns a car which she values at 1000. Bob values the same car at 1500. This difference in utility is the basis for trade between Alice and Bob. If Alice sells her car

---

4   An example of a situation when the value of money is practically zero is when you are on an uninhabited island where there is no one to sell to and nothing to buy.
5   A warning is in place here. Economists sometimes use the word 'currency' in the limited sense of the physical instantiations of money (typically coins and bank notes). *See*, for instance, www.thefreedictionary.com/currency (last visited on 31 December 2018). Here, we will also use the word 'currency' in a broader sense, for a valuta such as the dollar, the euro or the yuan.
      In Chapter 7, the existence of different currencies, with varying exchange rates, will play a central role.

to Bob for 1200, the price of the car is 1200, which is obviously not the same as the utility of the car for Alice or for Bob.

Utility, range and spread It is useful to have terms in connection with the difference in utility that an object has for two persons. Therefore, we will use the term 'utility range' for the range from the utility a good has for the person who values it least to the utility that the good has for the person who values it most. In our example, the utility range would therefore be from 1,000 (the utility for Alice) to 1,500 (the utility for Bob).

We will also use a term for the size of this range: 'utility spread'. The utility spread for Alice and Bob with regard to the car is 500. This is the upper value of the utility range minus the lower value (1,500-1,000).

The possibility of trade If Alice and Bob agree on a price for the car that lies within their utility range, that is between 1,000 and 1,500, they have a deal that is rational for both of them. In general, and ignoring transaction costs, trade of a good is (rationally) possible if there is a utility range between the owner of the good and a potential buyer and if the good belongs to the person who values it least.

Later we will see that transaction costs will change this general standard for the possibility of trade.

Personal utility A good has a particular utility for a person. This utility is the amount, expressed in some unit (e.g. euros), on which the person values the good. It is relative in two ways: first, it is relative to some good, which has the utility, and second it is relative to the person, for whom the good has this utility.

Normally, there will be many goods, material and immaterial, that a person possesses, and that also have utility for this person. Think, for instance, of a home, a bicycle, books, free time, a loving partner, good friends, a bad job, a nagging toothache, and so on… As this list illustrates, the utility that something has for a person may be positive but also negative. It is useful to have a term to denote the sum of all these utilities, positive and negative, taken together. We will use the term 'personal utility' for this purpose. Personal utility is the sum of all the utilities for some person P of the goods that P possesses. It is relative to a person – P in this case – but not relative to a good, as it is the sum of *all* the utilities connected to goods that this person possesses. So we may, for instance, write about the personal utility of Alice and the personal utility of Bob.

Welfare While personal utility is the aggregate amount of the utilities of all goods a person possesses, welfare is the aggregate amount of personal utility of all persons in a group. For example, we may write about the level of welfare of the Dutch, of the inhabitants of Maastricht, of all blue-eyed girls that were born on a Sunday afternoon in 1984 in Southside, Chicago, or of the group consisting of Alice, Bob and Carol. Welfare is, by definition, relative to such a group.

Pareto-improvement An exchange that makes at least one party better off and that does not make the other party worse off is called a Pareto-improvement.[6] In a typical Pareto-improvement, both parties will be better off: a win-win situation. This will, for instance, be the case if the price for which a good is traded lies within the utility range of the partners in the exchange. In that case, the personal utility of both partners will increase.

Suppose that Alice values her car at 1000, while Bob values this same car at 1500. If Alice sells her car to Bob for 1200, this is a Pareto-improvement. The personal utility of Alice increases with 200 (1200-1000), and the personal utility of Bob increases with 300 (1500-1200).

If a transaction influences the personal utility of the partners alone, a Pareto-improvement will raise the level of welfare of the group to which the partners belong. However, transactions often also influence the personal utility of persons other than the partners.

Pareto-efficiency Pareto-efficiency is a central notion in economic theory. A distribution of goods over a group of persons – for instance society as a whole – is called 'Pareto-efficient' if, and only if, every alternative distribution would result in at least one person becoming worse off. For example, a distribution of cars over the inhabitants of a small town is Pareto-efficient if it is not possible to devise a transaction between two or more inhabitants in which cars are exchanged, such that everybody will, at the end of the transaction, have a car that she prefers over her old car. Every exchange makes at least one person worse off.

Kaldor-Hicks efficiency Economists also use a different notion of efficiency: Kaldor-Hicks efficiency. A distribution of goods over the members of a group is Kaldor-Hicks efficient if, and only if, this distribution leads to a higher level of welfare in the group than any other distribution. The essential difference between Pareto-efficiency and Kaldor-Hicks efficiency is that the former focuses on the utility level of individual group members and is in that

---

6   Pareto-improvement and Pareto-efficiency are named after the Italian economist Alfredo Pareto (1848-1923).

sense individualist, while the latter focuses on the overall level of welfare and is in that sense collectivist.

5.3 Transaction Costs

5.3.1 Internal Costs and Benefits

Assume that Bob values the car that presently belongs to Alice at 1,500. Alice values the same car at 1,000. If Bob buys Alice's car for 1,200, Bob has a cost of 1,200 and a benefit in the form of the car, while Alice has a cost in the form of the car and a benefit of 1,200. Both have a profit: Bob has an increase in personal utility of 300 (1,500-1,200), while Alice has an increase of 200 (1,200-1,000). All the costs and benefits are internal to the transaction, as the cost for Bob (1,200) equals the benefit for Alice, and the cost for Alice (the car) is identical to the benefit for Bob.

Not all transactions have only internal costs and benefits. Often, there are disturbing factors, such as transaction costs and externalities.

5.3.2 Definition of Transaction Costs

If Felipe in Brazil wants to sell his bike for 150, and Caroline in the Netherlands wants to buy exactly such a bike for 170, it is not very likely that the sale will go on – in the first place, because Felipe and Caroline do not know (about) each other and their desires to trade a bike and, in the second place, because the transport of the bike from Brazil to the Netherlands costs too much. Of course, Caroline might hire a personal shopper in Brazil to discover the bike for her, but that would, again, be too costly. This means that the transaction costs are so high that they make the transaction irrational.

Costs like the ones mentioned in the example of Felipe and Caroline, which affect one partner in a transaction but are not beneficial to the other partner, are called 'transaction costs'. These costs may have as a result that transactions which would be rational if there were no transaction costs, become irrational and should not take place.

Transaction costs include[7]:
- *Search and information costs:* the costs that must be made to determine that the required good is available on the market and which product has the lowest price.
- *Bargaining costs:* the costs required to come to an acceptable agreement with the other party to the transaction, drawing up an appropriate contract and so on.
- *Execution costs:* the costs that must be made to perform a trade exchange, such as costs of transportation, insurance, taxes and custom tariffs. Execution costs also include costs of criminal sanctions such as fines and incarceration.
- *Policing and enforcement costs:* the costs of making sure the other party sticks to the terms of the contract and of taking appropriate action (often through the legal system) if this turns out not to be the case.

5.3.3 Taxation

A particularly important category of transaction costs is taxes that are connected to trade, such as value-added tax (VAT), transfer tax and tariffs on import and export. Here we will focus on transfer tax and its impact on trade.

Irene values her home at 200,000, while John values Irene's home at 210,000. The utility range is therefore from 200,000 to 210,000, and its spread is 10,000. In principle, any sale of the house for a price within the utility range should be rational for both parties.

However, if the government raises a 10% transfer tax on the sale of real estate, the transaction becomes irrational. If Irene wants to receive 200,000 for the house, she must ask for 220,000. Because John does not want to pay more than 210,000, the sale will not take place. The government does not receive any taxes, while Irene and John forego a seemingly attractive sale of the house.

Apparently, something has gone wrong, and it is worthwhile to study this foregone sale in some detail.

Gross transaction surplus Let us focus on sales transactions and ignore taxes for a while. If Seller sells a good to Buyer, there will typically be a utility range: Buyer values the good more than Seller.

---

7   *See* https://corporatefinanceinstitute.com/resources/knowledge/economics/transaction-costs/ (last visited on 1 May 2019).

5   The Economics of Trade: Basic Concepts

In the example about the sale of the house between Irene and John, the Seller utility of the house is 200,000, while the Buyer utility is 210,000. The utility range runs from 200,000 to 210,000.

The sales price will lie somewhere within the utility range, which means that both the seller and the buyer have an advantage. For the seller this advantage amounts to the difference between the sales price and the seller utility; for the buyer this will be the difference between the buyer utility and the price. We will call the advantage of seller the *seller surplus* and the advantage of buyer the *buyer surplus*. Together, seller and buyer have an advantage that equals the sum of the seller and the buyer surplus. We will call this the gross transaction surplus. See figure 5.1. Not surprisingly, this gross transaction surplus equals the utility spread between the seller and the buyer.

Let us assume that in the example about the sale of the house, Irene and John agree on a price of 204,000. In this case, the seller surplus amounts to 4,000 (204,000 minus 200,000) while the buyer surplus amounts to 6,000 (210,000 minus 204,000). The gross transaction surplus of this sale is 10,000 (4,000 plus 6,000). This amount is also the utility spread between John and Irene (210,000 minus 200,000).

Figure 5.1   Surpluses

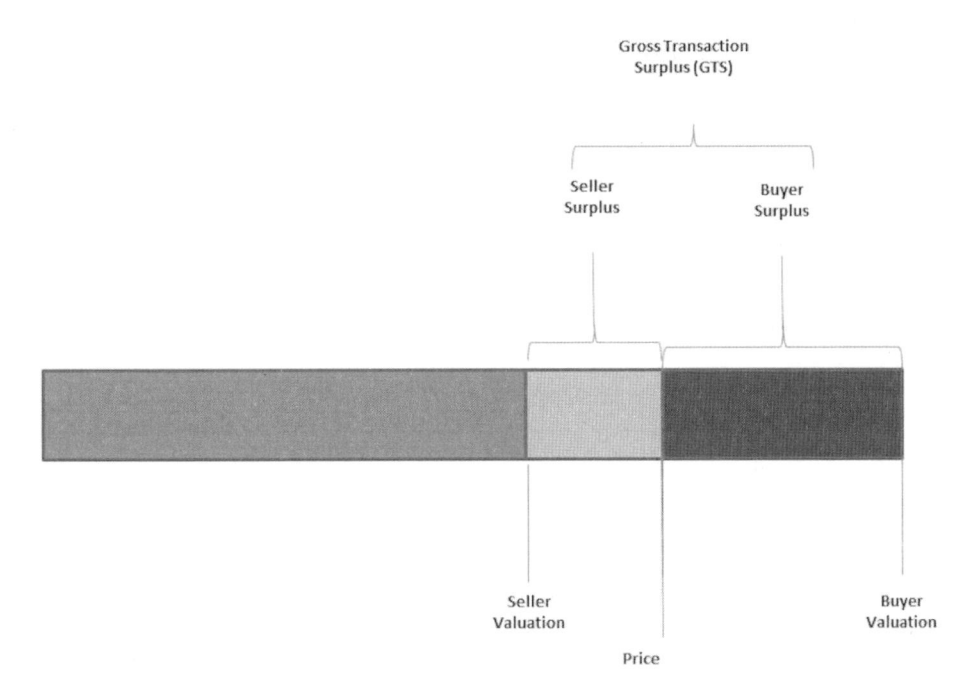

Net transaction surplus Often there are transaction costs. Buyer and Seller cannot take the full gross transaction surplus for themselves, because the transaction costs must be subtracted from the gross trade surplus. Then the remaining net transaction surplus equals the gross transaction surplus minus the transaction costs.

Suppose that the transfer tax in our last example was 2% of the Price. That would be 4,080. After the tax has been deducted from the gross trade surplus, the remainder of 5,920 is the net transaction surplus. This is the surplus that John and Irene together have gained. How this amount is divided between the two, depends on who must pay the tax. In any case, the State has an advantage that equals to the amount of the transfer tax (4,080).

Negative net transaction surplus When the transaction costs are less than the gross trade surplus, there is still an advantage to Buyer and Seller if the sale takes place. The net transaction surplus is more than zero. However, if the transaction costs equal or exceed the gross trade surplus, the net transaction surplus becomes zero, or even negative. Then it is not prudent any more for Seller and Buyer to go on with the transaction. They will forego the transaction, and with it the seller and the buyer surplus.

Suppose that the transfer tax in our example is 10% of the sales price of the house. That would be 20,400. After the tax has been deducted from the gross trade surplus, the net transaction surplus would become negative: -10,400 (10,000 – 20,400). There is no longer any gain (positive net transaction surplus) in the transaction for Irene and John, and if they are rational, the sale of the house does not go on. Irene misses her seller surplus of 4,000, while John misses his buyer surplus of 6,000. Moreover, the State has no tax income. This means that society as a whole (in this case: Irene, John and the State) has missed an opportunity for an increase of welfare, or – stated negatively – has suffered a welfare loss of 10,000.

5.3.4   Summary on Transaction Costs

Transaction costs are an important determinant of the issue of whether a transaction takes place. If we disregard externalities, a typical voluntary transaction contributes to welfare by adding the transaction surplus to the original level of welfare. If the transaction costs become so high that they exceed the gross transaction surplus, the transaction does not continue, and the transaction surplus is foregone. This is a loss for the welfare of society.

5.4 Externalities

5.4.1 Introduction

Definition Sometimes a transaction has costs or benefits that affect not only the parties, but also a third party (an outsider to the transaction). These costs and benefits, to the extent that they affect outsiders, are called 'external effects' of the transaction, or 'externalities'.[8]

Examples Suppose, for example, that Corrado has a farm that includes a barn with asbestos. Corrado is growing older and intends to sell his farm soon. He realizes that the asbestos in the barn will negatively affect the money he will receive for the farm and estimates the damage to be 1,000. Therefore, he makes inquiries about what it will cost him to have the asbestos removed.

Corrado receives two offers. One offer is from Asbestos Managers, who ask for 1,100 to do the job. For that price they will remove the asbestos and destroy it completely, according to the legal requirements. The second offer is from The Fixers, who ask for only 700. As everybody knows, The Fixers is a company run by the local mafia, and they will most likely dump the removed asbestos during night on a plot of land at the other side of the city.

Corrado reckons that the offer from Asbestos Managers is more expensive than the gain he expects from having the asbestos removed. Therefore, he decides not to accept this offer. The offer from The Fixers is more attractive. He will gain 1,000 from the money he will receive for his farm, and it will cost him only 700. Corrado prefers not to think too much about the way in which The Fixers will solve his problem. Therefore, he decides to contract with The Fixers for 700.

The Fixers dump the removed asbestos at night on a piece of land that belongs to Giulia. Giulia now has the costs of removing and destroying the asbestos, and these costs are external to the costs associated with the transaction between Corrado and The Fixers. Such costs are called externalities or external effects.

Externalities may also be benefits. Pedro contracts with a local builder to build a hotel. The hotel attracts tourists who buy goods in the local shops. The shopkeepers make a

---

8   See https://corporatefinanceinstitute.com/resources/knowledge/economics/externality/ (last visited on 1 May 2019).

profit, and this benefit is external to the contract between Pedro and the builder. The benefits are internal to the sales contracts between the visitors and the shopkeepers but would not have existed if the hotel had not been built. Therefore, the benefits are externalities to the contract to build the hotel.

5.4.2   Costs, Benefits and Decisions

If Bob considers buying Alice's car, then – if he is rational – he will balance his costs and benefits for the transaction. His costs are 1,200 and his benefit is the car, which he values at 1,500; his profit would therefore be 300. This buyer surplus makes it rational for Bob to buy the car from Alice. Alice will also balance her costs and benefits, and she will sell the car to Bob. The costs and the benefits of the transaction determine whether the transaction will take place, but this applies only to the internal costs and benefits. The costs for Nicky, the daughter of Alice who also used the car, are not taken into account. Neither are the benefits for Charles, the father of Bob, who is also going to use the car. From a welfare perspective, the additional costs and benefits are relevant, but they are not taken into account if Alice and Bob decide about the sale of the car solely on the basis of their own costs and benefits.

If Corrado decides whether to contract with The Fixers to solve his asbestos problem, he will balance the benefit of an increase in the value of his farm against the money that the mafia asks for removing the asbestos. Corrado will normally not take Giulia's costs into account. Therefore, if it is worth 1,000 to Corrado to have the asbestos removed and The Fixers are prepared to do the job for 700, The Fixers will have the job. The costs that Giulia must pay to have the asbestos destroyed – say 500 – do not play a role in the cost-benefit analysis that Corrado makes.

The transaction between Corrado and The Fixers has a positive transaction surplus. However, if we consider the small society consisting of Corrado, Giulia and The Fixers, the transaction and its execution decrease the welfare in this society. Giulia's loss is bigger than the surplus of the transaction between Corrado and The Fixers. We ignore the fact that The Fixers' practice is illegal and that Giulia may have a claim against The Fixers, and perhaps also against Corrado. By focusing only on Corrado, The Fixers and Giulia, we also ignore the fact that Giulia's costs will benefit the person who contracts with Giulia to remove the asbestos from her land.

5.5   SOCIAL DILEMMAS

5.5.1   Definition

Individual rationality, collective irrationality The asbestos story illustrates how externalities may lead to decisions that damage the overall welfare of a society. It also illustrates how individual rationality may lead to collective irrationality. If we ignore criminal sanctions and claims for damage, both Corrado and The Fixers made a rational decision. However, given that the welfare of the society decreased, the decision was, from a collective point of view, irrational. Both Corrado and The Fixers incurred costs, only to move the asbestos problem from Corrado to Giulia.

The phenomenon that some forms of behaviour are individually rational but collectively irrational is called a *social dilemma*.[9]

Mutual externalities The nature of the problem becomes clearer if we consider the reactions of other people who suffer from the externalities. Suppose that there are two neighbours who do not care much about each other and their mutual relationship. They have gardens, which share a border. On the border is a fence. One of the neighbours, Ziggy, removes the weeds from his garden and throws them over the fence into his neighbour's garden. For him this is the easiest way to dispose of the weeds, and his action therefore seems rational in a cost-benefit analysis.

The other neighbour, Peter, finds the weeds in his garden. He does not know where they came from, and he does not care either. As he does not like to have the weeds in his garden, he disposes of them in the way that is easiest for him: he throws them over the fence, into Ziggy's garden.

Ziggy finds the weeds in his garden. He does not know where they came from, and he does not care either. As he does not like to have the weeds in his garden, he disposes of them in the way that is easiest for him: he throws them over the fence, into Peter's garden.

Let us assume, slightly unrealistically, that this story repeats itself twenty times: Ziggy and Peter continue to throw the weeds over the fence into each other's gardens. At some

---

9   The definition that was offered here differs in formulation from other definitions, such as the ones given on http://faculty.washington.edu/jtenenbg/courses/tgh303/f12/socialDilemmaFormal.html: 'a social dilemma is a collective action situation in which the Nash equilibrium results in outcomes below the Pareto optimal'. Substantially, they are in agreement, however.

moment, the weeds are in Ziggy's garden again. The situation is exactly the same as when the story started, except for one thing. Both Ziggy and Peter have an aching back for collecting the weeds and throwing them over the garden fence. Both are worse off, and no problem has been solved.

Every time that either Ziggy or Peter threw the weeds over the garden fence, the action had more benefits than costs for the person performing it. However, every time, the external costs were the same as the internal gains. So from a collective perspective, the welfare perspective, every action was bad, since it had no net benefits but only net costs (the labour of throwing the weeds over the garden fence). That explains why the situation at the end of the story was the same, except for the cumulative cost of all the actions. This cumulative cost was the backaches of both Ziggy and Peter.

Let us also consider two more serious examples.

Air pollution The possibility that individually rational decisions may lead to collectively irrational results can lead to serious problems. One has to do with pollution. Pollution of the environment is often the result of small wrongs of individual polluters. For every individual car driver holds that the pollution caused by his car is negligible. If he stops driving his car, the overall pollution will hardly be less. For him individually, the costs of not driving a car are bigger than the gain of an unnoticeable decrease in air pollution. In a cost-benefit analysis the rational thing to do is clear: continue to drive his car. A car driver might also arrive at the same conclusion from the opposite direction: if everybody else stops polluting, the air will be clean anyway, and the minor contribution of his car will not change that. So he might just as well continue to drive his car.

Of course, for all other car drivers the same line of argument is valid. Everybody who stops driving their car acts irrationally. Since nobody wants to be irrational, everybody will continue driving their car, and the air pollution increases. It would have been much better if everybody had stopped: individual rationality leads to collective irrationality.

Tax dodging The second example has to do with tax dodging. Let us assume that it is possible to dodge taxes without being caught. For every individual it holds that she is irrational if she pays taxes while nobody else does it. Moreover, if everybody else is paying their taxes, one small contribution will not be missed. So, whatever the others may do, it is better not to pay taxes. This is individual rationality. Of course, if nobody pays taxes, there will be no tax income, and it is impossible to finance public goods such as roads, hospitals and schools. It would be much better if everybody paid their taxes. Not paying taxes leads to collective irrationality.

Social dilemma The phenomenon that some forms of behaviour are individually rational but collectively irrational is called a *social dilemma*. As the last two examples illustrate, social dilemmas can have very serious consequences. Moreover, they are difficult to control, because to stop them, individual agents are required to act against their own interests.

5.5.2   Internalizing Externalities

The solution to a social dilemma is to align the interests of society with the interests of the individual persons in it. This is done by making sure that interests that were originally only interests of third-party persons or organizations now also become interests of the parties to the transaction. Then these interests will be taken into account by the parties. This is called *internalizing externalities*.

Sanctions One way to internalize externalities is to attach sanctions to behaviour that negatively affects the interests of third parties. The asbestos case can illustrate this. Dumping asbestos waste is punishable, and therefore there is a cost attached to this behaviour. The cost is the amount of the punishment, multiplied by the risk that the sanction will actually be executed. For example, if there is a fine of 10,000 for dumping asbestos waste, and there is a 10% chance that the punishment will be executed, the additional cost of dumping the asbestos waste is 1,000. This cost has to be added to the costs of deconstructing the barn and transporting the waste to the land of Giulia. The external costs of dumping the waste are then internalized.

For example, if the original cost for The Fixers for deconstructing the barn and transporting the waste to Giulia's land was 200, the cost with the sanction included will be 1200 (200 + 1000). So The Fixers would need more than 1200 to make the transaction rational. Only if the sum of these costs is less than what Corrado will pay, it is rational for The Fixers to remove Corrado's waste and dump it. If Corrado will not pay more than 700, the transaction will not continue.[10]

By making the chance that the fine will be executed sufficiently high or by increasing the amount of the fine to a sufficient degree, the government can make The Fixers' practice irrational. When that has happened, the individual irrationality of the behaviour is in line with its collective irrationality, and the social dilemma has been solved.

---

10   Notice, by the way, that the cost of possible sanctions is transaction costs (execution costs). These costs are attached to the transaction and do not benefit the parties to the transaction. This shows how transaction costs can be created with the aim of internalizing externalities.

Sanctions are not the only way to modify the costs and benefits of a potential transaction. By subsidizing contracts with Asbestos Management, a community may shift the cost-benefit comparison in favour of transactions with legal asbestos handlers, thereby internalizing the benefit of a clean environment.

Finally, giving Giulia the possibility to claim damages from The Fixers or from Corrado can also internalize costs of pollution that might otherwise have remained externalities.

Third-party intervention Suppose that Giulia had been involved in the negotiations between Corrado and The Fixers. She does not want the asbestos to be dumped on her land, as this will cost her 500. She might offer The Fixers 400 if they do not dump the waste on her land but have it destroyed in the normal way. Let us assume that Corrado does not care how his asbestos is 'destroyed', so the question now is whether The Fixers will be willing to destroy the asbestos legally. By offering The Fixers 400, Giulia has made her problem the problem of The Fixers too. The 400 that Giulia is willing to pay is now a benefit that The Fixers must take into account when negotiating with Corrado. In this way, the costs of Giulia, which were originally external to the decision made by Corrado and The Fixers, have become internal and play a role in the decision-making process.

More in general, externalities can be internalized and can play a role in decision-making if the external parties who suffer the external costs are allowed to interfere in the decision-making process and are willing to pay to have a decision that is not (too) bad for them. If there are potential external benefits at stake, external parties can offer money to steer the decision in a direction that benefits them.

5.5.3 Externalities and Free Trade

Competition policy A realistic example of how internalizing externalities promotes welfare is the competition policy of the EU. Enterprises can boost their gains by limiting competition. If the two main producers of steel agree on a minimum price for steel that is higher than the market price would be if competition were in force, they can make bigger profits. In itself this is not bad. However, the bigger profits must be paid by the consumers of steel, and the problem is that these increased consumer costs are bigger than the increased profits of the steel producers. This means that society as a whole has a welfare loss, even though the steel producers have an increase in utility. For the steel producers, it is attractive to limit competition; for society as a whole it is unattractive.

To align the interests of the steel producers with those of society as a whole, the EU has attached monetary sanctions to the elimination of competition. With these sanctions in place, it is less attractive for enterprises to agree on minimum prices. If everything works out well, the costs that enterprises expect to have if they make competition-eliminating trade agreements with each other are bigger than the increased profits that they expect from the agreement. Then they will refrain from price agreements, and although the profits of the enterprises will drop, society as a whole will gain. The pursuit of Pareto-efficiency now promotes welfare.

Transaction costs as a means to avoid negative externalities Apparently, the level of the transaction costs is an important determinant of whether a transaction takes place. Since the State can influence the transaction costs by means of taxation or fines, it can use this tool to influence the transactions that will take place. In this way, the State can use transaction costs to avoid unwanted externalities.

6 The Economics of International Trade

6.1 Mercantilism and Free Trade

Many of us will recognize the phenomenon: we see an article advertised on the Internet for a price that is so low that we would love to buy it. It is really a bargain! However, we lack the money and have to forego the offer. This is a situation in which:
1. we value the article more than the seller does;
2. the price of the article is less than the value we attach to the article;
3. it is not possible to buy the article.

Apparently, the theory that a trade transaction will take place if it leads to a surplus for all parties to the transaction is too simple. That a transaction would be a Pareto-improvement does not always imply that the transaction will take place. Potential buyers must have enough money to buy things if opportunities present themselves. Having money is sometimes necessary to enjoy bargains and to reach even higher levels of welfare. This is one of the reasons why parents advise their children to save some money for when such opportunities arise. It is prudent to save; at least, so it seems. This kind of prudence underlies the economic policy of *mercantilism*.

6.1.1 Mercantilist Policies

Bullionism A country follows a mercantilist policy if it uses trade to accumulate national wealth. Originally, this wealth was measured in terms of the precious metals silver and gold, together also known as *bullion*. A simple mercantilist policy is to arrange international trade in such a way that the influx of bullion into a country exceeds its outflow. This is done by promoting a positive trade balance (more exports than imports). In a more sophisticated version, mercantilism would promote the net influx of durable goods, including not only bullion, but also finished products.

Policies A good impression of mercantilism can be acquired from the list of recommendations made by Von Hörnigk:
1. To inspect the country's soil with the greatest care and not to leave the agricultural possibilities of a single corner or clod of earth unconsidered.
2. All commodities found in a country, which cannot be used in their natural state, should be worked up within the country.

3. Attention should be given to the population, that it may be as large as the country can support.
4. Gold and silver once in the country are under no circumstances to be taken out for any purpose.
5. The inhabitants should make every effort to get along with their domestic products.
6. Foreign commodities should be obtained not for gold or silver, but in exchange for other domestic wares.
7. Foreign commodities should be imported in unfinished form and worked up within the country.
8. Opportunities should be sought night and day for selling the country's superfluous goods to these foreigners in manufactured form.
9. No importation should be allowed under any circumstances of which there is a sufficient supply of suitable quality at home.[1]

As can be seen from this list, international free trade is not high on the list of mercantilist priorities. Trade is a means for a country to obtain wealth in the sense of durable goods. If international trade contributes to this wealth, it should be promoted. To the extent that it impoverishes the country, it should be discouraged.

Criticism From the 17th century on, mercantilism has been criticized. We discuss two main lines of criticism. One line is that the amount of wealth in the world is not a fixed quantity that needs to be distributed over countries. Trade is not only a means of *distribution* of wealth in which everybody tries to get as big a share of the pie as possible; it is also a means to *create* wealth. The second line builds on top of the first line by detailing how international trade benefits all parties involved.

However, despite these criticisms, mercantilist ideas have not left the world stage. Developing countries still use mercantilist policies to protect their national industries against the leading competitive powers of developed international industries and nations. Moreover, some countries stick to mercantilist policies, even though it may be argued that they have left the stage of 'development'. Other highly developed countries, perhaps as defence against the protectionist strategies of others, reintroduce mercantilist policies to make their countries great again.

---

1   Taken from https://en.wikipedia.org/wiki/Philipp_von_H%C3%B6rnigk#cite_note-1 (last visited on 13 September 2018).

6.1.2   Is there a Fixed Amount of Wealth?

Although the list of mercantilist policies does not state it explicitly, it seems to have an underlying assumption. This assumption is that there is a fixed amount of wealth in the world, in the form of bullion or other durable goods, and that prosperity consists in having as big a part of this wealth as possible. Is this assumption correct?

Wealth The assumption is correct if wealth is defined as bullion and durable goods. At any moment in time, there is a fixed amount of gold, silver and other durable goods. Having as much of these goods as possible increases a country's power in the international arena, especially in the purchasing arena.

Welfare The assumption is incorrect if one focuses on the amount of welfare in a country. It is possible to increase the amount of welfare simply by moving a good within a country from one person to another who values it more. Since the redistribution is made within one and the same country, the amount of wealth of the country as a whole does not change. However, the amount of welfare increases. Here, the difference between wealth as defined in terms of durable goods, and welfare, as defined in terms of valuation, is crucial. Moving wealth within a country does not change the total amount of wealth in this country, but it may – and typically will – change the amount of welfare.

The same holds for moving goods from one country to another country. This does typically involve a change in wealth. If country A buys wheat from country B and pays with gold, country B has become wealthier. Country A has become poorer, as grain is not durable (it is meant to be eaten). However, if the population of country A was starving, they preferred wheat over gold, and the exchange of gold for wheat was an increase in welfare. Moreover, since country B had enough wheat, they preferred gold over wheat. So for both countries the exchange increased their welfare.

So if welfare is the 'real' wealth – and if we ignore externalities - every free exchange increases wealth. This observation lies at the basis of the pleas for free trade that at present are broadly supported. We will continue to study the theory behind these pleas in some more detail.

6.2 Absolute and Comparative Advantages

6.2.1 Absolute Advantage

One of the main critics of mercantilist policies was the Scottish moral philosopher and economist Adam Smith (1723-1790). In his book *The Wealth of Nations*, Smith argued that it was impossible for all nations to become rich simultaneously by following mercantilism because one nation's export is another nation's import. Instead, he stated that all nations would gain simultaneously if they practiced free trade and specialized in accordance with their absolute advantage.

To evaluate Smith's claim, we must first take a closer look at the idea of an absolute advantage. Country A has an absolute advantage in producing a good G over country B if it needs fewer resources to produce a certain amount of G.[2]

Let us take apple juice as an example. We assume that apples are the only resource necessary to produce apple juice. (So we ignore labour.) If Belgium can produce apple juice from fewer apples than the Netherlands, Belgium has an absolute advantage over the Netherlands in producing apple juice. Analogously, if the Netherlands can produce tomato juice from fewer tomatoes than Belgium, the Netherlands have an absolute advantage over Belgium in producing tomato juice.[3]

In this example, it would be advantageous for Belgium and the Netherlands to trade apple juice against tomato juice. To make this more concrete, we need a few more assumptions. Suppose that Belgium can make a litre of apple juice from six apples and a litre of tomato juice from twelve tomatoes, and that the Netherlands uses, respectively, eight apples and nine tomatoes. Suppose, moreover, that in both countries there are 24 million apples available and 36 million tomatoes. Without trade, the Netherlands would produce three million litres of apple juice and four million litres of tomato juice. Belgium would produce four million litres of apple juice and three million litres of tomato juice.

If both countries specialize in the production of the juice in which they have an absolute advantage and trade the surplus against a product of the other country, both countries benefit. If Belgium traded its tomatoes against four million litres of Dutch tomato juice, and four million litres of its apple juice against the Dutch apples, both countries would

---

[2] Mankiw and Taylor 2017, p. 388.
[3] We ignore the quality of the apple juice and the tomato juice here, or assume that it is the same in both countries.

end up with four million litres of both apple and tomato juice. Without the trade, Belgium would have only three million litres of tomato juice (and four million litres of apple juice) and the Netherlands would have only three million litres of apple juice (and three million litres of tomato juice). So the trade leads to an increase in the production of tomato and apple juice of both 1,000,000 litres and both countries benefit (enjoy a Pareto-improvement; Table 6.1).

Table 6.1 Absolute advantages

	Belgium		The Netherlands	
	Without trade	With trade	Without trade	With trade
Apples	24,000,000		24,000,000	
Tomatoes	36,000,000		36,000,000	
Apple juice	4,000,000	4,000,000	3,000,000	4,000,000
Tomato juice	3,000,000	4,000,000	4,000,000	4,000,000

Smith's claim The example of apple and tomato juice illustrates why Smith was right. If there is free trade, every country can specialize and produce what it does the best. If Belgium could not export its extra apple juice to the Netherlands or to another country, it would make little sense to produce more than what is necessary for domestic consumption. At some moment it would need to stop the production of apple juice and devote its remaining resources to a job at which it is not so good. The Netherlands would have to do the same, and the final result is a lower overall level of production. For the amount of goods produced, it is best if every country produces what it is best at, but this is only possible if the countries do not need to worry about overproduction. This worry is strongly decreased by the possibility of free international trade.

6.2.2   Comparative Advantage

It is quite obvious that international trade is advantageous if one country is better at producing one good and another country at producing another. If both countries specialize in what they are best at, the result is a useful division of labour, where trade prevents countries from overproducing.

However, what happens if one country is better than some other country in 'everything'? Is trade between the two countries still a good idea, or should the more productive country produce everything itself? The answer to this question depends on the circumstances. If the more productive country has a surplus production capacity, which would remain unused if the country imported goods, then it should not trade. However, if its production capacity does not suffice for domestic demand, and choices must be made on how to use the available capacity in the best possible way, things become different.

This was pointed out by the economist Ricardo (1772-1823) in his theory of comparative advantages. To explain this theory, we need an example where a production resource can be used for different products. Therefore, the example of tomatoes and apples in its original form is useless, and we choose an example where the only relevant resource is labour. Labour can be used to produce different kinds of goods, and a country that does not have sufficient labour to produce everything it needs must decide how much labour to allocate to the production of a good.

Example Let us assume that there are two kinds of labour necessary in the fruit sector: tomato picking and apple picking. There are also two countries involved: Norway and Spain. People in Spain are more experienced fruit pickers and are therefore better than Norwegian pickers, both for tomatoes and for apples. One Spanish picker can pick 1,200 apples in an hour, or 800 tomatoes. One Norwegian picker can pick 800 apples in an hour or 600 tomatoes. Both Spain and Norway have more apples and tomatoes than can be picked by their own workers, so it is not possible for Spain to ignore the Norwegian picking capacity.

To keep the example relatively simple, we assume that both countries have twelve pickers and that each of them can pick only 10 hours. If each country assigns half of its picking capacity to apple picking and half to tomato picking, Spain will have 72,000 apples and 48,000 tomatoes. Norway will have 48,000 apples and 36,000 tomatoes. Together they have 120,000 apples and 84,000 tomatoes.

If Norway used all of its labour capacity for picking tomatoes, it would produce 72,000 tomatoes (and no apples). That is 12,000 tomatoes less than the production of the two countries together devoting half of their capacity to tomatoes. If Spain spends 15 hours (one and a half pickers) on tomatoes, it compensates for this shortage. Spain still has 105 hours (10.5 pickers) left for apples, and this gives 126,000 apples. Together, the two countries produce 126,000 apples and 84,000 tomatoes, which is 6,000 apples more and the same amount of tomatoes than they would have had if Norway did not specialize in tomatoes. See Table 6.2.

Table 6.2 Comparative advantages

	Spain		Norway		Together	
	Without specialization	With specialization	Without specialization	With specialization	Without specialization	With specialization
Apples	72,000	126,000	48,000	0	120,000	126,000
Tomatoes	48,000	12,000	36,000	72,000	84,000	84,000

As this example illustrates, specialization leads to a higher aggregate production. In this example, the gain is 6,000 apples. In other cases, the numbers will be different, but the overall picture remains the same: specialization pays. As specialization requires trade to compensate for overproduction in one country and underproduction in another country, this argument for specialization is at the same time an argument for international trade.

Comparative advantage How is it possible that a country that is better at picking tomatoes benefits from importing tomatoes from a country that performs worse? The answer is that it is not the absolute advantage that counts, but the comparative advantage. Although Norway is worse than Spain in the absolute numbers for fruit picking, it is comparatively better than Spain in picking tomatoes than picking apples. In Norway the proportion *picked tomatoes/picked apples* is 36,000/48,000, or simplified 9/12. In Spain the numbers are 48,000/72,000, and simplified 8/12. It turns out that Norway is 1/12 better in the ratio of picking tomatoes to picking apples. So, comparatively speaking, Norway is better in picking tomatoes than Spain and this explains why picking tomatoes is better left to the Norwegians.

In a similar argument, it may be argued that Spain is comparatively better than Norway when it comes to picking apples versus picking tomatoes (1,5 vs 1,33). Therefore, picking apples is better left to the Spaniards.

6.2.3 Conclusion on Absolute and Relative Advantages

Absolute and relative advantages ensure that if the production of goods is assigned to those countries that have an advantage in producing them, the aggregate amount of produced goods can be higher for all goods. This does not automatically mean that all countries that participate in this production benefit, as it is possible that a country ends up with overproduction of one good and underproduction of another good. However, when the goods can be traded between the countries, it is possible that all countries end up with at least the same amount of every good as what they would have had without specialization, and sometimes even more. International trade makes specialization more attractive, and specialization leads to a higher overall production level and therefore to more welfare. That is what makes international trade attractive.

6.3 The (Dis)Advantages of Free International Trade

6.3.1 Consumer and Producer Surplus

Advantage of voluntary trade A voluntary sales transaction will normally benefit both seller and buyer. Such a transaction will be performed only if seller and buyer agree on a price that is within their utility range. This means that a sale at the agreed price will lead to both a seller surplus (the difference between the price and the seller utility) and a buyer surplus (the difference between the buyer utility and the price). If something prevents such a transaction from happening – high transaction costs in the form of a tax, for example – this leads to a loss (missing profit) for both parties.

If we consider trade within one country, every voluntary transaction will benefit both seller and buyer. Ignoring potential externalities, voluntary trade will lead to an increase in welfare within the country. This increase consists of two elements. One is the *consumer surplus*, which is the sum of the buyer surpluses of all domestic consumers. The other is the *producer surplus*, which is the sum of the seller surpluses of all domestic producers. (We assume here that sellers and producers are the same.) See Figure 6.1.

Offer, demand and equilibrium price To understand Figure 6.1, it is useful to first ignore the coloured elements. The figure contains two 'curves', which are, for the sake of simplicity, assumed to be straight lines. The offer curve represents the amount of goods that are offered given a particular market price. The curve goes up, indicating that the amount of goods offered increases with the market price. The demand curve goes down, indicating that the amount of goods demanded decreases if the market price increases.

At some price level, the amount of goods offered equals the demand. This will be the price at which the goods are actually traded, the domestic market price. It is also called an equilibrium, because the amounts of goods offered and demanded at this price level are equal.

Producer surplus The producer surplus is the dark triangle, directly above the line that represents the offers. Some producers are willing to sell for a price below the market price (equilibrium), and for them the price is higher than their utility. They have a seller surplus, and the sum of all the seller surpluses of all producers (who sell) is the producer surplus. The producer surplus does not extend above the price line, because above that line no products will be bought and no profits made.

Consumer surplus The consumer surplus is the lighter triangle, directly underneath the line that represents the demand. Some consumers are willing to buy for a price higher than the market price (equilibrium), and for them the price is lower than their utility. They have a buyer surplus, and the sum of all the buyer surpluses of all consumers (who buy) is the consumer surplus. The consumer surplus does not extend below the price line, because below that line no products will be sold and no benefits enjoyed.

Figure 6.1 Consumer and producer surplus

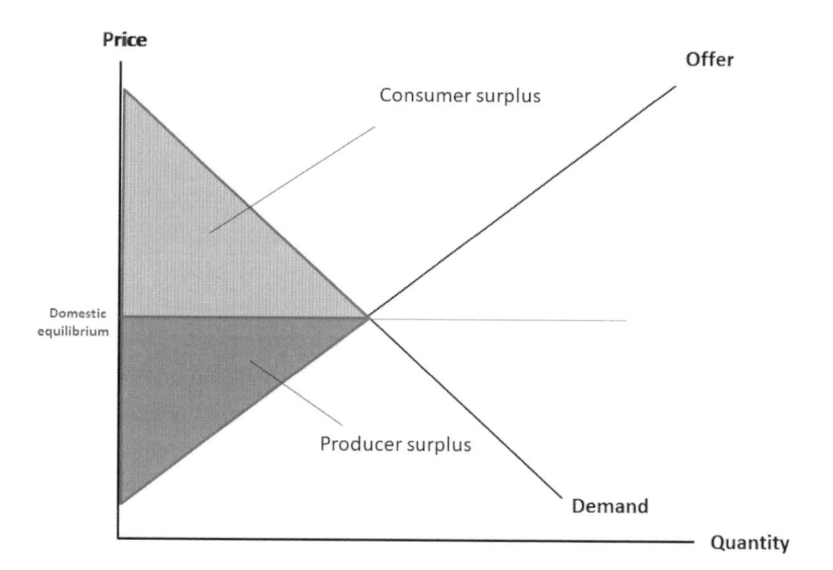

Welfare effect The sum of the consumer surplus and the producer surplus in a country is the effect of the sales on the welfare of the country. Because consumers buy only if this is to their advantage, the consumer surplus of voluntary transactions will always be positive (or at least zero). Because producers sell only if this is to their advantage, the producer surplus of voluntary transactions will always be positive (or at least zero). This means that the sum of the consumer surplus and the producer surplus will always be positive, and that voluntary trade makes a positive contribution to the welfare in a country.

European Integration: A Theme

International trade On the international level, a similar story holds true: every voluntary transaction will benefit both seller and buyer. However, this does not guarantee that international trade transactions will increase the welfare levels *of the participating countries*. For example, if consumers in the USA buy Huawei phones that were made in China, they buy fewer smartphones from local producers such as Apple. Is it possible that the gain in consumer surplus is less than the loss in producer surplus of the domestic producers?

To investigate whether allowing free international trade is also good for the countries as a whole that are involved in the trade – and not only the consumers in the importing countries and the producers in the exporting countries – we need to go into more detail. In this connection we will study the effects of:
- allowing free international trade in a country that is so small that it cannot influence the world market price;
- allowing free international trade in a country that is so big that it influences the world market price;
- the introduction of a tariff on international trade in a small country.

Figure 6.2   Import and export

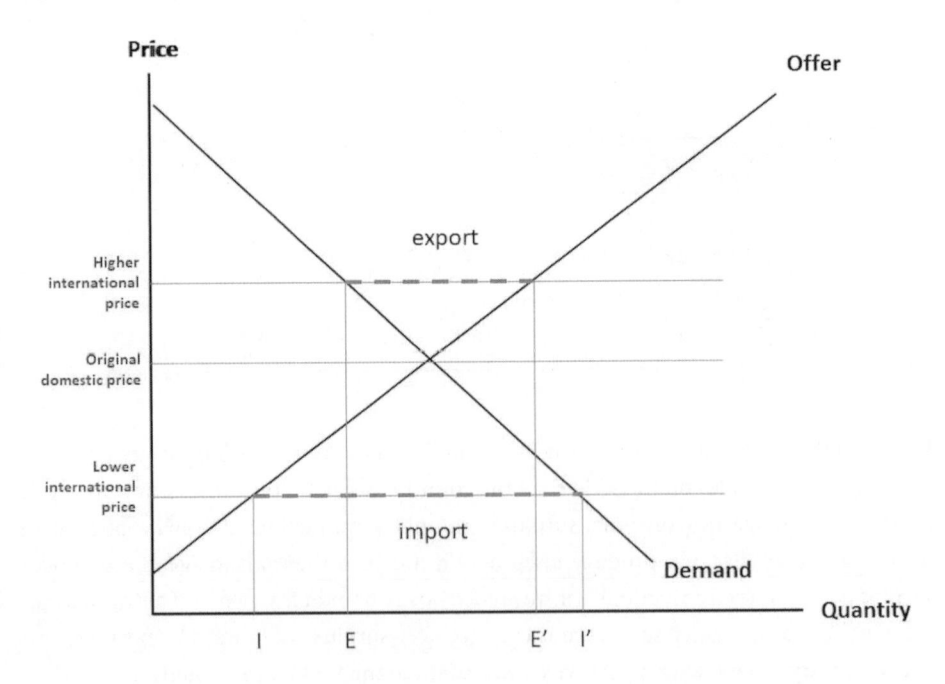

6.3.2 Allowing Free International Trade in a Small Country

Import and export If a country is not big, it typically does not influence the world market price if it opens its market to international trade. For example, if Luxembourg allows free international trade for mountain bikes, this will not change the price of mountain bikes on the international market. The main effect is that the price of mountain bikes in Luxembourg becomes equal to the international price. The price may drop and Luxembourg will become a net importer of mountain bikes. The price may also rise, and then Luxembourg will become a net exporter of mountain bikes. See Figure 6.2.

If the international market price – which has also become the local price – is high, the domestic offer of mountain bikes on the Luxembourgian local market will be higher than the demand. The surplus of bikes must be exported, and the amount of export equals what is offered at the market price minus what is demanded (E'- E). Obviously, the bikes will be exported at the (high) international market price.

If the international market price is lower than the domestic price, the domestic offer of mountain bikes on the Luxembourgian market will be less than the demand. The lacking bikes must be imported, and the amount of import equals the demand minus what is offered (I'- I). Obviously, the bikes will be imported at the (low) international market price.

Welfare effects of import Suppose that the world market price for mountain bikes is lower than the domestic price in Luxembourg. If Luxembourg opens its borders for the import of mountain bikes, the domestic price will drop to the level of the world market. Given this lower price, Luxembourg consumers will purchase more bikes. More purchases at a lower price means that the consumer surplus will increase. However, not all Luxembourg producers can afford to produce at such a low price, and some of them will leave the market. This means that at this lower price, less Luxembourg-made mountain bikes will be sold, and at the lower price. It also means that the Luxembourgian producer surplus will drop.

To compute the national effect of the open border for mountain bikes, we must balance the bigger consumer surplus against the smaller producer surplus. In Figure 6.3 we can see how this balance works out.

If the price of mountain bikes in Luxembourg drops from Home Price to World Price, the consumer surplus grows. Originally, it was only the area designated as A, but at the lower price level it consists of the areas A, B and C together. (It is the area under the Home demand line and above the price line.) This means that the consumer surplus has increased by B + C.

The same price drop decreases the producer surplus. Originally, it was the area designated as D and B together, but at the lower price level it consists only of the area D. (It is the area above the Home supply line, and below the price line.) This means that the producer surplus has decreased by B.

Since the increase in the consumer surplus (B + C) is more than the decrease in the producer surplus (B), the positive welfare effect of opening the border for mountain bikes is represented by the (surface of) area C.

Welfare and distribution effects Simply stated, if a small country opens its borders for import, the increase in consumer surplus is bigger than the decrease in producer surplus. This is a positive welfare effect. However, the gain is not equally divided over consumers and producers. The producers lose, while the consumers win (more). So the overall welfare effect is positive, but the distribution is to the disadvantage of the domestic producers.

That may be a reason why domestic producers of a good are not always in favour of allowing imports. Think, for instance, of the steel producers in the USA. They may be happy if steel imports are impeded by tariffs, because imports are not good for them. However, steel users in the USA pay for it, and they pay more than the producers gain.

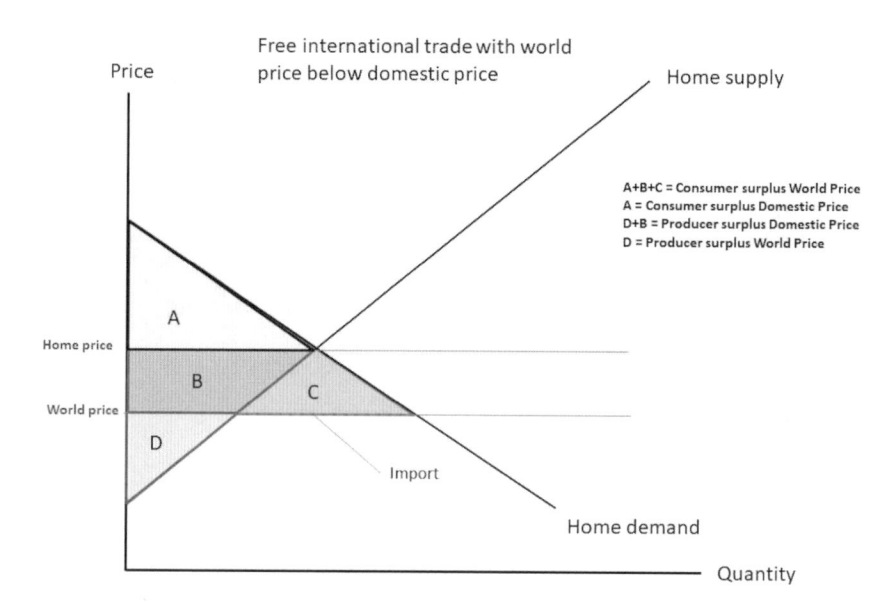

Figure 6.3   The welfare effect of imports

```
                Free international trade with world
Price           price below domestic price              Home supply

                                              A+B+C = Consumer surplus World Price
                                              A = Consumer surplus Domestic Price
                                              D+B = Producer surplus Domestic Price
                                              D = Producer surplus World Price

                    A
Home price
                B         C
World price
            D
                            Import
                                          Home demand
                                                        Quantity
```

Actually, the situation is even more complicated, because there are also externalities to take into consideration. Steel producers who can sell more on the local market will hire local workers, who earn an income and buy more on the local market, which boosts the economy. This is a positive externality of blocking imports. On the other hand, local consumers, and other industries that use steel, must pay more for steel products and will have less money left for buying other products. This hampers the local economy and is a negative externality of blocking imports. These externalities must be taken into account when computing the *overall* welfare effect of allowing or blocking imports.

When the international market price is higher than the domestic price Until now, we have only considered the effects of international trade on small countries if the world market price is lower than the domestic price. What if it is the other way around, i.e. the world market price exceeds the domestic price? Then the local price will rise to the level of the world price. The local consumers must pay more, but the local producers will earn more, both because of the higher prices and because they can sell more products on the international market. Figure 6.4 illustrates these effects.

The consumer surplus was A + B but drops to A. The producer surplus was D but increases to D + B + C. The welfare effect is positive and equals (the surface of) area C.

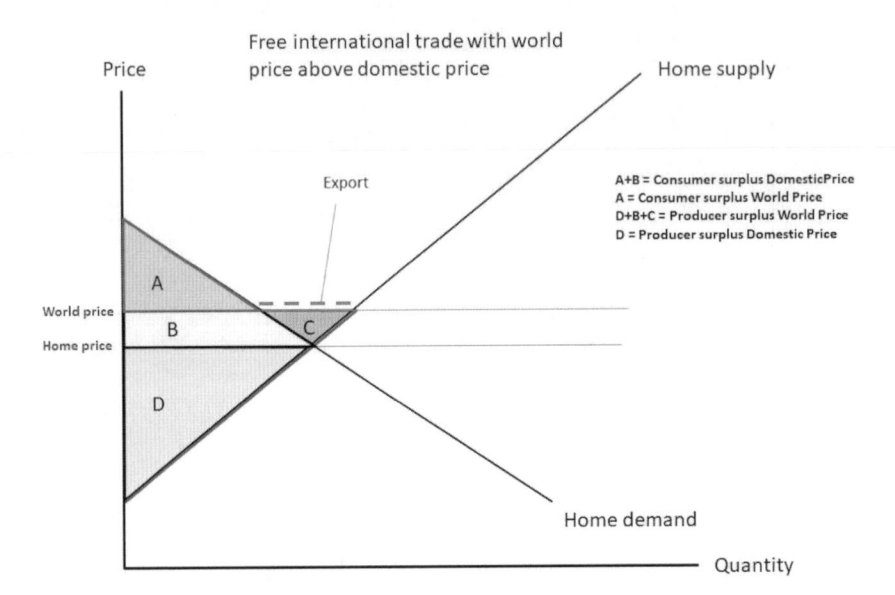

Figure 6.4   The welfare effects of exports

[Figure: Supply and demand diagram showing welfare effects of exports. Home supply curve slopes upward, Home demand curve slopes downward. World price is above Home price. Areas labeled: A (consumer surplus triangle at top), B (rectangle), C (small triangle near intersection), D (producer surplus triangle at bottom). "Export" arrow points to area between world price line and supply/demand intersection. Legend:
- A+B = Consumer surplus Domestic Price
- A = Consumer surplus World Price
- D+B+C = Producer surplus World Price
- D = Producer surplus Domestic Price*]*

6.3.3   Allowing Free International Trade in a Big Country

If a small country opens its borders for import and export, the immediate effect will be that the domestic price becomes equal to the world market price. If a big country opens its borders, the domestic price will move in the direction of the original world market price, but the world market price will also move towards the original domestic price. In the end, however, the domestic and the world market price will be equal. What are the implications for the domestic welfare effects?

Let us first consider the situation where the world market price was originally lower than the domestic price. In this situation, the domestic price will drop somewhat. The producers will lose, and the consumers will benefit, but the benefit of the consumers will exceed the loss of the producers.

If the world market price was originally higher than the domestic price, the domestic price will rise somewhat. The consumers will lose, and the producers will benefit, but the benefit for the producers will exceed the loss of the consumers.

Thus far, the story is not different from that about small countries. However, because the world market price is affected if a big country opens (or closes) its borders, there will be externalities for the consumers and producers elsewhere in the world as well. If the domestic price increases while the world market price drops, domestic producers will gain, but foreign producers will lose; and domestic consumers will also lose, but foreign consumers will gain. The domestic welfare effects are the same for big countries as they are for small countries; however, the external welfare effects are negligible if a small country opens its borders, but significant if a big country does so.

6.3.4 Tariffs

If a country wants to limit imports on specific goods, it typically does not prohibit these imports, but rather limits or taxes them. As the effects of limitations and taxation are similar in many important respects, we will discuss only taxes here. Such taxes are called *tariffs*.

A tariff raises the price of the imported good from the level of the world market price to some higher level.[4] This has several effects:
1. the State receives a tax income;
2. the amount of imported goods drops, as the domestic price has become higher;
3. consumers have to pay more for these goods;
4. domestic producers can sell more, as they do not have to pay the tariff;
5. domestic producers make a higher profit, as the price on the domestic market has risen.

The effects 2 and 3 lead to a smaller consumer surplus; while the effects 4 and 5 lead to a bigger producer surplus. (We are only talking about domestic producers; not those in other countries.) Effect 1 leads to tax income. The question that must be answered is whether the 'positive' effects of tax income and a bigger producer surplus together suffice to compensate for the smaller consumer surplus. The answer is negative, as can be seen from Figure 6.5.

In Figure 6.5, the box labelled D plays a central role. It represents the tax income. The width of this box is given with the amount of import if the tariff is in place, as the tariff is paid only over goods that are actually imported with this tariff. The height of the box represents the height of the tax, which coincides with the increase in the price.

---

[4] This higher level should still be below the domestic market price, because otherwise the goods would not be imported at all.

If the tariff is in place, the consumer surplus decreases with an amount represented by the areas B, C, D and E.

This loss is to some extent compensated by the increase in producer surplus (B) and by the new tax income (D).

However, the areas C and E are not compensated, and they represent the loss in welfare for the country.

We can conclude that a tariff has a negative effect on the total welfare of a country that uses the tariff and that 'gains' the tax income. The local consumers pay for this tax income in the form of a higher local price for the imported goods and loss of potentially advantageous transactions. (The tariff will function as a transaction cost that blocks a number of transactions.)

Figure 6.5   The effects of a tariff

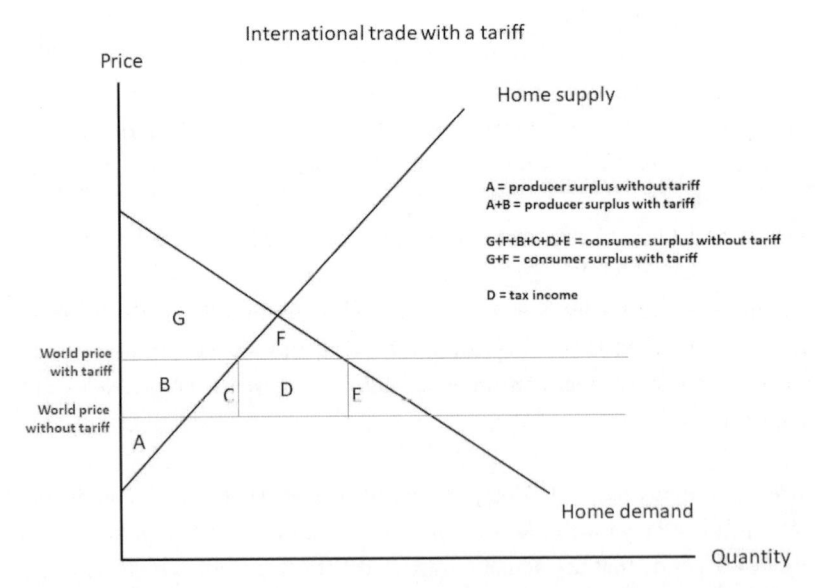

International trade with a tariff

A = producer surplus without tariff
A+B = producer surplus with tariff

G+F+B+C+D+E = consumer surplus without tariff
G+F = consumer surplus with tariff

D = tax income

6.4   Conclusion

If we only look at the internal effects in a particular country when it opens its borders for international trade, we find that the overall welfare effects are always positive. If the consumers lose, the producers gain more, and if the producers lose, the consumers gain more.

However, if the distribution of welfare is taken into account as well, we see that free international trade is good for domestic producers if the world market price is higher than the domestic market price (before trade was made free). However, then it is bad for the domestic consumers. If the world market price was lower than the domestic price, opening the borders for trade benefits only domestic consumers.

The foregoing does not take the external effects on other countries into account. If a small country opens its borders, this does not affect the world market price, and the external effects on foreign countries will be negligible. However, if a big country opens its borders, the world market price moves in the direction of that country's domestic price, and external effects on foreign countries will typically be the opposite of the local effects.

It is not easy to give a general answer to the question of whether the opening of trade borders of a large, industrialized country will have a positive welfare effect on the world as a whole. However, we do know that the introduction of a tariff leads to a loss of welfare in the country that uses the tariff. This means that if a country considers raising a tariff, it should realize that the tariff will have an overall negative welfare effect for the country itself. However, distribution effects may ensure that the producers in the country gain if the world market price is lower than the domestic market price would have been without open borders.

7 Money

7.1 What Is Money?

7.1.1 Coincidence of Wants

Example Mary is sailing her one-person boat on the Pacific, when she is surprised by a heavy storm. Because she is an excellent sailor, she manages to land her boat on an uninhabited island. The boat is severely damaged, and she cannot leave the island without help from outside. When Mary sets out to discover the island on which she landed, she finds to her surprise that the island is not completely uninhabited. The same storm that brought her to the island also brought four other pleasure yachts. These four boats are also not seaworthy, and several people are now stranded, possessing only the goods that were on their boats.

The persons on the island are from five different countries with five different currencies: dollars, euros, reals, roubles and rupiahs. Since there is no guarantee that they will ever reach the inhabited world again, their coins and banknotes are of little use to the castaways. The only method that seems left to exchange goods is barter (exchange without money). Mary would like to have some cigarettes, and she is willing to offer the compass from her ship in exchange for them. However, Raoul is the only person in possession of cigarettes, and he is not interested in a compass. Natacha is interested in the compass but has no cigarettes, and nothing else that would interest Raoul. Kevin has an old-fashioned watch that can be wound up, and Raoul would like to have it, but Kevin is not interested in cigarettes or anything else that Raoul is willing to trade. And so on …

Coincidence of wants The people on the island face what economists call the 'coincidence of wants' problem.[1] If you want to exchange a good G for some good H, you need to find a partner who has H and wants G. Such a person may be hard to find. Of course you might barter G against M with a third person, in the expectation that it is possible to barter M against H again, but that is complicated, unless M is something that everybody wants.

Enter money Here is where money enters the play, because money is exactly something that everybody wants, not because it has any intrinsic value but because everybody else

---

1 Mankiw and Taylor 2017, p. 553.

will accept it in exchange for goods. Money is, by definition, something that is accepted by 'everybody' as a means of payment, and derives its value precisely from this function.

7.1.2   Overview

Money is the central topic of this chapter. Section 7.1 deals with questions such as what money is, what its functions are and what forms it takes. Section 7.2 addresses the creation of money and the role of the central bank in this connection. Because the value of many things is often expressed in terms of money, it is not easy to see that money itself also has a value. This value of money, including inflation and deflation and interest and exchange rates is the topic of Section 7.3. Section 7.4 makes a slight detour by discussing how the value of money can be manipulated for the purpose of indirect taxation. Section 7.5 returns to the value of money in a short discussion of trade equilibria and what maintains them. This leads to the possibility, or rather the impossibility, to conduct monetary policies, a topic discussed in Section 7.6. This chapter is concluded in Section 7.7.

7.1.3   The Functions of Money

Money has three functions; anything that fulfils these three functions is, for that reason, money.[2] The three functions are:
1. a medium of exchange;
2. a unit of account; and
3. a store of value.

Medium of exchange The example about the uninhabited island illustrates that money functions as a medium of exchange. If barter is the only means to exchange goods between people, it may be difficult to find a partner who is offering what you want and who wants what you have to offer. This is the problem of the coincidence of wants, and it inevitably leads to high transaction costs (search costs).

A primitive way to overcome this problem is to make multi-person deals, where person A exchanges one thing for something else that is expected to be exchangeable against still something further, which can once more be exchanged for the item person A really wants. It is difficult to organize such multi-person deals, and the transaction costs will often exceed the utility spread of the exchanges. More plainly said, it is not worth the trouble. Therefore,

---

2   Mankiw and Taylor 2017, p. 554.

multi-person deals will not often take place. This situation changes if there is something that everybody wants. This 'something' is money in its role of an exchange medium.

Commodity money Money can be intrinsically valuable. For instance, many people think that gold is intrinsically valuable and that that would make gold coins also intrinsically valuable. Such money is called 'commodity money' for the reason that the money itself is also a commodity.

Legal tender In the end, money can function only as a medium of exchange if it is widely accepted as such. This acceptance can be promoted if some authority – typically a State – declares the money to be 'legal tender', that is an official means of payment. If this has happened, people will be more disposed to accept money for payment. In turn, this strengthens the reliance of people that money will continue to fulfil this function, thereby making it again possible for the money to do so.

Fiat money Neither intrinsic value nor governmental support is necessary for the existence of money. In the end, the only thing that is required is that 'everybody' accepts the money as a medium of exchange. When that is the case, even the name of the exchange becomes different: sale. Money that is money only because everybody accepts it as a medium of exchange is called 'fiat money'.

A nice historical example in this connection is that while the USSR was dissolving in the 1980s, people in Moscow lost their faith in the rouble as money. Instead, they started to use cigarettes as a means of exchange, as a unit of account and as a store of value. This means that cigarettes fulfilled the functions of money and therefore had become money. Of course, cigarettes were not legal tender, but that does not mean that they were not money.

The so-called cryptocurrencies are a more recent example of money that exists outside the realm of State control. The bitcoin is a well-known example.

Unit of account The main function of money is to be a medium of exchange. However, as soon as money starts to be used in this function, it can also be used as a unit of account. The value of goods can be expressed in terms of money. For example, the value of a car is 10,000 units of some currency.

Store of value Money can fulfil its role as medium of exchange only if it has some durability. If you sell a book for 10 units of money, and the day after you cannot use the money any more to buy something else, then the money has not fulfilled its function. You would not accept money in exchange for a book if there were a serious risk that it would end up worthless. Therefore, functional money must be durable, and because of its durability, it can be used to store value. For example, you can put money in your bank account and save it for the future. Saved money is a store of value.

7.1.4 The Forms of Money

Requirements for money Given the three functions that money fulfils, not everything can be money. Functional money must meet the following requirements[3]:

1. *Fungibility:* Individual units must be interchangeable. For example, a €1 coin is 'the same' as any other €1 coin, and practically the same as two coins of 50 eurocents.
2. *Durability:* If something physically spoils in the short term, it cannot be used as money, as it cannot function as a store of value.
3. *Portability:* If something is to be used as currency, it must be portable. Money in the bank may not always be portable in a strict sense, but it is still money as it can easily be transferred.
4. *Cognizability:* It must be possible to recognize money, because recognition is essential for the acceptance of money as money.
5. *Stability of value:* If the value of money changes frequently, it cannot be used as a medium of exchange or as a store of value. Something can be a medium of exchange only if it can be accepted as money today without any fear that it cannot be used a few days from now. This is why high inflation is so destructive for a particular currency.

7.2 THE CREATION OF MONEY

A substantial part of the money that is in circulation was created by States. For example, the United Kingdom issues English pounds, and China issues yuan. However, anything can function as money if it is only recognized and used as such. This opens the possibility for agents other than States to create money. Coins, banknotes and deposits on demand with banks are the most common forms of money, and, in particular, the deposits give banks the power to create money. As this power is crucially important for the amount of money that is in circulation, and therefore also for the value of money, we will pay some attention to this power of banks to create money.

---

3   See https://en.wikipedia.org/wiki/Money (last visited on 16 October 2019), referring to: Desjardins, Jeff (15 December 2015). 'Infographic: The Properties of Money'.

7.2.1 Money Creation by Banks

Assets, liabilities and reserves If a client deposits money in a bank account, the bank will have a *liability* (debt) towards this client. It also has *assets* for the same amount in the form of a *reserve*.

For example, if A, B and C each deposit 1,000 in the bank, the bank has assets of 3,000 and liabilities towards A, B and C of 1,000 each. If the bank keeps all of its assets stored in a vault, the full amount functions as reserve to meet the bank's liabilities.

Figure 7.1 Assets and liabilities

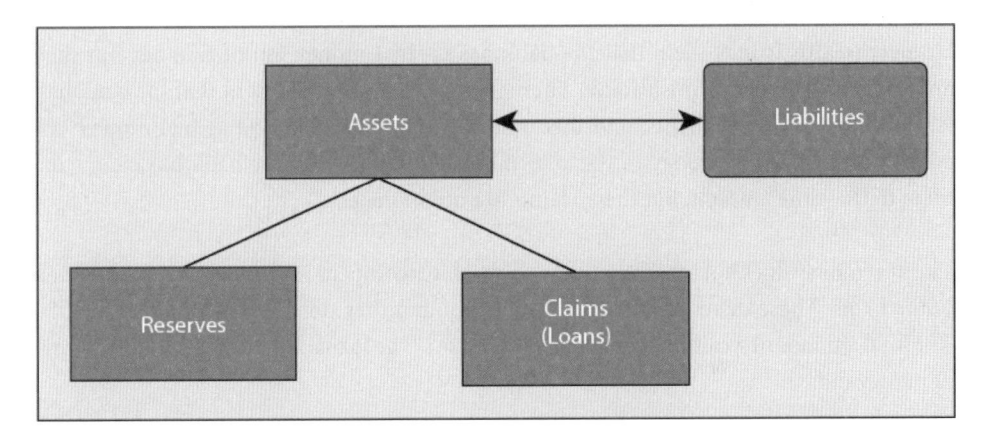

Reserves and loans It is possible for a bank to keep all of its assets as reserve, but that is not necessary. Normally, not all clients will ask for their money back at the same time. Perhaps in an ordinary month, at most 5% of the money is demanded without corresponding new deposits. (E.g. 8% is demanded, but 3% new deposits are made.) That would mean that 95% of the deposited money is waiting in a vault for demands that will never occur. This money could be put to better use, and that is what banks typically do: they lend the money to others who need it, against interest. As compensation they have claims against their debtors (the borrowers) totalling the amount of the loaned money and the expected interest. See Figure 7.1.

Following the preceding example, the bank lends 90% of the deposited money, that is 2,700. Now it has liabilities for 3,000, reserves of 300, and claims to the amount of 2,700. The reserve and the claims together are the assets of the bank, and they still are 3,000, precisely the amount of the bank's liabilities.

New money The clients who deposited their money with the bank still have their money in a bank account. They can demand the money overnight and use it for electronic payments. In short, the deposited money can and will be used as real money, and therefore it is real money. This means that the clients who deposited money in the bank still have 3,000.

The clients who took a loan from the bank now also have bank accounts, totalling the amount of 2,700. They can demand the money overnight and use it for electronic payments too. The money in their accounts can and will also be used as real money, and therefore is real money. This means that the borrowers have 2,700. So the total amount of money now is 5,700 (3,000 + 2,700). By lending money, the bank has created new money.

No new wealth It may seem that the bank has created money out of thin air, but that appearance is somewhat misleading. There is new money, to the extent that the bank has lent money to its new clients, and this money can and will be used as real money. As compensation for the money in the accounts of the borrowers, the bank has claims on them to the same amount, but these claims are not money.

The new money does not represent new wealth, as it is compensated by debts to the amount of the loans. These debts do not count as money, but they do count as negative wealth. The total amount of wealth did not change because of the loans, although the total amount of money did.

Perhaps this appears strange. How is it possible that there is more money without there being more wealth? Borrowed money can function as a medium of exchange. It can be used to buy things, for example. If that happens the borrower has new things, but that is not new wealth as there is still the debt that must be repaid. When the debt is repaid, the money leaves circulation and therewith disappears *as money*. The debt also disappears, and therefore the total amount of wealth still remains the same. The 'only' thing that happened during the loan was that there was temporarily more money in circulation, representing the original amount of wealth.

7.2.2   The Role of the Central Bank

The banks of a country fall under the responsibility of the country's central bank, or – in the case of the EU – under the responsibility of the European Central Bank (ECB). Central banks play an important role in the execution of a country's monetary policies and, in particular, in determining the amount of money in circulation.

Outright monetary transactions There are at least two ways in which a central bank can influence the amount of money. The first way is direct: the central bank itself operates on the financial market by buying bonds (loans) from the public or by selling them to the public. These transactions are called *outright monetary transactions*.

Ignoring some technical complications, an example of outright monetary transactions is the bond-buying program of the ECB that started in 2012. In this program, the ECB bought government and company bonds to support the European monetary system.

Bonds are not considered to be money, but the central bank pays for them with (new) money. This means that if the central bank buys bonds from the public, it brings money into circulation, thereby increasing the amount of money. When the central bank sells bonds to the public, it takes the money paid for the bonds out of circulation, thereby decreasing the amount of money.

Reserve requirements The second way in which the central bank can influence the amount of money is indirect; it may influence the lending policy of 'ordinary' banks. We have seen that banks that receive money in deposit keep their assets in the form of reserves and claims. The reserves are what banks keep stored in their vaults, while banks have claims on the organizations and persons that borrowed money from them. The more banks lend, the bigger the amount of money in circulation.

Central banks can often impose duties on ordinary banks to keep some percentage of their assets, for instance 10%, in their reserves. This money does not enter into circulation and is, from the perspective of society, non-existent. The higher the percentage of their assets that a bank must keep in reserve, the less money will be available for society and the smaller the total amount of money.

The use of a reserve requirement is an indirect method of influencing the amount of money in circulation, as banks are not obligated to lend all the money they are allowed to. For example, if a bank has a reserve requirement of 10%, it is allowed to lend 90%. However, it may decide to lend only 70%, thereby keeping a reserve of 30%. It is the actual lending by banks that influences the amount of money directly. The influence of the central bank through reserve requirements is indirect, as the central bank can only impose boundaries on the lending behaviour of ordinary banks.

7.3 The Value of Money

Consider a country C, where the people earn plenty of money but where there are too few homes. People will bid against each other to buy one of the few homes available for sale, and the prices of the homes will rise to a level that exhausts the available money. Although people in country C have plenty of money, they cannot buy much when it comes to housing.

If there is also a shortage of many other things people need, all prices will rise, and people will not be able to buy much for their money, even though they have plenty of it. In practice, people do not have wealth at all: they have money that used to have a high purchasing power a decade ago but that is almost worthless now.

7.3.1 Inflation

The real value of money is not what is printed on the bank notes, but what can be bought with it. The rise in the prices of goods and the drop in purchasing power – and therefore also the value – of money are two sides of the same coin. The value of money rises or falls as the general price level falls or respectively rises.

When the general price level rises, and the value of money drops, we speak of inflation. This may, for instance, happen when the value of a particular currency has dropped and all imports become more expensive. Then the price level of the imported goods rises, and with it the general price level. People can buy fewer (imported) goods for their money, and the value of their money has decreased. This happened in the first half of 2018 in Turkey, when the Turkish Lira depreciated.

The same happens when there is a sudden and substantial rise in people's earnings. If everybody suddenly earns 10% more and – this is an important condition – the offer of goods does not change accordingly, the main effect will be that people compete for the scarce goods and that the general price level rises. People may nominally earn 10% more, but as a matter of fact, their purchasing power has not changed substantially. The value of what people earn has remained more or less the same, even though the amount expressed in currency has increased.

The price of homes The present situation in the Netherlands with regard to the prices of homes is a case in point. There are too few homes in the Netherlands, and their prices are high. In the long run, this problem can be solved if more homes are built, but in the short term people have to compete for the scarce homes that are available.

The income that people receive from labour rises, but this does not mean that people can more easily afford to buy a home. Since 'everybody's' income rises, everybody is able to pay more for the scarce homes, and the price level of the homes rises with the rise in the salaries. This is inflation.

An increase in money lending – for example, when people can take out higher mortgages – may have the same effect. Then too the amount of money in circulation increases. If there is no corresponding rise in the offer of homes, the prices of homes will rise and inflation occurs.

The same holds for the tax deductibility of interest paid on mortgages. If there is a shortage of homes, this deductibility does not lead to more affordable homes, but only to higher prices (and higher debts).

7.3.2   Deflation

Deflation is the opposite of inflation: the purchasing power of money rises, or – in other words – the goods that are being sold become cheaper.

This may happen when the earnings of people decrease and shopkeepers are forced to lower their prices to match the capacity of their customers. A decline in moneylending has the same effect, as it shrinks the amount of money in circulation.

It may also happen when the currency of a country appreciates, and all imports become cheaper (expressed in the domestic currency). People's power to purchase (imported) goods increases, and the value of the money therefore also increases.

7.3.3   Interest Rates

Interest is the amount of money that must be paid to borrow money. In this sense, the interest rate is an indicator of the value of money.

Typically, the interest rate is expressed as a percentage of the borrowed amount. For example, if a State borrows 10,000,000 against an interest rate of 3%, it must pay 300,000 interest each year.

The amount of interest depends on the market for loans, and several factors play a role. Here we will focus on only one factor: the amount of money that is available. The more money people save, the more money is available for lending purposes. This has a negative effect on the interest level: it becomes more affordable to borrow money. The same effect occurs if the central bank of a country creates more money. Money then becomes less scarce, and a debtor needs to offer less interest to be able to borrow.

Quite recently, we encountered the phenomenon of negative interest rates. The supply of money in some European countries is so big that people must pay to store money with banks, and banks must pay to deposit their money with the ECB.

'Cheap money', money that can be borrowed against a modest interest rate, will increase the demand for money. More loans will be taken out, and the total amount of money increases.

The opposite effect also occurs. If less money becomes available because people save less, or because the central bank creates less money, or even destroys some, the interest rate will rise.

A higher interest rate will decrease the demand for money. Less loans will be taken out, and the total amount of money decreases

Apparently, there is a close relationship between the interest rate and the amount of money that is available. A higher interest rate takes money out of the market, and the amount of money decreases. At the same time, the existence of 'superfluous' money will make money cheaper and will cause interest rates to drop.

We have seen that the central bank of a country, or – in the case of the Eurozone – the ECB, can influence the amount of money that is available. By creating money, central banks can push interest rates down, and by destroying it, they can make the interest rates rise.

7.3.4 Exchange Rates

Gold standard There is more than one monetary unit or 'currency'. Well-known currencies are the euro, the dollar, the yuan and, now, the bitcoin. Until 1971, a currency unit such as a physical dollar stood for a fixed amount of gold. This was the so-called gold standard.

However, in 1971 this link with gold was abandoned, and the value of money became completely conventional and a matter of offer and demand.

When currencies were still linked to an amount of gold, the relative values of the currencies were fixed, unless their associated amount of gold was changed. For example, if the English pound stood for three units of gold, while the dollar stood for one unit, the exchange rate would be $3 for £1. If the pound were to be devaluated from three units of gold to two units, the exchange rate between dollars and pounds would change accordingly: $2 for £1.

When the link between currencies and gold was abandoned, the value of currencies became a matter of offer and demand, and the exchange rates would fluctuate. As we will see later, this variability of exchange rates has both advantages and disadvantages.

Because an exchange rate expresses the value of one currency in terms of another currency, it is an indicator of the relative value of a particular currency. Changes in exchange rates reflect changes in the value of a currency relative to other currencies. Inflation and deflation reflect changes in the value of a currency relative to goods.

7.4 Indirect Taxation

By manipulating the value of money, it is possible to raise 'taxes' from those who have much money, in favour of those who have debts. We discuss three possible forms of this indirect taxation: taxation through inflation, through low interest rates and through exchange rates.

7.4.1 Inflation Tax

If you borrowed a lot of money, for instance for financing the home you live in, chances are that the amount of money you have to pay back is worth less than the money you borrowed. The cause is inflation. If after 20 years all nominal prices have doubled, as has your salary, the amount of money you have to repay on your mortgage has remained the same, but its value is half of what it used to be. In terms of the number of hours you have to work for the money, your debt has halved. For the bank this means that the money it will receive back on the loan is worth less than the money it lends. Of course, the interest the bank charges on the loan is, among others, meant to compensate for this loss of value of the money.

Private persons can borrow a substantial amount of money to pay for their homes, but the biggest money lender is usually the State. For example, the sovereign debt of Germany in January 2018 exceeded €2,000 billion. At an inflation level of 2% a year, the value of this debt in terms of goods has halved after 36 years. The people and banks who bought government bonds will lose half the value of their money during these 36 years. This means that inflation functions as a kind of tax on money lenders, for the benefit of borrowers, prominently including States. This kind of 'tax' is therefore called 'inflation tax'.

7.4.2   Interest Tax

Money lenders want compensation for their temporary loss of money and also for the inflation tax they will 'pay'. This compensation consists in the interest that money borrowers must pay to the money lenders. If the interest rate is kept low, this is a benefit for those who borrow money, including States, and a loss for those who lend money, including pension funds who must save for future pension payments. The long period of extremely low interest rates in Europe has brought financial troubles to many a pension fund, but has, at the same time, saved many a State from even more serious financial troubles. If pension funds cannot guarantee their future payments to pension beneficiaries any more – as is the case in the Netherlands – these beneficiaries indirectly pay for the State debts. The name 'interest tax' would adequately describe this phenomenon.

7.4.3   Exchange Rates

If the euro depreciates relatively to the dollar, American products will become more expensive in the Eurozone. More in general, if the currency of country A depreciates relative to the currency of country B, products from B will become more expensive in A. This higher price means that people with the depreciated currency become somewhat poorer: nominally, they still have the same amount of money, but they can buy less foreign products with it. Devaluation leads to inflation.

At the same time, people from the country with the appreciated currency can buy products from the other country at a lower price: appreciation leads to deflation. Nominally, the people from the appreciated country (to state it briefly) have remained as rich as they used to be, but in terms of the goods they can buy they have become richer, richer at the cost of the people from the depreciated country.

We will encounter this mechanism again when we discuss the role of depreciation as a means to dampen the effects of 'asymmetric shocks'.

7.5 Trade Equilibria

Suppose that two countries have a fixed exchange rate. That is, in a sense, the case within the Eurozone, where all members share the same currency: the euro.[4] Then there is a mechanism operative that promotes an equilibrium in trade relations between these two countries.

Price-specie flow mechanism Let us use Germany and France as an example and assume for the sake of argument – and unrealistically – that the rest of the world has no impact on the trade relations between these two countries. Suppose that Germany buys a lot of French goods, while France does not buy so many German goods. The trade balance between Germany and France is therefore negative for Germany and positive for France. Goods flow out of France into Germany, and money flows from Germany to France. Let us assume that the German Central Bank does not create extra money. Then the amount of money in Germany decreases and the price level in Germany will drop, as German people cannot afford the higher prices any more. This makes it more attractive for French people to import goods from Germany, and this restores the trade balance.

At the same time, the amount of money in France increases, thereby raising the general price level as French people have more to spend. This makes it less attractive for German people to import goods from France, which also restores the trade balance.

We see that a disturbance of the trade balance between countries that have a fixed exchange rate sets a mechanism in operation that 'automatically' restores the trade balance. This mechanism is called the 'price-specie flow mechanism' or also Hume's mechanism, after the Scottish philosopher/economist David Hume (1711-1776).

Interest rate The effect of the price-specie flow mechanism is even strengthened by the interest rates in Germany and France. If money flows out of Germany, there will be less money to borrow, and the interest rate in Germany rises. As it becomes more expensive in Germany to borrow money, the amount of money that Germans can use to buy French products decreases, the import of French products diminishes, and the trade balance moves towards equilibrium. The opposite story holds in France: there are more euros available, and the interest rates drop. This creates even more money to spend on German products and also leads to a restoration of the trade equilibrium.

---

4 Strictly speaking, countries with the same currency have no exchange rate at all, but from an economic perspective sharing a currency boils down to the same as having a fixed exchange rate.

Exchange rate If two countries have currencies with a flexible exchange rate, the tendency towards equilibrium is even stronger. Take the Eurozone and the United States. If the United States runs a trade deficit with the Eurozone, there will be a net flow of dollars from the United States to the Eurozone. As a result, there are too many dollars in the Eurozone and the dollar will depreciate relative to the euro. This makes products from the Eurozone more expensive for the Americans and American products more affordable for Europeans. As a result, the trade balance will shift in the direction of equilibrium.

Fixed amount of money It should be pointed out that all three mechanisms presuppose that there is a fixed amount of money available. Money must become scarce in some countries and abundant in other countries as result of trade imbalances; otherwise the mechanisms will not work. With the arrival of paper and electronic money, which can be created at a low cost, the amount of money can grow and shrink easily, and this hampers the functioning of the three mechanisms.

However, there are reasons not to be too lax about the amount of money; think of the desire not to have too much inflation. Therefore, although the amount of money is theoretically unlimited, there are, nevertheless, boundaries on the amount of money that is available, and the three mechanisms will continue to play a role.

Summary If two countries share a currency, or have a fixed exchange rate, there are 'automatic' mechanisms, based on price levels and on interest rates respectively, that restore the equilibrium of the trade balance between these countries if one country runs a trade deficit with the other. If the countries have a flexible exchange rate, the price levels will not be adapted any more to the same degree, but instead of the price level, the currency of the country with a deficit will depreciate. This has a similar effect on the trade balance as a drop in the price level.

7.6 THE IMPOSSIBLE TRINITY

There are close relationships between the financial policies of a country, including the amount of 'sovereign debt', the price level and the interest rate in that country, the trade balance of this country with other countries, and the exchange rate between that country's currency and the currencies of other countries. An important factor in this connection is the possibility to freely move money and financial products between countries. These relationships give rise to what has been called the 'impossible trinity' principle.

Definition Briefly stated, this principle boils down to the impossibility of having
- full capital mobility,
- fixed exchange rates, and
- autonomous monetary policy

together.

Because the impossibility of having the three elements of the trinity together plays such a central role in the process of monetary integration in Europe, we will discuss the principle in some detail.

7.6.1   If There Were No Full Capital Mobility

Suppose that a country closed its borders to the flow of capital and that no capital could flow into the country or move outside the country, or could do so only with special allowance. Then that country could conduct a monetary policy without the need to take the 'outside world' into account. To see what this means, we will consider two policies and see how they work out without and with free flow of capital.

Stimulation by money creation If a central bank creates more money and the money cannot 'escape' from the country, there are two short-term effects and, possibly, one long-term effect. One short-term effect is that the general price level will rise (inflation), because there is more money available for the same amount of goods and services. A second short-term effect is that the interest rate will drop, because more people can lend money (put it in a savings deposit in a bank) and fewer people will need to take a loan. Both effects will in the longer term lead to the expansion of the economy. If there is more money, people can buy more. At first there are not sufficient products to buy and the price level will rise, but in the long run the production of goods and services will increase to accommodate the higher demand. This effect is strengthened by the lower interest rate, which makes it easier to borrow money for investment in the production of more goods and services. By creating more money, which cannot escape the country, a central bank can stimulate the economy, which leads to higher production and a higher level of employment.[5]

What happens if the borders of the country are opened to capital flow? The answer depends on the situation in the rest of the world, but the following scenario is plausible: People who have more money will invest that money in other countries, where the interest rate does

---

5   This assumes that the economy still has room for growth. If, for example, there was already full employment, the increase in money will only lead to higher salaries (and then higher price levels).

not drop. This means that the pressure on the national price level and interest rate is much smaller, and the desired stimulation of the national economy does not take place.

A brake on government spending If the government of a country spends more money than its income allows (runs a deficit), the State has to borrow the money. If there is no transborder flow of capital, the money must be borrowed locally. This means that the State takes money out of the local economy.

Now there are two possibilities. One is that the government spends the money locally, for example on social security benefits. Then the money returns into the economy and there will be no lack of money.

The other possibility is that the government spends the money elsewhere, for example by buying arms from foreign producers. In the latter case, the money is withdrawn from the local economy. Now the effects are the opposite of money creation: in the short term there will be deflation and the interest rate will rise. In the longer term the economy will shrink. The higher interest rate will force the government to pay more rent, which is a brake on more money borrowing and spending. The shrinking economy will cause the tax income of the State to drop, which causes the direct effect of money borrowing (the State having more money) to be partially undone. This is also a brake on too much money borrowing and spending.

If the State can borrow on the international market, the effects of this borrowing on the local market will be weaker, at least in the short term. Because the borrowed money comes from abroad, the local amount of money will not drop immediately. There will be less deflation, and the interest rate will not rise immediately, or so strongly. That is good for the local economy, but the brake on too much government spending is less strongly felt. In the long run, the money must still be repaid, but then the sovereign debt may already have increased much.

Summary We see that the free flow of capital dampens the effects of local monetary policies. This is sometimes attractive and sometimes unattractive, but in all cases the free flow of capital diminishes the control of the State over the local economy. As a result, it is no longer possible to conduct any monetary policy the government would like, and to combine this with fixed exchange rates.

7.6.2 Exchange Rates, Interest Levels and the Free Flow of Capital

The existence of fixed exchange rates has effects that are similar to those of borders open to the flow of capital: States have less influence on what happens in their local economies, and the effects of monetary policies are dampened. To see why this is the case, it is best to reconsider an earlier example.

Suppose that the EU wants to stimulate the European economy by conducting a policy of ample money. The ECB buys bonds on the open market, thereby creating more money. We have seen that if there is a free flow of money, much of this additional money may flow away, for instance to countries with a higher interest rate than is available in Europe. However, exchange rates may influence the money flow. Suppose that a money lender can receive 1% interest in Europe and 3% in the USA. We assume that the money will be certainly repaid in time, so this is not a factor that should have any influence. However, to receive 3% interest in the USA, the money lender must exchange his euros for dollars and later exchange the dollars back for euros. There is a risk that the dollar meanwhile has depreciated relative to the euro and that the money lender will receive less euros back than he invested in the USA.

This valuta hazard causes the flow of capital over the world to be less than might be expected if exchange rates were ignored. Fixed exchange rates facilitate the free flow of capital and therefore negatively influence the effects of local monetary policies. Flexible exchange rates make it less attractive to invest money in foreign countries and therefore increase the effects of local monetary policies.

7.6.3 Why the Trinity Is Impossible

By now we have all the building blocks to explain the impossibility of the trinity. If money can flow into and out of a country without any impediments – and now we count flexible exchange rates as an impediment – national monetary policies will not work. Measures aimed at increasing the amount of money will fail because the money will flow out of the country. It is like trying to raise the water level in a small part of the sea without means to prevent the water from flowing away to the rest of the sea. Measures aimed at limiting the amount of money suffer from the opposite complication: foreign money will easily flow into the country, frustrating the policy. This is like trying to make the level of the water lower in a small part of the sea, without any means to stop water from the rest of the sea flowing in.

Giving up autonomy To continue the metaphor a little more: if you want to manage the local sea water level according to your wishes and you cannot stop the water from flowing in and out, the only thing you can do is to adapt your wishes to what will happen anyway. You should strive for a water level that is equal to the level around your area. In monetary terms this is comparable to conducting a monetary policy that amounts to following the money market. This means giving up monetary autonomy.

Summary of the impossible trinity In order for local monetary policies to be efficacious, the free flow of money into and out of the country must be stopped or at least limited. This can be done by prohibiting this free flow (no full capital mobility) or by making it less attractive (having flexible exchange rates). However, it is not possible to have autonomous monetary policies, free flow of capital and fixed exchange rates at once.

7.7 Conclusion

Money fulfils different functions. Perhaps its main function is to be a medium of exchange. Because everybody accepts money as a means of payment, money can solve the problem of the coincidence of wants. Because of its function as a medium of exchange, money can also function as a unit of account and as a store of value.

Money is a social phenomenon, and, like other social phenomena, its existence depends on acceptance. Everything that is accepted as money is money. Being created in an official way, or officially recognized as money (being 'legal tender'), may promote acceptance, but it is not necessary, as is very clearly reflected by the existence of cryptocurrencies. Therefore, anybody, in principle, can create money.

However, in practice, most money is officially issued, or created by banks that lend money. If a bank lends money, more money enters into circulation and therefore also in existence. Central banks can influence the total amount of money, among others through outright monetary transactions and – indirectly – through reserve requirements on ordinary banks.

Not only is money used to express the value of goods in its function of unit of account, but it also has a value itself. The value of goods can be expressed in terms of money, but the value of money can also be expressed in terms of goods. The value of money increases if it becomes possible to buy more goods with it. This is called 'deflation'. The value of money decreases if goods become more expensive. This is called 'inflation'.

It is also possible to compare money with other money, or – more precisely – one currency with another currency. The exchange rate between currencies expresses the value of one currency in terms of the other. After the gold standard was abandoned, the exchange rates between currencies is often a matter of offer and demand.

Money has a price. This price can be expressed by means of the exchange rate with some other currency (in international transactions), but also by the rate of interest that needs to be paid to borrow the money (often a local affair). By manipulating exchange and interest rates, or the amount of money that is in circulation, it is possible to influence the value of money. This makes it possible to 'tax' people who have money in favour of people who are in debt.

Finally, the close relationship between the amount and value of money and exchange rates makes it impossible for a State to conduct autonomous monetary policies and to combine this with fixed exchange rates and open borders for money. This is called the 'impossible trinity', and this trinity had a strong influence on the development and structure of the European Monetary System.

8 Monetary Integration

8.1 Attempts at Fixed Exchange Rates

The gold standard There is a long history of different currencies existing next to each other, and most of that history there was hardly any issue with regard to exchange rates. There is a simple explanation. All coins – bank notes did not exist yet – were money because they contained a certain amount of gold (or silver). Their value was determined by this amount, and therefore all coins had a common denominator in the form of their gold content. This meant that there was a fixed exchange rate, determined by how much gold a coin contained. This was called the 'Gold standard'.[1]

In the 19th century, this gold standard was replaced by the 'Gold Exchange Standard'. Individual countries could create their own money, but this money was explicitly linked to gold: a bank note entitled its owner to a specific amount of gold. From the point of view of exchange rates, this made no difference as every piece of money still represented a fixed amount of gold.

The Bretton Woods system After World War II, the link between money and gold was further loosened. According to the Bretton Woods system,[2] currencies had a fixed – but changeable – exchange rate with the dollar, and the dollar was linked to a fixed amount of gold.[3]

This meant that indirectly all involved currencies were still linked to gold. It also meant that this link depended on the guarantee of the USA that there was sufficient gold available to cover all the claims that could be based on money. In 1971, the USA ended the convertibility of the dollar into gold, and in 1973 the fixed, but changeable, exchange rate between the dollar and the other involved currencies was given up. Exchange rates between currencies came to be determined by the exchange market, and were a matter of offer and demand. As a matter of fact, the Bretton Woods system collapsed during the 1970s.

---

1 This section is based on Baldwin and Wyplosz 2015, chapter 14.
2 This system derives its name from the 1944 Bretton Woods conference, where it was adopted.
3 A currency can have an exchange rate with another currency that is both fixed and changeable if changes need to be made explicitly. Such an explicit change is, for example, made by the central bank through a decision to devaluate or revaluate a currency. In the absence of such a decision, the exchange rate remains the same. This means that the rate is not directly determined by the money market, as is the case with a fully flexible exchange rate.

EUROPEAN INTEGRATION: A THEME

8.2 THE ROAD TOWARDS THE EUROPEAN MONETARY UNION

8.2.1 Drawbacks of Flexible Exchange Rates

The collapse of the Bretton Woods system meant the end of semi-fixed exchange rates between currencies; exchange rates became flexible. For the process of European integration, the existence of flexible exchange rates between the currencies of the Member States has several drawbacks. One of them is the increase in transaction costs attached to intra-European trade; another one is uncertainty about the profitability of trade transactions.

Transaction costs Suppose that, before the arrival of the euro, a producer in France wants to sell a particular kind of wine to German consumers. The French wine must compete with German wines, and its price plays a role in this competition. The producer needs a particular price for the wine expressed in French francs. The German consumers are willing to pay a particular price expressed in German marks. At some stage of the trade process, German marks need to be exchanged for French francs, as the producer wants to receive francs for his wine, while the consumers will pay marks. This exchange costs money, and these costs are transaction costs; they make the French wine more expensive for German consumers. In a number of cases, the additional transaction costs will tip the balance: the German consumers find the French wine of their liking too expensive and will buy German wine instead. Since they would have bought French wine if there were no transaction costs, there is a negative welfare effect.

Transaction costs may make exchanges, which would in principle benefit the parties, unattractive. The existence of different currencies, which leads to transactions costs connected to the need to exchange currencies, are an impediment to intra-European trade. They may prevent transactions that would otherwise be beneficial and have negative welfare effects.

Uncertainty Suppose that a German trader buys wine for 10,000 French francs. At the conclusion of the sales contract this amounts to 3,300 German marks. If the franc appreciates relative to the mark in between the closure of the contract and the time of payment, the trader may have to pay more for the wine, for instance 3,500 marks.

The possibility that exchange rates will fluctuate during a contract creates uncertainty. This uncertainty is unattractive and may have the effect that fewer contracts will be concluded. Trade transactions normally have positive welfare effects, and these positive effects are sometimes foregone as a result of uncertainty about exchange rates.

8.2.2 The Snake in the Tunnel and Other Failed Attempts

At the beginning of the 1990s, steps were taken to complete the Single European Market. The impediments that flexible exchange rates impose on trade within Europe explain why monetary integration was an important item on the agenda.

The snake in the tunnel As a matter of fact, there had already been earlier attempts in Europe to limit the damage created by the collapse of the Bretton Woods system. The earliest was a local imitation of the Bretton Woods system. The currencies of European countries were pegged to the dollar in a fixed exchange rate (a separate rate for every currency, to be sure), and the exchange rates were allowed to fluctuate around this pegged rate within a certain bandwidth. This regime was maintained by controls on the flow of capital between countries. At first, currencies were only allowed to have fluctuations of 1% above or below the fixed rate, but when this turned out hard to maintain, the allowed bandwidth became 2.25% in 1971. This resulted in a 'tunnel' of allowed exchange rates inside which the range of a single currency was allowed to crawl up and down like a snake. Hence the name 'snake in the tunnel'.

The European Monetary System and the Exchange Rate Mechanism The snake in the tunnel did not last. Different economic circumstances in different countries caused some currencies to be undervalued, even if they were at the top of the tunnel, and other currencies to be overvalued, even at the bottom of the tunnel. Remember that the 'real' value of a currency depends on offer and demand and that the trade balance and the monetary policies of a country determine this offer and demand to a large extent. Keeping the exchange rate of a currency within boundaries that do not match its market value is like keeping sea water in a small part of the sea on an artificial high or low level. That is no easy job, and in the long run it is bound to fail.

The link between the European currencies and the dollar was given up, and it was decided, in 1978, to link the European currencies only to each other. This was called the 'European Monetary System'. The heart of this system was the 'Exchange Rate Mechanism', in which the exchange rates between European currencies were fixed. The participating countries and their central banks undertook the responsibility to support these rates by selling currencies on the brink of becoming overvalued and buying currencies on the brink of becoming undervalued. Changes in the exchange rates between currencies were still possible, but only with the approval of all participating countries.

In between 1979 and 1987 there were a total of twelve changes in the European exchange rates. Apparently, this system for keeping exchange rates stable did not function well either.

The reason for this failure may be sought in the tendency of the participating countries to conduct their own monetary policies. (Think of the impossible trinity.) As a result, the strength of the different currencies did not develop in similar ways. To return to the sea metaphor: because of the differential policies, the water level between different parts of the sea was bound to become increasingly different, and the required efforts for keeping the levels fixed kept increasing.

Ultimately, countries started to realize that the combination of stable exchange rates and free flow of money (within Europe) would be possible only if the monetary policies of countries were harmonized. In practice this meant that the monetary policy of the German *Bundesbank* would be followed by the central banks of most European countries.

8.2.3 The Euro

The time had arrived to ensure a closer monetary integration between European countries. This monetary integration would include fixed exchange rates between the currencies of the Member States, ultimately by introducing a single European valuta, the euro. The euro was introduced non-physically (checks, electronic banking) in 1999, and as a currency (bank notes and coins) in 2002.

Implications of a shared currency If different countries share a currency, this has implications for what these countries can do on the monetary level. We have seen that there is a close relationship between the amount and direction of international trade, government loans and exchange rates. If the government of a country runs a big budgetary deficit, it must borrow money, which positively affects the exchange rate of this valuta and negatively affects the trade balance with other countries, and indirectly also domestic employment. However, if a country has a negative trade balance, the demand for its valuta will drop with the exports. This in turn has a positive effect of the trade balance and on employment. This is a feedback mechanism which in the long run tends towards trade balances in equilibrium.

This feedback mechanism does not exist, or does so only to a much smaller extent, if the country shares its valuta with other countries. For instance, the international demand for the euro does not decrease substantially if the Greek exports fall. The price of Greek products as expressed in another valuta – say English pounds – will not drop, and the Greek export is not supported by a lower value of the valuta (euro).

Influence of budgetary deficits of one country on exports of (and employment in) other countries Another implication of having a single valuta is that the policies of one country influence the welfare in other countries. For example, if France runs a big budgetary deficit, it must borrow euros on the international money market. The offer of euros on that market decreases, and the value of the euro as expressed in, say, the dollar, increases. The exports of all euro countries to non-euro countries will drop, not only the French exports. Because the amount of exports influences employment, a big budgetary deficit in one country may negatively affect employment in other countries that use the same valuta.

8.2.4 The Stability and Growth Pact

As a result of the use of a common valuta, what happens in one country affects the welfare of other countries. This explains why the decision to introduce a common valuta for the EU Member States was accompanied by rules that would limit the negative effects that a single currency might have. These rules were included in Articles 121 and 126 TFEU and elaborated in the Stability and Growth Pact. Essentially, they boil down to the requirements that a government deficit in a year may not exceed 3% of the country's Gross Domestic Product (GDP) of that year and that the national debt may not exceed 60% of the GDP.

The *government deficit* is the negative difference between the income and the spending of a government (income – spending).

The *Gross Domestic Product* is the value in money of all the products and services produced in a country in – typically – one year.

The *national debt* is the amount (of money) a State owes to its creditors.

Six-Pack As big countries such as Germany and France did not comply with the requirements of the pact, the requirements were relaxed in 2005. Following the financial crisis in Europe, the requirements were made stricter again in 2011, in the Six-Pack measures. The following quotes from a press release in December 2011 by the European Commission[4] clearly capture what was at stake:

> On 13th December 2011, the reinforced Stability and Growth Pact (SGP) enters into force with a new set of rules for economic and fiscal surveillance. These

---

4   See http://europa.eu/rapid/press-release_MEMO-11-898_en.htm (last visited on 19 June 2019). *See also:* https://ec.europa.eu/info/business-economy-euro/economic-and-fiscal-policy-coordination/eu-economic-governance-monitoring-prevention-correction/stability-and-growth-pact_en.

new measures, the so-called 'Six-Pack', are made of five regulations and one directive proposed by the European Commission and approved by all 27 Member States and the European Parliament last October. This change represents the most comprehensive reinforcement of economic governance in the EU and the euro area since the launch of the Economic Monetary Union almost 20 years ago. In line with 8-9 December European Summit agreements, the legislative package already brings a concrete and decisive step towards ensuring fiscal discipline, helping to stabilise the EU economy and preventing a new crisis in the EU. [...]

From 13 December 2011 onwards, financial sanctions will apply to euro area Member States that do not take adequate action. Member States currently in excessive deficit procedure should comply with the specific recommendations the Council addressed to them to correct their excessive deficit. In case a euro area Member State does not respect its obligations, a financial sanction can be imposed by the Council on the basis of a Commission recommendation, unless a qualified majority of Member States vote against it. [...]

The new rules of the amended Stability and Growth Pact make the debt criterion of the Treaty absolutely operational, since it has been largely neglected over the past years. Another major element of the new rules is that a new numerical debt benchmark has been defined: if the 60% reference for the debt-to-GDP ratio is not respected, the Member State concerned will be put in excessive deficit procedure (even if its deficit is below 3%!), after taking into account all relevant factors and the impact of the economic cycle, if the gap between its debt level and the 60% reference is not reduced by 1/20th annually (on average over 3 years). [...]

Effective enforcement of the rules is as important as the rules themselves. This equally applies to the preventive arm. The amended SGP allows stronger action when the budgetary execution of a Member State deviates significantly. In order to enforce this rule, deviations have been quantified and can lead to a financial sanction (an interest-bearing deposit of 0.2% of GDP as a rule) in case of continuous non-correction. Such a sanction is proposed by the Commission and adopted by 'reverse qualified majority' voting in the Council.

Furthermore, if its budgetary plans do not comply with the provisions of the preventive arm, a Member State can be requested to present new plans that do comply. Member States not in EDP will have to demonstrate compliance with the provisions of the preventive arm in their next stability or convergence programmes as of next Spring 2012, in the context of the European Semester. Member States under EDP should show compliance after the correction of their excessive deficit. [...]

Over the past decade, the EU has registered serious gaps in competitiveness and major macroeconomic imbalances. A new surveillance and enforcement mechanism has been set up to identify and correct such issues much earlier: the Excessive Imbalances Procedure (EIP), based on Article 121.6 of the Treaty. It will rely on the following main elements:

Preventive and corrective action: The new procedure allows the Commission and the Council to adopt preventive recommendations under Article 121.2 of the Treaty at an early stage before the imbalances become large. In more serious cases, there is also a corrective arm where an excessive imbalance procedure can be opened for a Member State. In this case, the Member State concerned will have to submit a corrective action plan with a clear roadmap and deadlines for implementing corrective action. Surveillance will be stepped up by the Commission on the basis of regular progress reports submitted by the Member States concerned.

Rigorous enforcement: A new enforcement regime is established for euro area countries. It consists of a two-step approach whereby an interest-bearing deposit can be imposed after one failure to comply with the recommended corrective action. After a second compliance failure, this interest-bearing deposit can be converted into a fine (up to 0.1% of GDP). Sanctions can also be imposed for failing twice to submit a sufficient corrective action plan.

8.3   EXCHANGE RATES AND ASYMMETRIC SHOCKS

The combination of fixed exchange rates, including a common currency, free flow of capital and independent monetary policies, is impossible. This means that if the Eurozone countries, which share a currency, allow free flow of capital between them, as they should because they are also EU members, they cannot conduct independent monetary policies any more. Although countries typically do not like to give up their autonomy, harmonized monetary policies should not be an insurmountable problem, unless ... the circumstances 'force' countries to follow their own monetary policies. That might be the case if the economic circumstances in one particular country suddenly change in a way that invites monetary measures, while such a change does not occur in the other countries. Such a sudden change, which hits one country or area but not the others, is called an 'asymmetric shock'.

Example: agricultural disease The occurrence of asymmetric shocks is a test case for whether a common currency such as the euro is feasible. To see why this is the case we will have a closer look at the ensemble of valutas, exchange rates and trade balances. We will do so by means of the example of German traders who imported French wine during the period preceding the adoption of the euro, when the French still used francs and the Germans marks.[5]

Suppose that because of a disease that hit the German vineyards, the German wine production suddenly dropped by 70%. In the upcoming 10 years not much improvement is to be expected. As a result of the production drop, German customers want to drink more French wine. German wine traders have to buy more French wine, and the French wine producers can export more wine to Germany. As the wine buyers must pay for the wine in marks and the wine sellers must receive francs, an exchange from marks to francs is necessary. Let us assume that the German wine traders buy French francs and pay for them in German marks. Because the import of French wine soars, the demand for francs increases. At the same time, the offer of German marks for buying francs will also increase, as the Germans needs the francs to buy French wine. As a result, the price of the franc rises (the franc appreciates), while the price of the mark drops (the mark depreciates).

If the franc appreciates, the price of French wines, as expressed in German marks, rises. The depreciation of the German mark has the same effect. This means that French wines become more expensive in Germany and that the Germans will drink less (French) wines. At the same time, German wines become more affordable in France. The demand for the remaining German wines increases, and their price in marks can be raised, because the marks themselves have become cheaper.

If the Germans drink less French wines because they become too expensive, the demand for French francs will drop, as will the offer of German marks. As a result, the exchange rate between the German marks and the French francs changes again, this time in favour of the mark. And then the French wines become more advantageous again, and the exchange rates change again …., and so on. At the end, this process of mutual adaptation of French wine imports and fluctuations in exchange rates will end in an equilibrium in which the

---

5 We assume that the amount of trade is big enough to influence the exchange rate between the two valutas and that there are no other relevant factors than the ones mentioned.

price of the French franc as expressed in German marks will have risen somewhat, but not as much as initially seemed to happen. The import of French wine in Germany also has increased somewhat, but not as much as initially seemed to happen.

The general message of this example is that, on the one hand, the level of imports and exports, and, on the other hand, the exchange rate between the involved valutas influence each other. A trade surplus (more export) leads to appreciation of the exporter's valuta. A trade deficit leads to depreciation of the valuta. This also works the other way around: the higher value of a valuta leads to less export and more imports, while the lower value leads to more exports and less imports.

Asymmetric shocks Economists call an event like the disease in the German vineyards that did not hit France an 'asymmetric shock'. It is a shock because the event seriously affects (part of) the German economy. It is asymmetric, because the shock does not hit every country, but only Germany.

The example illustrates how the exchange rate mechanism mitigates the effects of the shock. Without the depreciation of the mark, the negative effects would be limited to the German wine traders and drinkers, who must pay more for their wine, and to the producers of German wines, who are in no way compensated for their production loss. If the mark depreciates, the damage is distributed over all users of the German mark, who have lost some of their purchasing power. Moreover, the German wine producers can raise the price in marks of their remaining wines, thereby compensating a bit for the loss of production.

On the other side of the border, in France, the opposite happens. As the franc appreciates, all users of the franc see an increase in purchasing power, because imports become cheaper (in terms of francs). The price of the French wines as expressed in francs must drop a bit to keep the French wines competitive in a market with a higher price for the French franc. The profit that in the first instance benefits the French wine sellers alone is thus redistributed over all possessors of French francs.

The example illustrates how a change in the exchange rate of currencies mitigates the effects of asymmetric shocks by distributing the costs and the benefits of these shocks over all users of the involved currencies.

8.4 Optimum Currency Areas

We have seen that the use of a single valuta diminishes transaction costs and uncertainty and thereby increases welfare. We have also seen that exchange rate fluctuations are part of a mechanism that mitigates the effects of asymmetric shocks. If exchange rates are fixed, as is the case with a single valuta, this mitigating effect cannot be invoked anymore. This raises the question pertaining to the circumstances under which the positive effects of having a single valuta outweigh the negative effects.

Conditions for an OCA This question has been addressed in economic theory under the heading of an Optimum Currency Area (OCA). An OCA is an area that derives more benefits than costs from having a single valuta. The OCA theory is based on the idea that a country in a monetary union must maintain competitiveness in the hard way – by keeping costs and prices low – rather than by devaluation of its valuta.[6] In the economic literature several conditions are mentioned that, if met, would call for the use of a single valuta. These criteria include:[7]
1. Labour mobility
2. Homogeneity
3. Fiscal transfers

Labour mobility If a country in a monetary union is hit by an asymmetric shock, this means that in that country there will be hardship, including lowering wages and unemployment, while conditions in the other countries will be better. This unevenness can be redressed if the workers from the country that was hit move to the countries that remain spared.

Returning to our example of the German vineyards that were hit by a disease, recall that the German wine production drops and Germans in the production process lose their jobs. Moreover, they compete for the remaining jobs, which means that the wages of those who can still work also go down. On the other side of the border, in France, wine production soars, and more labourers are needed to harvest and process the grapes. Vacancies will remain unfilled, and because of the competition to hire workers, wages will rise. Both the problems on the German side of the border and the problems on the French side will be solved without exchange rate fluctuations if only the German workers would move to France to work there.

---

6   Baldwin and Wyplosz 2015, p. 366 (textbox).
7   Baldwin and Wyplosz 2015, Chapter 15, Section 4.

However, labour mobility is not very high in the EU. Although there are exceptions, people generally prefer not to leave their families and work with other people who speak another language. Therefore, from this perspective, the EU is not an OCA.

Homogeneity If asymmetric shocks cannot occur within an area, this area is more likely to be an OCA, because there is less of a need to deal with such shocks.

For example, if France and Germany had the same kinds of vineyards, a disease that would hit the German vineyards would most likely hit the French ones also. Then both countries are hit, and one single economic policy can be used to help both countries overcome their problems. Moreover, if Germany and France were the only members in a monetary union, this policy might include depreciation of their common valuta.

More in general, if countries are, from an economic perspective, highly similar, it is not likely that they will be hit by asymmetric shocks, and then there is no need for the exchange rate mechanism to mitigate the shocks, and the countries can just as well become members of a monetary union.

From an economic perspective, some EU Member States are quite similar, while some other Member States are not. This makes it more attractive for some Member States to participate in the euro than it is for some other Member States to do so.

Fiscal transfers If a shock occurs within a country that belongs to a monetary union because the demand for the goods of that country drops, often (some of) the other countries of the union will experience an opposite shock, as they will produce more of the good that the first country does not deliver any more. By transferring money from the countries that experience the positive effects of the shock to the country that experiences the negative effects, the impact of the shock can be alleviated in all countries.

For example, if France (indirectly) paid for the unemployment benefits that the German State must pay its unemployed workers, the amount of money, and with it the inflationary pressure, would decrease in France, while the amount of money in Germany would drop less severely, and the deflationary pressure would remain limited.

However, fiscal transfers mean that one country 'pays for' the problems of another country. This requires solidarity between the countries that is not always available, especially not if one country believes that the asymmetric shock in another country is that other country's own fault.

8.5 Conclusion

There are obvious advantages to having a single European valuta. Countries with the same valuta experience a sense of unity that would be less without the common valuta. Moreover, trade between the countries is not hampered by the transaction costs of changing money and by the uncertainty of exchange rate fluctuations. These advantages are offset by the impossibility of using monetary policies to mitigate the effects of asymmetric shocks. How the balance between the advantages and the disadvantages must be struck depends on factors like labour mobility, economic homogeneity and the possibility of fiscal transfers. A complicating factor in this connection is that the presence of a monetary union may itself influence the factors that make such a union (un)desirable. For instance, the feeling of unity that a common valuta promotes can contribute to the willingness to pay for the asymmetric shocks that hit another Member State.

At present it is not obvious that the EU as a whole is an OCA, but it is quite possible that the existence of a monetary union between many Member States contributes to the creation of such an area.

9 SOVEREIGNTY

9.1 INTRODUCTION

Causes of the discussion One of the groundbreaking decisions of the European Court of Justice (ECJ) was in the Van Gend & Loos case. The issue at stake was whether nationals from the EEC Member States could derive rights from the law of the EEC. As is well known, the answer to this question was affirmative, but the most important aspect of the decision was the proclamation that EEC law was an independent legal order:

> The Community constitutes a new legal order of international law for the benefit of which the states have limited their sovereign rights, albeit within limited fields and the subjects of which comprise not only member states but also their nationals.[1]

Apart from announcing a new legal order, the ECJ also wrote that the EEC Member States had limited their sovereign rights for the benefit of the EEC. That sounds impressive, but it is far from clear what it means if a State 'limits its sovereign rights'. However, in the aftermath of the Van Gend & Loos decision, authors also started to write about the 'transfer' of, or giving up, sovereignty from EU Member States to the EU.[2]

This chapter deals with this so-called 'transfer of sovereignty' from the EU Member States to the EU. First, it illustrates the alleged phenomenon by means of two recent crises in the EU. Then it offers a historical and legal-theoretical analysis of what sovereignty is and argues that a transfer of sovereignty is, as a matter of fact, impossible and should therefore not be a cause for concern.

---

1 CJEU Case 26-62; https://eur-lex.europa.eu/legal-content/EN/TXT/HTML/?uri=CELEX:61962CJ0026&from=NL (last visited on 19 August 2019).
2 An example is the comment on the BBC website about the English Parliament giving up some of its sovereignty when it passed the European Communities Act 1972. *See* www.bbc.com/news/uk-politics-eu-referendum-35630757 (last visited on 22 October 2019).

9.2 Two Crises

9.2.1 The Migration Crisis

Numbers During the last decade, the EU Member States have received hundreds of thousands of applicants for asylum. According to statistics provided by the EU,[3] the influx of asylum seekers in the EU developed as follows (Figure 9.1):

2008	2009	2010	2011	2012	2013	2014	2015	2016	2017	2018
225,150	263,835	259,630	309,040	335,290	431,095	626,960	1,322,845	1,260,910	712,235	646,060

Figure 9.1   Numbers of asylum seekers

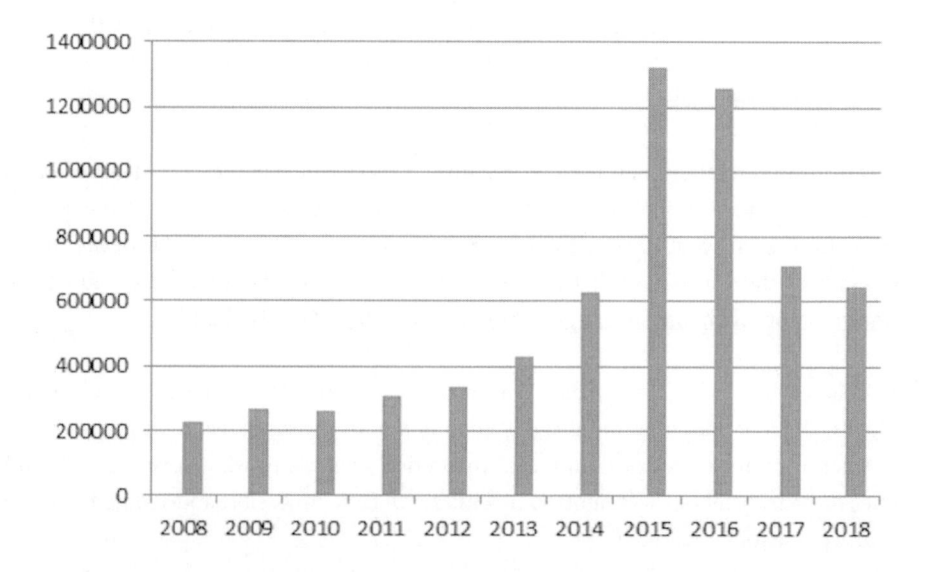

Many of these applicants are refugees who fled terrible conditions in their home countries, such as civil wars, terrorism and discrimination on religious or gender-related grounds. Many others are economic refugees seeking better job opportunities or better welfare provisions than are available in their countries of origin. The asylum procedure has also become a means to circumvent the ordinary migration policies of the EU.

---

3   The Eurostat website:
    https://ec.europa.eu/eurostat/tgm/table.do?tab=table&init=1&language=en&pcode=tps00191&plugin=1 (last visited on 19 August 2019).

Whatever people's reasons are for applying for asylum in the EU, the annual migration to the EU is large, and it is important that the needs of asylum seekers are somehow taken care of while they are on EU territory. Most asylum seekers arrive on EU territory through one of the countries bordering the Mediterranean, giving a leading role to Greece and Italy in managing the influx.

Schengen zone Most EU Member States, including Greece and Italy, are also part of the Schengen zone, in which there are in principle no border controls.[4] This had the effect that asylum seekers who entered a Schengen territory could move freely within Europe, going to the country that seemed most promising to them. The result was large streams of migrants moving from East and South Europe in the direction of Germany and the UK. Because the UK is not part of the Schengen zone, substantial groups of people became stranded east of the Canal, looking for any opportunity to cross into the UK. As a reaction to these migrant streams, some members of the Schengen zone, including Austria, Belgium, Denmark, France, Germany, Norway and Sweden, introduced temporary border controls, thereby somewhat 'spilling back' the process of European integration.

Dublin III According to the Dublin III regulation presently in force, the Member State in which an irregular immigrant enters the EU is the state responsible for the shelter of the immigrant and the procedure for handling the asylum application. This means that Greece and Italy would bear most of the burdens of the immigrant stream. However, as the European Commission formulates it,[5]

> The large-scale, uncontrolled arrival of migrants and asylum seekers has put a strain not only on many Member States' asylum systems, but also on the Common European Asylum System as a whole. The volume and concentration of arrivals has exposed in particular the weaknesses of the Dublin System, which establishes the Member State responsible for examining an asylum application based primarily on the first point of irregular entry.

Dublin IV For these reasons, the European Commission proposed in May 2016 to reform the Dublin system. The proposed – but not yet adopted – Dublin IV regulation, aims to:

---

4   See   https://ec.europa.eu/home-affairs/sites/homeaffairs/files/e-library/docs/schengen_brochure/schengen_brochure_dr3111126_en.pdf last visited on 18 October 2018.
5   *See*   https://ec.europa.eu/home-affairs/what-we-do/policies/asylum/examination-of-applicants_en   (last visited on 19 October 2019).

- enhance the system's capacity to determine a single Member State responsible for examining the application for international protection, shortening time limits for take-charge requests and transfers;
- ensure fair sharing of responsibility between Member States by complementing the current system with a corrective allocation mechanism in cases of disproportionate pressure;
- discourage abuses and prevent secondary movements by requiring proportionate procedural and material consequences in case of non-compliance.

According to the Commission, this

> ...new system would automatically establish when a country is handling a disproportionate number of asylum applications. It would do so by reference to a country's size and wealth. If one country receives disproportionate numbers above and beyond that reference (over 150% of the reference number), all further new applicants in that country would (regardless of nationality) be relocated, after an admissibility verification of their application, across the EU until the number of applications is back below that level. A Member State would also have the option to temporarily not take part in the reallocation. In that case, it would have to make a solidarity contribution of €250,000 for each applicant for whom it would otherwise have been responsible under the fairness mechanism, to the Member State that is reallocated the person instead.

Other measures This proposal for relocation of asylum seekers fits within a broader programme of measures proposed by the Commission.[6] Another measure in this package is the introduction of the European Border and Coast Guard Agency. This is a refurbished version of the already existing Frontex, which should be more effective in protecting the external borders of the Schengen zone. If necessary, the Agency can intervene in the border protection of a country if the country does not succeed in doing so itself.[7]

The Commission also proposed to create its own list of 'safe countries' to which asylum seekers may be sent back. However, it turned out difficult to reach agreement on which countries should be on the list, and the negotiations about the list have been suspended in 2019.[8]

---

6   Buonanno 2017.
7   *See* http://europa.eu/rapid/press-release_MEMO-15-6332_en.htm (last visited on 19 October 2019).
8   *See* www.europarl.europa.eu/legislative-train/theme-towards-a-new-policy-on-migration/file-european-list-of-safe-countries-of-origin (last visited on 19 October 2019).

Crisis The influx of asylum seekers and migrants into Europe has caused a crisis in Europe. People from different Member States reacted differently to the new inhabitants of their countries, with much resistance in Central and East-European countries in particular. In some countries the 'threat' of incoming migrants and the number of incidents in which migrants were involved have caused large-scale protests and demands to close the national borders to asylum seekers. This dissatisfaction may also be a breeding ground for populist political parties.[9]

The stark increase in the number of asylum seekers in 2015 and 2016 has brought to light the disagreement between EU Member States on how to deal with the asylum seekers, which is clear from the fact that neither the Dublin IV regulation nor the EU list of safe countries of origin nor the proposal for relocation has been adopted. The solidarity between the Member States in taking care of the incoming people has until now turned out to be mainly verbal. The relocation of people that landed in Greece or Italy has taken place only on a small scale. As a reaction, the Italian Prime Minister threatened in August 2018 that Italy would stop its contribution to the EU.[10]

A common denominator of the elements of the migration crisis is, first, the difference in outlook between the EU Member States on how to deal with the issues and, second, the unwillingness to cooperate in a common solution. The external pressure caused by the stream of migrants asks for close cooperation between the EU Member States, but rather than accomplishing this, the task seems to drive the Member States further apart. Member States hold more tightly to their sovereign powers, rather than grant the EU the powers that are necessary to deploy a common policy.

9.2.2 The Financial Crises

Sub-prime crisis Around the year 2010, the EU, and in particular the Eurozone, was hit by a series of financial crises. One source was the collapse, in the US, of the Lehman Brothers bank in 2008. As with many other banks, Lehman Brothers was involved in providing credit to private borrowers too easily. The collateral for these loans, often mortgages on homes, turned out to be insufficient to cover the defaults on repayments. Further, the claims that were already insufficiently secured by collateral were not the best claims to own: they were 'sub-prime'. Because the debts and their collateral were repackaged in financial products that were subsequently traded all over the world, the problem of over-

---

9 Buonanno 2017.
10 www.thelocal.it/20180824/italy-will-stop-paying-into-eu-unless-bloc-takes-in-stranded-migrants-deputy-pm (last visited on 18 October 2018).

financing, which had its origin in the US, also hit banks in many other countries. This became the 'sub-prime crisis'.

It turned out that the players in the financial world were closely connected through the trade of financial products and that a substantial crisis that hit one country or bank would soon spread to other countries and banks too. The reserves of many banks turned out to be insufficient to compensate not only for the money that these banks had lent to the public, but also for what they had lent to States.

Eurozone crisis The loans from banks to States connect the sub-prime crisis to the Eurozone crisis. During the period before the Eurozone countries were united by the euro, countries had to pay substantially different interest rates if they borrowed money on the financial market. If a country was seen as less creditworthy, or if there was a risk that the currency of that country would depreciate, they would have to pay more interest than a creditworthy country with no risk of currency depreciation (e.g. Germany). After the euro was introduced, the interest rates of the countries in the Eurozone converged. Because the currency part of the risk had disappeared, this made it easier for countries in Southern Europe to borrow relatively cheaply. As a result, their sovereign debts (the debts of the State) increased. Theoretically, this should not have been possible, because the rules of the Eurozone forbade large deficits. However, the enforcement of these rules was lax, and some countries tried their best to hide deficits from the European Commission. Further, the sub-prime crisis forced States to 'rescue' banks, which cost large amounts of money and, in combination with already large sovereign debts, this caused the financial load on some States to become too heavy.

In a number of cases, the financial position of States became grave, as they were forced to bail out banks that were also in financial trouble. In other cases, the relationship between banks and States went the other way around: banks had to depreciate the bonds of States that had large budgetary deficits. As a result, the reserves of the banks shrank, and banks themselves had to be 'rescued' by (other) States. The general picture is that financial institutions and the finances of States were so closely intertwined that a problem on one front immediately led to a problem on the other.

When a new Greek government revealed in 2009 that the Greek sovereign debts were much larger than was previously admitted, this was the beginning of a new phase in the financial crisis: it turned out that more countries, for different reasons, had deficits that were too big to bear. Several countries, including Greece, Spain, Portugal and Ireland, had to be supported financially. This was done by means of loans that were negotiated and supervised by the 'troika', a cooperation of the International Monetary Fund, the ECB and the European Commission.

Austerity measures As a condition for receiving these loans, the receiving countries were obligated through 'memoranda of understanding' to take 'austerity measures', such as limitations on social security spending. These measures would allow the financial situations of the receiving countries to recover. The measures hit the populations of these countries very hard. People protested and voted for political parties that opposed the measures. Moreover, economists disagreed about whether the measures were, in fact, the proper solution to the crisis. However, as the austerity measures were imposed as a condition for receiving much needed loans, all countries accepted them in the end, although some felt as though they were forced to do so against their will. This may be regarded as another cause of Euroscepticism and populism.

New rules In order to avoid a recurrence of something like the Eurozone crisis, new rules were adopted by the Eurozone ministers of the European Council in the form of legislation packages termed the 'six-pack', the 'two-pack', and the Treaty on Stability, Coordination and Governance. These rules further limited the possibilities for Eurozone members to pursue their own fiscal policies, and – what is possibly more important – they increased the power of organizations such as the Commission and the ECB to supervise the financial behaviour of the Member States.

Sovereignty As a result of the financial crises, the EU Member States, in particular those that belong to the Eurozone, have lost a portion of their freedom to conduct their own financial policies.

In a sense, this outcome was anticipated. Until the experiment in the EU, monetary integration was typically the outflow of independent economic and political integration. Economies of countries were already strongly integrated, and the adoption of a common currency was a natural consequence. In the EU this was different. Here, monetary integration was adopted as a means to promote further economic and political integration. The EU was not an OCA, but the introduction of the euro should have made it into one. Ironically, the Eurozone crisis did contribute to the integration of Europe. The crisis made it essential that in the short term important measures were collectively taken. Those measures (six-pack, two-pack, introduction of a European banking union) contributed even further to the integration of Europe.

However, many countries are not happy with this 'loss of sovereignty'. For example, at the moment this text is being written (summer 2019), Italy is in conflict with the European

Commission. The Italian government, which enjoys large popular support, is not willing to keep its budgetary deficit within the limits required by European rules.

Reliable predictions are hard to make, especially when they concern the future, and therefore it is difficult to predict the outcome of the ongoing events. There is a saying – not very truthful – that anything that does not kill you only makes you stronger. The EU may come out stronger after the financial crisis. However, it is far from certain that the solutions to the Eurozone crisis and other developments that are perceived as threats to the sovereignty of the EU Member States will not kill the EU in its present form. In this connection, the fact that the reforms are seen as a threat to the sovereignty of the Member States plays a role.

However, as we will soon see, it is questionable whether the reforms do threaten the sovereignty of the Member States, first, because it is not very clear what sovereignty involves, and, second, because it is dubious whether the Member States can lose their sovereignty because of these reforms, considering the true character of sovereignty.

9.3 Introducing Sovereignty

The notion of sovereignty entered legal discourse in the 16th century, when two major developments began to take place simultaneously.

Absolute rulers One development was that countries came to be governed by absolute rulers. During the Middle Ages, rulers were assumed to be bound by natural or divine law and had to share their power with the nobility and the clergy. From the 16th century onwards, rulers became more powerful and also claimed to be entitled to rule without limitations or checks by rules or by peers. The rulers claimed to be 'free from laws' (*legibus absolutus*); hence the expression 'absolute ruler'. The Hobbesian theory that the ruler should not share his power with others, as this would lead to disagreements and a return to the state of nature and a war of everybody against everybody, illustrates this shift. Another illustration can be found in the booklet 'The Prince' (*Il Principe*), written in 1515 by a public servant in Firenze, Machiavelli, as advice to his ruler. At the time, the book was considered a scandal, because Machiavelli advised the ruler to only pretend to obey higher law but to ignore it in favour of keeping power.

Independent states The second major development was that States became independent. This development was, in particular, important in continental Europe, where the Holy Roman Empire *de facto* split up into a large number of smaller states. It was legally confirmed in the Westphalian peace treaties, which are often seen as a decisive step towards the recognition of independent States. For the German States this meant that they were no longer dependent on the Emperor as ruler of the Holy Roman Empire, and neither were the States connected by the same religion.[11] Moreover, because the States were independent, this meant that it had become possible to distinguish between international law as the law that regulated the relations between States and national law as the law that is in force within States. This distinction between two kinds of law has become known as the 'Westphalian duo'.

External and internal sovereignty The creation of the Westphalian duo is closely related to a distinction between two kinds of sovereignty. External sovereignty concerns the relationship between States as such, and means, by and large, that States are not allowed to, or cannot, meddle in the internal affairs of other States. This is the kind of sovereignty that is referred to in Article 2, Section 1 of the Charter of the United Nations:

> The organization is based on the principle of the sovereign equality of all its members.

Internal sovereignty concerns the question of who is 'the boss' in an independent State. This question is best understood in a historical context. For quite some time, there had been an ongoing debate (if everything went peacefully) about the relative power of worldly rulers (emperors, kings, princes and dukes) in relation to church authorities (bishops, including the Pope). A similar debate on power existed between the allegedly highest rulers (emperors and kings) and allegedly subordinate persons and bodies (high nobility, people's representatives and courts). During the period of absolutism (17th and 18th centuries) this battle was often decided in favour of the absolutist rulers,[12] but as the idea of the separation of powers became more popular, the discussion about the highest authority was revived.

Popular sovereignty Next to the notions of external and internal sovereignty, we also encounter popular sovereignty. Popular sovereignty, as it is traditionally conceived, is not a third form of sovereignty, next to internal and external sovereignty, but rather an answer to the question of who is the internal sovereign in a State. According to the theory of popular sovereignty, the people are the internal sovereign and the source of all competences

---

11 The emphasis on the German States here should be interpreted as an indication that the development towards independence was particularly important for the German States, as they were officially still parts of the Holy Roman Empire. Other States, such as England, had already taken this step towards independence.
12 A famous exception is England, in which Parliament is since the 17th century considered the internal sovereign.

exercised by State authorities. Public servants are assumed to act on behalf of the people. The view that the people are sovereign is an alternative to the view that the King or the Emperor is the ultimate source of authority (or the penultimate source if it is assumed that the King or the Emperor derived his authority from God).

Later in this chapter, it will be argued that the traditional theories of sovereignty previously described suffer from a lack of conceptual clarity. To restore the required clarity, the set of our conceptual tools needs to be expanded, and that is the topic of the next section.

9.4 Social Reality: Basics

We will use the analytical tools of legal theory to obtain a better grasp of what is at stake in the discussions about external and internal sovereignty. We begin at the bottom, with the question of how facts and things can exist in social reality, and work ourselves up to the notion of sovereignty.

9.4.1 Three Kinds of Facts

Objective facts Facts can exist in two or three ways. They are objective if they do not depend on what humans think about their existence. They can also exist in social reality, where their existence depends on whether people believe in their existence.

Objective facts are easy to understand. Mount Everest is the highest mountain on earth, whether we believe it or not. The same holds for the fact that adult elephants are bigger than adult mice, that Australia is surrounded by sea and that 3 + 4 equals 7. Objective facts are assumed to be the same for everybody: if two people disagree on an objective fact, at least one of them must be wrong.

Subjective 'facts' Objective facts can be contrasted with subjective 'facts'. Examples of such subjective 'facts' are the 'fact' that chocolate tastes better than cauliflower or that it rains too often. These subjective 'facts' are a matter of taste (chocolate tastes better than cauliflower) or rest on a standard that is not widely shared (too much rain). Subjective 'facts' need not be the same for everybody, and, therefore, many people will even refuse to use the word 'facts' for them.

Social facts It may seem that the room for possible facts is exhausted by objective facts and subjective 'facts'. Something is either objective and real, or merely subjective and in that sense unreal. However, this simple opposition between objective and subjective overlooks an intermediate group of facts, those facts that exist in social reality. We will call these latter facts 'social facts'. Social facts are very important for lawyers, as most facts with which lawyers work are social facts. Moreover, an important subset of the social facts is the result of rules. (Figure 9.2)

Figure 9.2 Three kinds of facts

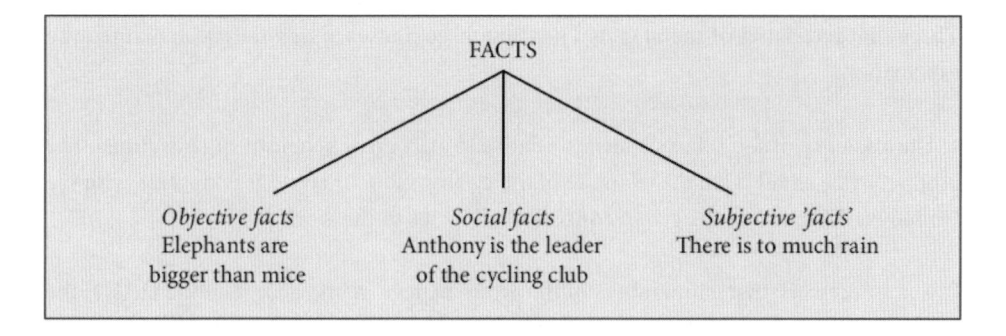

```
                            FACTS
              /               |               \
      Objective facts      Social facts      Subjective 'facts'
       Elephants are     Anthony is the leader   There is to much rain
       bigger than mice  of the cycling club
```

9.4.2   The Existence of Social Facts

Social facts exist if, and to the extent that, people believe them to exist and accept them. Suppose that a small group of five persons have a cycling club. Each Saturday afternoon they meet at Anthony's home, from where they set out on a tour of their extended neighbourhood. At the beginning there was no leader, but after some time it turned out that if Anthony proposed a destination, this was typically accepted by everybody else. On the way, Anthony would also make proposals about when to stop for a break and when to resume, and these proposals were typically also adopted without substantial discussion. After some time, the members of the cycling club would actually count on Anthony to propose destinations and stops. If somebody else wanted to make a stop, she would ask 'Anthony, is it not time for a break?' and then Anthony would take a decision. Moreover, if somebody else proposed a break, he would be corrected by the others, who would agree that it is Anthony who should decide.

This would amount to the adoption of Anthony as the leader of the cycling club, without any official decision to make him into one and without an official description of the tasks and powers of the leader. The leadership of a group consists in the acceptance by the others of the decisions that the leader makes and a refusal to follow the decisions of anybody else. What has happened in our example is that everybody believes that Anthony is the leader of the group, accepts his leadership and believes that the others also believe in and accept his leadership.

Definition of social facts This example can be generalized into the following provisional definition of when a fact exists in social reality. Fact F exists in a social group G as a social fact if and only if sufficiently numerous members of G:
1. believe and accept F,
2. believe that sufficiently numerous other members of G do the same, and
3. consider such beliefs and acceptances as ground for the existence of F.

Three characteristics of social facts There are three clauses in this definition that require explanation:

1. The existence of social facts is always relative to a group of people or organizations. The group may be small, as in the example of the cycling club, or large, as is the case with the United Nations, where the group consists of all States in the world.

It is not necessary that all members of the group believe in and accept all the facts. If the cycling club consisted of twenty members, and only one of them did not accept Anthony as the leader, Anthony would still be the leader. However, if only Anthony accepted himself as the leader, he would be mistaken about his leadership. Similarly, the United Nations still exists as an organization of States, even if one or two States do not accept its existence. Clearly there can be boundary cases, for example if 70 States did not accept the existence of the United Nations, while 125 States did, the existence of the United Nations as a social fact may be called into question. The existence of social facts is often a matter of degree.

2. It is necessary that the members of the social group themselves consider acceptance as a ground for existence. Suppose, for example, that all members of a group believe that 3.13 multiplied by 4.38 equals 13.6094 and also believe – for instance because this is taught in all schools – that everybody else also believes this. However, they also believe that the fact does not depend on beliefs or acceptance, but that it is objective. In this case, it is not a social fact that 3.13 multiplied by 4.38 equals 13.6094. If it were a fact, it would be an objective fact. However, since the calculation is objectively wrong, it is not an objective fact either. It is not a fact at all.

Notice that all of this would have been different in the case of Anthony's leadership of the cycling club. If everybody believes and accepts that Anthony is the leader, it does not make sense to say that everybody is wrong. The very fact that everybody believes and accepts that Anthony is the leader *makes* Anthony the leader. The beliefs make themselves true, and this is characteristic of facts in social reality.

3. Not only is it necessary that sufficiently numerous members of a social group *believe* that some fact exists, but often they must also *accept* it. For instance, if Christian is a member of the cycling group, it does not suffice that he believes that Anthony is the leader; he must also accept Anthony as the leader. This means that if Anthony takes a decision, Christian will typically comply with that decision. He will follow Anthony to the chosen destination, stop when Anthony decides to take a break and pick up his bicycle again when Anthony decides that the break is over.

Whether acceptance is necessary next to the mere belief that a social fact exists depends on the type of fact in social reality. If all members believe that it is best (but not obligatory) to arrive at the final destination after Anthony, there is no need for acceptance. The mere fact that everybody believes that this is the best makes it the best. However, if all members believe that nobody ought to arrive at the destination before Anthony, this requires acceptance, as this fact requires a particular kind of behaviour (do not arrive before Anthony).

The crucial point here is that the existence of some social facts requires more from the group members than merely believing that these facts exists. Sometimes it requires a particular kind of behaviour. The fact must not only be believed, but must also be accepted, and this acceptance manifests itself in compliance and in criticism of those who do not comply.

9.5 Social Reality: Rules and Rule-Based Facts

9.5.1 The Main Function of Rules

Different subordinate functions People often think that all rules prescribe behaviour. For instance, we have the rule that cyclists must cycle on the right-hand side of the street. This rule seems to prescribe cycling on the right. However, rules also fulfil other functions. Some rules give persons the competence to perform some kind of juridical acts. For example, there is a rule that owners of goods are competent to alienate – e.g. sell or donate – their goods. This rule does not prescribe anything, but empowers owners to alienate. Another example is the rule that the President of the US is the commander-in-chief of the US army. This rule does not prescribe anything either but attaches the status of being the commander-in-chief to the status of being the President of the US.

One main function As these examples illustrate, rules fulfil many different functions, and it would be a misunderstanding to assume that all rules prescribe behaviour. However, on

a more abstract level, it is possible to find one main function that all rules have in common: all rules attach facts of one kind to facts of another kind. Let us look at some examples:
- The rule that forbids the growing of marihuana attaches the duty not to grow marihuana to being a legal subject.
- The rule that cyclists must cycle on the right attaches the duty to cycle on the right (but not the duty to cycle) to being a cyclist.
- The rule that grants owners the competence to alienate attaches the competence to alienate to the status of being the owner.
- The rule that skateboards count as vehicles for the Traffic Act attaches the status of being a vehicle in the sense of the Traffic Act to being a skateboard. (Other rules attach consequences to being such a vehicle.)
- The main rule of tort law attaches to the event that a tortuous act caused damage an obligation for the tortfeasor to pay damages.

Sometimes the legal consequence of a rule is that some duty or obligation exists. In these cases, but only in these cases, the rule may be said to be prescriptive or mandatory. Many rules are not mandatory.

Structure of rules Because rules have their main function in common, all rules share a common structure: they have a condition part and a conclusion part. The conclusion part specifies which fact is created (attached) by the rule. This fact is called the *consequence* of the rule. If the rule is a legal rule, the consequence is the legal consequence. The condition part of the rule specifies the facts to which new facts are attached. These facts are called the *operative facts* of the rule. They determine whether a rule is applicable to a case.

Take for example the rule that the President of the US is the commander-in-chief of the US army. The operative fact of this rule is that somebody is the President of the US. This fact makes the rule applicable. The legal consequence of the rule is that this person is the commander-in-chief of the US army. Other rules attach consequences to the possession of this latter status.

9.5.2 How Rules Exist

It is a frequent mistake among lawyers to assume that all rules must have been created. As a matter of fact, most rules were not created. The rules of meaning of natural languages illustrate this well. There is a particular kind of animal that is called 'dog' in English, 'chien' in French and 'Hund' in German. If you call such an animal 'cat', you make a mistake because the word 'cat' does not stand for dogs. If you call a dog 'cat', you violate a rule of meaning. This rule of meaning has grown together with the English language, but it was never created.

There are very many rules of meaning, and hardly any of them were created.[13] The same holds for most rules of arithmetic – they were 'discovered' – or moral rules. At the same time, many rules were created, and legal rules illustrate this phenomenon of rule creation well, even though there are also many legal rules that have not been created ('unwritten' law). For a proper understanding of law, in general, and of sovereignty, in particular, it is important to understand the differences and the relationships between rules that were explicitly created and rules that have 'grown' spontaneously.

Social rules Social facts exist because their existence is recognized by the members of a social group. Often there is system in this recognition. If a man over a particular age is not married, people recognize him as (call him) a bachelor. If one particular member of a cycling club 'always' determines where to go and when to have breaks, people will recognize him as the leader of the group. If a person is in danger, other people will recognize that they have a moral duty to assist.

A more extensive example would be the following. The cycling club has the rule that its leader determines when a break is over. This means that (almost) every time the leader decides that it is time to continue the trip and announces this, the members of the club pay for their drinks, get up from their chairs in the café and continue the cycling trip. They believe that the break is over, and that the others believe the same, they accept that they should go on and believe that the others accept this too. In other words, each time that the leader declares that the break is over, it becomes a social fact that the break is over. As the connection between the announcement of the leader and this effect always exists, it can be said that the group has a rule that the leader can (has the competence to) call an end to the break.

Notice that the relationship between the existence of a social rule and the belief and acceptance of social facts is bidirectional. The facts exist, because they are attached by the rule to other, already existing facts. The rule exists in a social group because the members of the group tend to recognize the facts that are created by the rule. In the case of social rules, it does not make sense to ask what comes first, the rule or the consequences of the rule.

---

13   There are a few exceptions, as with artificial words such as 'laser'. This word originated as an abbreviation for 'Light Amplification through the Stimulated Emission of Radiation'.

There are also social rules in law, and they are called 'customary law' or 'unwritten law'. Next to treaties, customary law plays an important role in international law. Unwritten law is often used for determining whether a duty of care exists in tort law. Violation of such a rule counts as unlawful behaviour, and this may lead to the liability to pay damages.

Created rules Many legal rules have been created explicitly, in the form of legislation, treaties or – in the common law – in the form of judicial decisions. If a rule is explicitly created, the rule is valid because of the way it was created. This means two things:
1. If the rule is recognized as valid, the consequences of the rules must also be recognized. For example, if the legislature makes the rule that cyclists must cycle on the right, this rule is recognized as valid. The validity of this recognition means that legal subjects also recognize that cyclists must cycle on the right.
2. If a rule is recognized because of its origin (pedigree), rules with the same origin must normally also be recognized as valid. So if the rule that cyclists must cycle on the right is recognized as a valid legal rule for the reason that it was created by the legislature, other rules created by the legislature must also be recognized as valid. In other words, if rules are created through decision-making, as is the case with most legal rules, there must be other rules, meta-rules about rules, that attach the validity of rules to the outcomes of decision-making processes.

9.5.3   Rule-Based Facts and Rules

Rule-based facts Many social facts are the result of some rule. That may be a legal rule, such as the rule that underlies the duty to compensate the damage of a tort. It may also be a non-legal rule, such as the rule of the cycling club that a new leader must buy all group members a drink at the club's favourite pub. Such facts, which exist because they are attached by some rule to other facts, are called 'rule-based facts'.

Normally, rule-based facts come into existence every time the conditions of the relevant rule are satisfied and this rule is applicable. For example, if there is a rule that makes criminals punishable, the fact that somebody is a criminal makes this rule applicable, and the rule 'automatically' attaches the fact that this person is punishable.

Rule-based rules Interestingly, one kind of fact that is often based on a rule concerns the existence of a new rule. For instance, the cycling club may have the rule that the leader can make rules on the departure time of cycling tours. (Saturdays at 14h00; Sundays at 10h00.)

The phenomenon of rule-based rules occurs most frequently in law. Almost all legal rules have been created explicitly, and the power to create new legal rules is typically granted by an already existing rule of (constitutional) law. For example, a country – which counts as a social group – has the rule that:

IF Parliament makes a statute

And IF Parliament follows the rules for making legislation in doing so

THEN all the rules in the statute are valid law.

Suppose, moreover, that Parliament adopts the Traffic Act according to the official legislative procedure and that one of the rules in the Traffic Act reads that for the purpose of this Act skateboards count as vehicles. Then, on the basis of the mentioned rule of recognition, the rule that for the purpose of the Traffic Act skateboards count as vehicles is a valid law. This boils down to the fact that the rule about skateboards exists as a legal rule.

This example illustrates that the fact that a particular rule is a valid legal rule is in itself the consequence of another rule. This other rule makes that legislation is a means to create valid legal rules; it makes legislation into a legal source. Let us suppose that the mentioned rule was itself not created by means of legislation, and that it was instead a social rule. This would mean that the citizens of the country in question tend to recognize rules that were officially made by Parliament as legal rules; they recognize legislation as a source of law. Further, this recognition means that these citizens recognize the legal consequences of these rules. In our example this would mean that the citizens, when they must apply the Traffic Act, recognize skateboards as vehicles.

9.5.4 Popular Sovereignty

Legal rules can, and most often do, exist for the reason that they were explicitly created. However, in order for a rule to exist because it was created, another rule must have existed that made it possible to create legal rules. This other rule may also have been created explicitly, but then still another rule must have existed that made it possible to create this rule. Also, that rule may have been created, but then … and so on. A legal system may be a pyramid of rules that were created on the basis of other rules, but at the top of this pyramid there cannot be a rule that was explicitly created. If that were otherwise, the rule 'at the top' could not really have been at the top, because there must have been a still higher rule making the creation of the alleged top rule possible.

Kelsen and the Basic Norm Hans Kelsen (1881-1973) was a famous Austrian constitutional lawyer. He wrote the Constitution of Austria, but also developed a well-known theory about the nature of law, the *Reine Rechtslehre* (Pure Theory of Law). According to this theory, a legal rule could be valid only if it was created by a person or a body that was empowered to do so. Moreover, this empowerment could take place only by some valid legal rule. It is easy to see that if one asks whether a particular legal rule is valid, one ends up regressing infinitely to ever higher rules and authorities. Every rule presupposes the validity of some higher rule, and the chain never ends. Kelsen recognized this problem and 'solved' it by assuming that every legal system has one 'highest' rule, the validity of which has to be assumed because otherwise the whole legal system would be invalid. This highest rule, which Kelsen called the Basic Norm, does not really exist but must be assumed to exist to explain why the rules of a legal system are valid.

State sovereignty Most people find Kelsen's theory about the Basic Norm unsatisfactory. It is strange to base the validity of a whole legal system on a highest rule that admittedly does not even exist. Nevertheless, a similar construction is accepted by those who argue that there must be a basis for the authority of the officials of a legal system who create rules and who impose duties on (other) citizens. This basis, some claim, is the sovereignty of the State. The State is sovereign, meaning that it has the power to make rules on any subject and that it has the power to impose duties and to empower state officials to do the same. Moreover, a State must be sovereign in this way, because otherwise the rules of the State would be invalid and the officials of the State would be powerless. That sounds very much like Kelsen's view, namely that we must presuppose a Basic Norm, because otherwise valid law could not exist. Happily, both Kelsen's argument and the described theory of State sovereignty are based on a false presupposition.

Two modes of existence Kelsen and the adherents of State sovereignty assume that the validity of a rule can be based only on creation by an agent who had the legal power to do so. We have already seen that this is not correct. Rules can also exist (be valid) if their consequences are by and large accepted in a social group. In other words, rules can exist as social rules.

We have also seen that a system of created rules cannot consist of created rules alone, because then it would, so to speak, 'hang in the air'. That is the problem Kelsen encountered when he tried to base the validity of all legal rules on other legal rules. It is also the problem of the theorists of State sovereignty, who believe that the sovereignty of States is necessary to explain the validity of the State rules and the legal powers of the State officials. These theorists have a hard time explaining why States are sovereign.

Any system of rules that really exists must somehow be based on recognition by the members of a social group. The only thing needed for this recognition is the existence of one single *social* rule that empowers some authority to create legal rules.[14] This social rule founds the legal system in social reality, and the rest can be a pyramid of explicitly created rules. That is all a legal system needs.

This does not show that every legal system is based on such a single social rule. There must at least be one social rule, because otherwise the system hangs in the air. However, there may very well be other social rules in a legal system, and as a matter of fact (almost) all legal systems have many more social rules. One need only think of the unwritten rules that impose duties of care in tort law or of the unwritten rules of criminal law to exclude the punishability of criminals (justifications and excuses).

Popular sovereignty If the above argument is correct, and if all legal systems presuppose at least one social rule, it shows that all legal rules *in the end* depend on recognition by the people to whom the rules apply. Individual legal rules may exist whether people like them or not, because they were validly made by the legislature or a court. However, this is possible only if legislation and court decisions are generally recognized as official legal sources, and that in turn depends on what people believe and accept. The basis of positive law lies in social reality and the beliefs and recognition of the people. In this sense, people are sovereign; there exists popular sovereignty.

However, it does not mean that the people have a special competence within the legal system, a competence that might, for example, be realized through elections or referenda. Such a competence is not excluded by the notion of popular sovereignty defended here, but it is a different subject. The popular sovereignty that necessarily exists is nothing other than the necessity that a legal system is in the end a phenomenon in social reality. It does not depend on the content of a particular legal system. Popular sovereignty in the sense of special competences of the people in political procedures depends on the content of a legal system. Such sovereignty may exist in some jurisdictions and not in others.

9.6 Legal Consequences

The legal consequences of rules are very diverse, but most of them can be categorized under one of four headings:

---

14 This is the view propagated by the English legal philosopher H.L.A. Hart. *See* Hart 1961, Chapters V and VI.

European Integration: A Theme

1. Duties and obligations;
2. Permissions;
3. Competences;
4. Legal status.

Duties A duty exists if somebody is legally obligated to do something, or to refrain from doing something, without there being another person who has a claim that this behaviour is actually performed. For example, if it is forbidden to drink alcohol on the street, this is a duty to refrain from some kind of behaviour. However, there is nobody in particular who can claim that you do not drink alcohol in public. A police officer can inform you that you are behaving illegally, or can even impose a fine for doing so, but there is no right-holder corresponding to your duty.

Obligations In the case of obligations there are corresponding right-holders. For example, if David contracted with Dorris that Dorris will clean David's car, Dorris is under an obligation *towards David* to clean David's car, and David has a claim *against Dorris* that she will clean his car. Obligations are always the result of an obligation-creating event, such as a contract or a tort. This event determines the content of the obligation (what should be done), the person who is obligated to do something and the person who has the corresponding claim.

Permissions If there is a duty or an obligation, somebody is obligated to do something or to refrain from doing something. If a person is *not* obligated, they are *permitted* to do or to *refrain* from doing something. Most often, no rule is needed for a permission, as permission is the default situation. For example, if there is no rule forbidding parking in front of your home, you are permitted to do so without the need for a special rule that gives you this permission.

However, a permissive rule is necessary to make an exception to an existing prohibition. In general, it is forbidden to kill human beings, but perhaps there is a permissive rule that gives secret agents such as James Bond a license to kill. In general, it is forbidden to run a red traffic light, but there may be a rule that permits this in case of an emergency.

Competences Juridical acts make it possible for legal agents to intentionally change the legal position of themselves or of others, or to bring about other legal consequences. For example, the sale of a car is a juridical act. Depending on the jurisdiction, such a sale leads either to an obligation to transfer ownership, or directly to the passing of ownership from the old to the new owner. Granting a building permit for a house is also a juridical act, and if a public servant grants a citizen such a permit, they create an exception to the general prohibition to build, and the citizen is now permitted to build the house. Legislating is also a juridical act. In doing so, the legislature creates new legal rules, or repeals existing rules.

For all these juridical acts it holds that not everybody can perform them. Only the owner of a good can transfer ownership through a sale; only designated public servants can grant building permits and only official legislators can make new rules through legislation. For all juridical acts it holds that the agents performing them must have the relevant competence. Without such a competence, the juridical act will typically be null and void and have no legal consequences.

A legal competence is a special case of a legal status. It is a fact to which law attaches a further legal consequence and that derives its legal relevance from that consequence.[15]

9.7 Legal Status

Legal rules often operate as follows: There is a legal status such as being an owner; there are rules that specify when this status exists and rules that specify what the consequences of this status are. In legal reasoning, we are often interested in whether one of the consequences of the status exists. To establish this, we must first determine whether the status exists and to that purpose we must apply the rules that define when the status is present.

Examples Let us make this more concrete. Jeannette has bought a painting from Bernard, but suddenly Pierre claims that the painting belongs to him. To determine whether Jeannette has become the owner of the painting, it is necessary to find out whether Bernard was competent to transfer the ownership. Bernard says he was competent, because he was the owner. When pressed, he argues that he became the owner because he made the painting himself.

Both being competent to transfer and being the owner are examples of legal status. There are no physical counterparts for being competent and being owner; both characteristics are purely immaterial. However, ownership and the competence to transfer do exist as rule-based facts, and the law attaches consequences to the presence of these facts.

---

15   This idea of legal status was inspired by the influential article Tû-tû, in which Alf Ross argued that ownership as such does not really exist but merely has a function in legal arguments that lead from the conditions of ownership to the consequences of ownership (Ross 1957).

Status makes sense in law, because the law attaches consequences to the possession of status, typically even more than one consequence. For instance, if Bernard owns the painting, not only is he competent to transfer it, but he also has permission to destroy the painting and to use it. Moreover, nobody except Bernard is allowed to destroy the painting. However, as the owner, Bernard can give permission for its destruction.

Another example: Juliette is the Mayor of Tinseltown. As the Mayor, she has both the duty and the competence to preside over the town council; she is also competent to make emergency regulations for her town and is permitted to use the Mayor's office.

Legal status plays an important role in law as it intermediates between, on the one hand, duties and obligations and, on the other hand, the non-legal facts to which the law indirectly – via the status – connects these duties and obligations.

The 'logic' of status Because there are several consequences attached to the possession of a status, these consequences typically go together. For instance, as soon as Bernard has transferred the ownership of his painting to Jeannette, Jeannette has permission to use and destroy the painting, and she is competent to transfer the ownership of the painting to somebody else. Moreover, if the status is lost, all the consequences of the status are also lost. For instance, if Juliette gives up her function as Mayor, she no longer has the duty or the competence to preside over the town council, and she has also lost the permission to use the Mayor's office.

The pincushion metaphor To understand how status operates in law, it may be useful to use the pincushion metaphor of status. Legal status can be compared to a pincushion, and the consequences that law attaches to a status can be compared to the pins in the cushion. At one moment, the cushion may contain more pins; at another moment there may be fewer.

For example, if the State introduces a real estate tax, homeowners will have a duty attached to their ownership. Metaphorically speaking, the new tax inserts an extra pin into the cushion. However, the cushion itself, the right of ownership, remains the same. If the owner creates a usufruct on a house, he loses the competence to transfer the house free of limited rights. Metaphorically speaking, a pin has been removed from the cushion. The cushion has remained the same: the owner of a house with a usufruct is still the owner of the house. He has not given away a portion of the ownership; only a competence that was attached to the ownership. However, if an owner transfers the ownership to somebody else, the whole cushion, including the pins inserted into it, moves from one holder to another.

The pincushion metaphor is particularly useful because it illustrates the fundamental difference between changing the consequences of a legal status (changing the pins in the cushion) and moving or ending the status (the cushion belongs to somebody else or is thrown into the waste bin with all the pins in it).

9.8 External Sovereignty as Legal Status

In the development of international relations over the last five centuries, a legal framework has come into existence with States as the main actors and relations between States as the core issue. The rules in this framework are partly social rules (customary law), which means that they exist because they are used by States to attach legal consequences to fact situations. They are also based on treaties between States. After World War II, part of this legal framework was codified in the Charter of the United Nations, particularly in Article 2, Section 1.

It is important to consider what the rule of Article 2, Section 1 actually does: it attaches a legal status – sovereign equality – to another status, being a State. The Charter itself does not specify what this sovereign equality entails. In terms of the pincushion metaphor: all States possess the same kind of pincushion, but the Charter leaves unspecified what the pins in the cushion are. The pins are provided by unwritten and customary law.

External sovereignty is a legal status, which means that it is attached by a legal rule to some other factual situation. In the case of external sovereignty, this other situation is that some organization is a State. If an organization is a State, it possesses for that reason external sovereignty, and the 'rights' that go with it (the pins in the cushion). Logically speaking, the pincushion of external sovereignty comes first, while the consequences attached to external sovereignty – the pins in the cushion – depend on the existence of external sovereignty. If States have 'sovereign rights', they have them because they possess external sovereignty, not the other way round.

Sovereignty and competences The expression 'sovereign equality' suggests that all cushions contain the same pins. However, in the course of time the pins in the cushions may change. After a lapse of time, some States have sovereignty with more pins in the cushion and other States have sovereignty with fewer pins. For instance, if the EU Member States have transferred some of their competences to the EU, these States have fewer competences attached to their sovereignty than other States that did not transfer competences.

However, a change in the number of pins in a cushion does not change the cushion itself. Less metaphorically, if States give up some of the consequences attached to their sovereignty, they do not give up part of their sovereignty. After all, as pins may be placed back in the cushion that they came from, competences may return to the sovereignty that they were extracted from. Sovereignty is a pre-condition for having the consequences that are attached to sovereignty; it is not the collection of all these consequences. In terms of our metaphor, the pincushion is not identical to the collection of all the pins.

Transfer of competences As has become clear in the history of the EU, it is possible that States transfer some of the competences attached to their sovereignty to some other body such as the European Commission.

It is important to realize that it is not always the case that when the EU receives some competence, it was transferred by the Member States. It is also possible that Member States give some competence to the EU and at the same time also retain this competence themselves. Take Article 2, Sections 1 and 2 of the Treaty on the Functioning of the European Union:

Section 2 explicitly makes it possible that States confer a competence on the EU while at the same time retaining this competence. It also indicates that in that case, States can exercise their competence only if the EU did not exercise its competence. Apparently, the possessor of a competence – in this case an EU Member State – can create a similar competence for the EU, without thereby losing its own competence. An example of such a shared competence is the field of consumer protection. See Art. 4 TFEU, Section 2 sub f.

> Article 2 TFEU
>
> 1. When the Treaties confer on the Union exclusive competence in a specific area, only the Union may legislate and adopt legally binding acts, the Member States being able to do so themselves only if so empowered by the Union or for the implementation of Union acts.
>
> 2. When the Treaties confer on the Union a competence shared with the Member States in a specific area, the Union and the Member States may legislate and adopt legally binding acts in that area. The Member States shall exercise their competence to the extent that the Union has not exercised its competence. The Member States shall again exercise their competence to the extent that the Union has decided to cease exercising its competence.

However, as Section 1 indicates, it is also possible to transfer a competence, by granting the EU an exclusive competence. An example of such an exclusive competence is the field of the customs union. See Art. 3 TFEU, section 1 sub a. The difference between an exclusive and a shared competence is not between kinds of competences, but rather between transferring a competence and making a duplicate competence for another agent.

Transfer of sovereignty It is possible to transfer or duplicate competences that are attached to sovereignty, but is it also possible to transfer sovereignty itself? It may be useful to consider other examples of status to see how this works, for instance ownership and the right of privacy. It is possible to transfer ownership, but it is not possible to transfer the right to privacy.[16] Apparently, it depends on the status at issue, whether it can be transferred.

It is very unlikely that sovereignty, which has historically been strongly connected to statehood, can be transferred. All States are already sovereign, and have little to gain from receiving the sovereignty of another State, if we can even imagine what that would amount to. It is also unclear what it would mean if a non-State agent would somehow receive the sovereignty of a State, resulting in a non-State entity having sovereignty. Sovereignty appears to be a good example of a legal status that cannot be transferred.

This means that the transfer or duplication of the competences that originally belonged to EU Member States cannot amount to the transfer of actual sovereignty. In becoming EU members, the Member States may have given up some of their competences or permissions, but they have not given up their sovereignty. Even if the Member States had intended the transfer of actual sovereignty, they even could not in fact give up, or transfer, their sovereignty. Assuming otherwise is to make a conceptual mistake.

Giving up statehood States cannot give up their (external) sovereignty, but they can give up their independence as States. When the States of Northern America decided to form a federation, they gave up their independent statehood, and by doing so, they lost their external sovereignty. However, it is important to distinguish giving up of statehood and the loss of external sovereignty connected to it from giving up of permissions or competences attached to sovereignty. Conceptually speaking, these are quite different things.

Sociologically speaking, however, it may happen that if sufficient permissions and competences are given up, the sovereignty to which they were attached loses its relevance and

---

16 Giving permission to do things that would normally count as violations of privacy, such as reading your electronic address book, is not giving the privacy away but merely suspending a prohibition to do something. It is an exercise of a competence attached to the right.

has, as a matter of fact, disappeared. At that moment we can say that the State whose sovereignty was lost has lost independence and has stopped existing as a State. However, even if that has happened, the State did not transfer its sovereignty. The sovereignty was lost because the statehood to which the sovereignty was attached was lost.

9.9 Internal Sovereignty Is No Legal Status

External sovereignty is a status assigned by international law to States. It cannot be transferred, although it is possible to transfer competences that are attached to sovereignty. What about internal sovereignty? Can it be transferred? Is it somehow involved in the process of European integration?

What is internal sovereignty? These questions cannot be answered easily, because it is far from clear what is meant by internal sovereignty. It is possible to distinguish three different ideas, all of which are sometimes denoted by 'internal sovereignty':

1. The idea that in a particular territory, the State is the organization that has the supreme power. We may call this form of internal sovereignty 'State sovereignty'. The traditional candidate for a non-State organization limiting the power of the State was the Roman Catholic Church. A modern candidate might be large, multinational enterprises or syndicates of workers.

2. The idea that some organization within the State apparatus has a power that is not limited by any other State organization. This form of internal sovereignty may be called 'sovereignty as supremacy'. In the United Kingdom it is assumed that Parliament is in this sense sovereign.

3. The idea that some organization within the State apparatus has a power that is not confined to a limited set of topics. Historically, it was, for instance, important that a sovereign could prescribe a religion for her or his people. More recently, a contested topic might be whether the sovereign can obligate parents to vaccinate their children. This form of internal sovereignty may be called 'sovereignty as unboundedness'. Presently, it is generally assumed that this form of internal sovereignty does not exist because human rights demarcate an area that is free from State intervention.

If the discussion of whether States give up their sovereignty when they transfer competences to the EU is interpreted as a discussion of internal sovereignty, only the first two of these ideas of internal sovereignty can be at stake. Perhaps the national State is not the supreme authority in its own territory any more, or an organization within the State gives up its internal sovereignty in favour of the EU.

As history has shown, it is not obvious that a State, being a particular kind of organization, does not exercise the supreme power on its territory. Even at present, there are countries where the supreme power is exercised by religious authorities, with only a subordinate role for the State. Moreover, many countries operate some system of division of powers between State organizations, and these countries lack an internal sovereign in the sense of supremacy. So it is possible that a State has no internal (supreme) sovereign or that a State does not possess State sovereignty. But does this possibility imply that a State or a State organ can transfer internal sovereignty to the EU?

Powers and competences An important distinction in this connection is between power and competence. Other than the related concept of competence, power is not a legal concept. There are no rules that grant somebody or something any power, although the existence of power can be influenced by rules. For example, if Parliament has the competence to legislate and exercises this competence by following the procedure for legislation, then the immediate result is a validly passed Bill. Because a meta-rule says that the rules in validly passed Bills are valid legal rules, an indirect result of Parliament's exercising of its competence is that Parliament has made new rules. Apparently, the combination of the rule that grants Parliament the competence to legislate, the rules that specify the procedure for legislating, and the meta-rule that grants rules in a validly passed Bill the status of valid legal rules gives Parliament the power to create new legal rules. However, there is no single legal rule with as its conclusion that Parliament has the power to make rules. The power – which is very real – is the side effect of rules that confer competence, specify procedure and grant the status of valid legal rule. Some powers are the result of legal rules, but the possession of those powers is not a legal status itself, but merely a side effect of existing rules that primarily fulfil different functions.[17]

Legal power is no legal status If the possession of a legal power is not a legal status, then having supreme or unrestrained powers is certainly not a legal status. This means that there is no rule that grants somebody or some institution the status of internal sovereign in the first or second sense. Moreover, if a country has an internal sovereign, this conclusion can only be drawn from the power this sovereign actually has *on independent* grounds. The internal sovereign is the internal sovereign because she has supreme or unrestrained powers, and not the other way round.

---

17   *See* Hage 2018, pp. 209-212.

Internal sovereignty cannot be transferred Internal sovereignty has to do with the possession of legal power, in particular the possession of supreme power, or of unlimited power. Such powers are the result of legal rules but are a side effect of rules that grant competences, specify procedures or grant legal status. Having a legal power is itself not a legal status. This means that it is not possible to directly transfer legal power to some other person or organization.

Legal competence, by contrast, is a legal status and can be transferred. As a result, a legal power moves from the person who, or organization that, originally had the competence to the person who or organization that has received the competence. For example, if a national State delegates the power to legislate about municipal affairs to the council of the municipality, the legislative power on these topics has moved from the national state to the municipality council. So it is possible to cause legal power to move from one person or organization to another. However, this cannot be done by transferring internal sovereignty. The possession of internal sovereignty is the result of the possession of legal power and competence, and not the other way round.

This means that it is not possible to transfer internal sovereignty from national States or State organs to (organs of) the EU. Internal sovereignty cannot be transferred.

9.10 Conclusion

The movement towards supranationality in the EU meets with much resistance, and this resistance is often framed as a resistance against the transfer of sovereignty. In this chapter, we have moved from the description and analysis of two crises in the EU via a legal-theoretical analysis of the notion of sovereignty to the conclusions that neither external nor internal sovereignty can be transferred to the EU. What is possible is the transfer, or the duplication, of competences. The discussion of whether and to what extent such a transfer or duplication is desirable makes sense. Disguising this discussion as one about the transfer of sovereignty is at best mistaken and at worst misleading.

10 Euroscepticism

10.1 Introduction

At the time this text is being revised (autumn 2019) it may seem that the popularity of the EU is at an all-time low. Brexit is approaching, Italy has announced that it will not comply with European budgetary rules, Poland and Hungary are having problems with the acquis on the rule of law, and Central and Eastern European Member States are not accepting the relocation of refugees entering the EU through its southern border.

Figure 10.1   Did your country benefit?

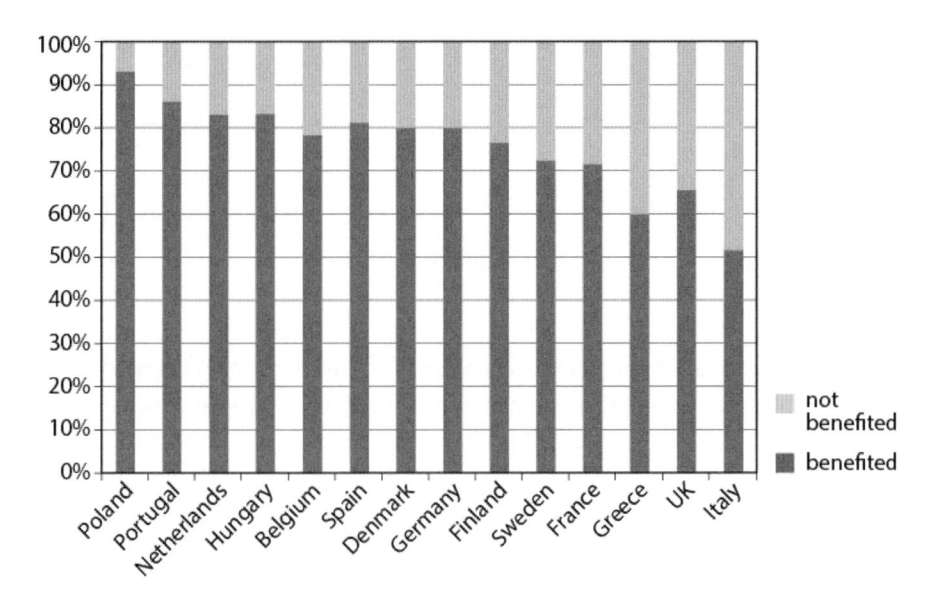

[Bar chart showing percentages of respondents who felt their country benefited vs. not benefited from EU membership, for the following countries (left to right): Poland, Portugal, Netherlands, Hungary, Belgium, Spain, Denmark, Germany, Finland, Sweden, France, Greece, UK, Italy. Legend: benefited / not benefited.]

Surveys However, it is wise not to confuse disagreement on the future course of the EU with discontent about the EU in general. In 2018, the European Parliament conducted a Eurobarometer Survey, in which 89.2% of EU inhabitants responded positively to the question of whether they believed their country had benefited from its participation in the EU. The results for some of the countries are shown in Figure 10.1. As the overview shows, there are big differences between Member States, but overall, inhabitants in most countries believe that their countries have benefited from EU membership.

It is clear that despite the noise, the EU's popularity is not waning. Figure 10.2 gives an overview of the answers that were given to the question of whether the experience of EU membership was positive or negative in the country of the interviewee. The answers were collected from 2007 until 2018.[1]

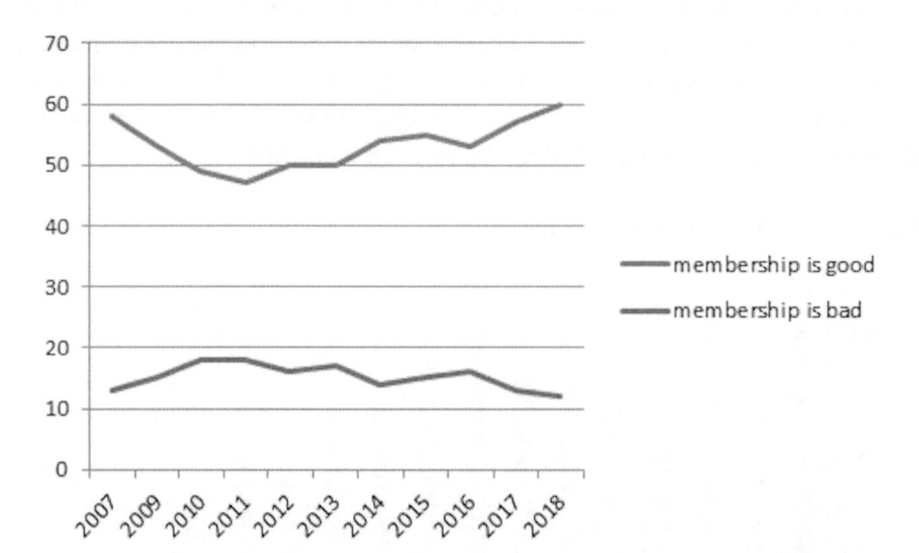

Figure 10.2   Was EU membership good or bad for your country?

As can be seen from the graph, the EU's popularity was at a low in 2011, when only 47% of those interviewed thought that the membership of their country was good. However, even in that year, only 18% believed the membership to be bad, a much lower number. Moreover, since 2011, the EU's popularity has been rising, with only one minor dip in 2016. In the 2018 survey, 60% of those interviewed thought the EU membership of their country was good, and only 12% thought it bad.

Distribution, rather than welfare The overall picture of the EU's popularity looks good if it is approached from the angle of whether Member States benefit from their membership. However, readers should notice that the questions were asked from a state-centred perspective. The questions were:

---

[1]   The information was taken from www.europarl.europa.eu/at-your-service/files/be-heard/eurobarometer/2018/public-opinion-monitoring-at-a-glance-september-2018/en-plenary-insights-september-2018.pdf (last visited on 29 October 2018).

'Generally speaking, do you think that (OUR COUNTRY)'s membership of the EU is...? (A good thing/A bad thing /Neither a good thing nor a bad thing/Don't know)'

And:

'Taking everything into account, would you say that (OUR COUNTRY) has on balance benefited or not from being a member of the EU? (Benefited/Not benefited /Don't know)'

Questions that might have received different answers are: whether it is a good thing that the EU exists, whether the average inhabitant of an EU Member State benefits from the existence of the EU, or whether the worst-off inhabitants of the EU benefit from the existence of the EU.[2] The questions tended to focus on the benefits for Member States of the EU, rather than on the EU as a whole, or – to state it in economic terminology – on distribution effects, rather than on welfare effects.

Economic and other welfare In an economic study, it was found that almost all countries that joined the EU in the 1980s or in 2004 had, on average, a 12% larger actual increase in GDP than they would have had if they had not joined the EU.[3] Only Greece was worse off because it joined the EU. However, it should be noted that in this study, being better or worse off was defined in terms of the GDP, a unit that falls within the same category as money. The GDP of a country can be measured relatively easily, but it is not necessarily a measure of what is valuable to people. For example, it does not measure whether people feel comfortable and at home in their own countries or – even more in general – whether they are happy with their lives.

Perhaps other effects of EU membership are relevant to the question of whether people are happy with the EU. After all, the UK benefited strongly from its EU membership,[4] but nevertheless on 23 June 2016 a small majority of UK voters chose to leave the EU. How could this have happened if the people believed the economy of the UK benefited from the EU and that EU membership was good for their country?

---

2   This last question was inspired by Rawls' second principle of justice. *See* Rawls 1971, p. 60.
3   Campos, N., Coricelli, F., & Moretti, L. 'How Much Do Countries Benefit from Membership in the European Union?' (9 April 2014), https://voxeu.org/article/how-poorer-nations-benefit-eu-membership (last visited on 29 October 2018).
4   *See* Campos, N., Coricelli, F., & Moretti, L., 'The Eye, the Needle and the Camel: Rich Countries Can Benefit From EU Membership' (27 April 2016), https://voxeu.org/article/how-rich-nations-benefit-eu-membership (last visited on 29 October 2018).

This question can be generalized. Many inhabitants of EU Member States seem to be sceptical about the Union, even though the EU brings them economic benefits and even though on reflection – that is: when they are interviewed on it – they believe the EU to be good for their countries. This phenomenon is called 'Euroscepticism', and the central question of this chapter is how Euroscepticism can be explained. Because the EU brings, from an economic perspective, mainly benefits, the focus will be on a non-economic explanation.

10.2 Anywheres and Somewheres

In 2017, David Goodhart's book *The Road to Somewhere* was published. The book addresses the background of British politics, and, in particular, Brexit. Its main claim is that we can distinguish between two main groups of people, which Goodhart called 'Anywheres' and 'Somewheres' and that the differences between the members of these two groups explain why the majority of the Brits voted for Brexit.

Anywheres are the people who tend to do well at school and who dominate British culture and society. After secondary school, they typically move, first, to a residential university in their late teens and thereafter to a career in professions that takes them to London or even abroad. They have 'achieved' identities, based on what they have achieved with respect to education and career success. They are comfortable and confident with new places and people,[5] and this explains their name 'Anywheres'. According to Goodhart's estimate, Anywheres constitute about 25% of the British population.

Somewheres In contrast to Anywheres, who can live anywhere, Somewheres are more rooted. Their geographical mobility is low. Goodhart mentions that 60% of the British people still live within 20 miles of where they lived when they were 14. This explains their name 'Somewheres'. They also have 'ascribed' identities, such as 'Cornish housewife' or 'Scottish farmer', based on group belonging and particular places from where they come and continue to live. They possess these identities not only in the eyes of others, but also in their own eyes: they identify themselves with their ascribed identities. Rapid change in society destabilizes these identities, and that is why Somewheres often find rapid change unsettling. According to Goodhart's estimate, Somewheres constitute about half of the British population. They therefore form a substantially larger group than the Anywheres, which nevertheless dominate British culture and society.

---

5   Goodhart 2017, p. 3.

Somewheres and immigration Goodhart emphasizes that most Somewheres are not xenophobic or racist but also that a large proportion of them find the size of migration to the UK too large. Many of them do not feel at home in their country any more. This resistance to mass immigration is a major, or perhaps even the main reason, why the British voted for Brexit.[6]

10.3 Reason and Passion

From an economic perspective, immigration can benefit a society. Newcomers become both producers and consumers and they contribute to the growth of the economy in a given society. If people were completely rational, they would support immigration, at least so it seems. However, either the situation is more complicated than it seems or people are not always fully rational. In his book *The Righteous Mind: Why Good People Are Divided by Politics and Religion*, the social psychologist Jonathan Haidt contrasts the views of Plato and Hume on the relative role of reason and emotion (passion) in the human mind.[7]

Reason and passion. According to Plato, the passions drive people to all kinds of behaviour, much of which is not wise. It is the role of reason to rein in the passions and to lead people to rational behaviour. According to Hume, reason is the slave of the passions. Passion determines what people will do, and reason fulfils two subservient functions: it provides people with the means to achieve the goals that passions dictate, and it provides people retroactively with reasons why their behaviour was right. Haidt claims that Hume was right: the passions (emotions) dictate what people will do, and reason has at best a limited role in steering human behaviour. So even if economists are right and immigration is beneficial to society, it is still the irrational emotions that determine what people will do. This would explain why the British voted for Brexit, and also the widespread Euroscepticism, even though, rationally speaking, EU subjects benefit from the EU.

Why are people often so irrational? Perhaps they are not irrational at all; perhaps we only use a wrong definition of what counts as rational? These are the questions that will be addressed in the rest of this chapter. They are crucially important, if we want to know whether the policies of the EU – which often have an economic underpinning – are wise.

Proviso The following argument is based on recent findings in evolutionary and social psychology and even expands these findings. This means that the conclusions are most

---

6   Goodhart 2017, pp. 117-145.
7   Haidt 2012, pp. 32-36.

likely not all correct. However, it would be a mistake not to use recent scientific results for the reason that these results may still be falsified.

We begin our argument noting that the following conclusions must be drawn cautiously. There are two argument lines:

Argument 1 For biological reasons, animal, and therefore also human, decision-making systems, favour relatives and people that live nearby over strangers. This means that there is more solidarity with people in the neighbourhood and with relatives than with people from elsewhere. As the UK, as well as many other EU Member States, are net payers to the EU, this preference for the 'own' people may be a cause of why the British and many inhabitants of other Member States want to exit the EU.

Argument 2 For biological reasons, which involve the structure of our minds and their evolutionary roots, human minds are more suitable for dealing with standard situations about which there exists consensus than they are for dealing with new, complicated cases. Although minds can handle complex cases, people find this annoying and fatiguing. For this reason, most people do not like complexity and the diversity that is one of its causes. Immigration brought about more diversity in society than people could, or were willing to, handle. Many people were therefore in favour of Brexit, as they expected that this would halt large-scale immigration. The same fear of mass immigration partly explains the Euroscepticism in some other Member States as well.

10.4 The Genetic Basis of Altruism

Struggle for life The mechanism that underlies evolution is rightly described as 'Struggle for life and survival of the fittest'. However, this slogan is easily misinterpreted. It is tempting to think of individual animals fighting with each other, with the strongest animal surviving. However, if this were the mechanism of evolution, lions would survive and zebras would be extinct. The concept of survival that evolution deals with is not the survival of the individual animal or plant, but of a species (kind) of animals or plants. Actually, as we will soon see, it is more complicated still.

However, let us first focus on the survival of a kind. If a mother sacrifices herself for her child, this is not good for the survival of the mother, but it may be useful for the survival of the child and of the human species, as this allows the child to procreate. A species in which the parents are willing to sacrifice themselves for their children may have a greater chance of survival than a species in which parents do not undergo such sacrifices. The struggle for life does not take place at the level of individuals but on the level of the genome. Individuals are 'merely' instruments for the genome (the genes) to replicate itself. In this connection, survival of the individual may be useful as the individual can still procreate, but survival of its progeny is even more useful. A species of animals in which all individuals are able to procreate before they die, will continue forever.

Kin-directed altruism For the continued existence of the genome, it is valuable not only if parents are willing to sacrifice themselves for their children, but also if siblings and other close relatives are willing to do the same. Siblings and close relatives share a lot of genes with each other, and for the continued existence of these genes, altruistic and even self-sacrificing behaviour may be useful.

Before continuing, it is important to avoid a possible misunderstanding. If a mother sacrifices herself for her child, she does not do so for the reason that this promotes her genome. She does so, we may assume, because she loves her child. The point of the argument is not that the motives for self-sacrifice have to do with survival of the genes. It is that animals, again including humans, that for some reason are willing to self-sacrifice for close relatives will promote the survival of their genes. Such a species of animal will be selected in the process of the struggle for life and survival of the fittest. Loving your children is thus good for the propagation of your genes.[8]

A related point is that evolution does not operate only on the physical aspects of species: how fast an animal can run or how much sunlight a plant can transform into fuel. It also takes place at the level of psychology, and at the level of the brain to the extent that this has psychological implications. If two species are completely equal, except that the first kind has parents who love their children, while the second has egoistic parents, the first species is more likely to survive. Psychological traits, such as love of children and of close relatives pay off in the struggle for life.

Reciprocal altruism The evolution of mankind is a process that has been in motion for quite some time. By far, the major part of this process took place when human beings still lived in small groups of hunters and gatherers. The members of such a group would typically be close relatives of each other, and therefore the care for other group members would have survival value for the genome of the group members. Groups in which the members

---

8   Perhaps some find this analysis of why parents love their children debasing. However, a scientific theory is not bad because it is debasing; it is bad if it is false and if its predictions turn out to be wrong. There are good, empirically supported, reasons why this theory that individuals are instruments for the propagation of genes is correct. *See*, for instance, Dawkins 2016 and Wright 1994, and the primary literature discussed there.

took care of one another would be more successful in the struggle for continued life than groups in which the members did not cooperate. As such, genes that make people altruistic towards people in their near environment were selected in the struggle for life. Kinds of people who are not altruistic in this sense will go extinct.

Moreover, this does not hold only for groups in which people are genetically related. If the members of a group assist one another, all members will have a better chance to procreate and to pass their genes on to future generations.[9] The only condition is that if you help another group member, it is to be expected that this other group member will return the favour when an opportunity presents itself. Support for relatives works better, as they share your genes, but support for group members who are not relatives is still advantageous for the propagation of the involved genes.

Conversely, support for other individuals who are not genetically related and who cannot be expected to give reciprocal support is, genetically speaking, a bad idea. Those individuals are competitors for the scarce means of survival, and supporting them decreases your chances of procreation and your children's chances of survival until they can procreate. Genetically speaking, altruism is good to the extent that it increases the propagation of your genes, and it is bad if it decreases this propagation value. Notice that we are not talking about morally good or bad here, but merely of good and bad for the survival of genes. It should be noted that nature is selective on survival value, and not on moral value, unless being moral has survival value.

Solidarity within the EU We are all willing to support other people, but not all other people. Relatives – people who share a large proportion of our genes – and people in our neighbourhood – who are expected to reciprocate the support they receive – are attractive beneficiaries for assistance. This does not mean that we use genetic proximity and the expectation to receive something in return as reasons to justify our willingness to support. Unbeknownst to ourselves, these factors play a role in determining whether we sufficiently 'like' others enough to be willing to support them. Our judgments concerning whom to help are made intuitively, and our reasoning rationalizes these intuitive judgments. If our relatives take stupid decisions, we reproach but also help them. If strangers take stupid decisions, we do not help them, allegedly because the consequence will teach them a lesson. If people from our own country suffer as a result of bad government decisions from the past, we are in solidarity. If the same happens to people from Greece, we are hesitant to assist because this creates a moral hazard. If the EU forces us to assist, this may be viewed as a reason to leave the EU.

---

9   *See* Bowles and Gintis 2011.

10.5   Dual System Decision-Making

Systems 1 and 2 Human beings operate with a dual system for decision-making. One system works very quickly and provides intuitive judgments. For example, if you see a drowning child, you will immediately try to rescue her. The decision on what to do will be taken without elaborate thinking or balancing costs and benefits. In a different setting, if a lawyer hears about a case, he will almost immediately know how the case should be solved; the lawyer's 'feeling of justice' operates instantaneously. Because this system works fast and intuitively, without taking the time to balance costs and benefits, this system – although developed in evolution – is not fully rational, and its resulting decisions may sometimes be suboptimal. The psychologist Daniel Kahneman called this 'system 1'.[10]

The other system was called 'system 2'. This system is rational, and its outcome is not intuitive but based on reasoning. Its operation takes more time, varying from many seconds to sometimes even weeks. The latter will, for example, be the case with court decisions, which are carefully considered.

Both systems have their advantages and disadvantages. The main advantage of system 2 is that its outcomes are more rational. Its main disadvantage is that it is time-consuming. When you are in traffic and you must decide whether to brake because a pedestrian is crossing the street, you lack the time to consider the pros and cons of your decision carefully; you must decide *now*. The possibility to decide quickly is the main advantage of system 1, and its corresponding weakness is that it is less accurate.

Implementation The two systems are associated with different parts of the brain. System 1 is mostly realized by the so-called 'limbic system',[11] while the implementation of system 2 is for a substantial part in the dorsolateral prefrontal cortex (DLPFC).[12] From an evolutionary perspective, the limbic system is relatively old and also exists in many other species of animals as well. The DLPFC is part of the brain cortex, a relatively recent addition to the brain, which is characteristic of humans and non-human primates (e.g. chimpanzees and gorillas).

The elephant and the rider The social psychologist Haidt also distinguished two decision-making systems, closely parallel to Kahneman's systems 1 and 2, and he called them the

---

10   Kahneman 2012, Part I.
11   *See* https://qbi.uq.edu.au/brain/brain-anatomy/limbic-system (last visited on 8 August 2019).
12   The vague formulations 'mostly' and 'for a substantial part' are there to account for the fact that our knowledge of how the brain implements the mind is far from perfect yet and that the attribution of functions (system 1 and system 2) to brain regions is most likely only a coarse approximation.

elephant and the rider, respectively.[13] The rider is the rational part and the elephant the intuitive one. An important point that Haidt adds to this distinction between the two systems is that the rider is not an independent mental agent. Although it may sometimes try to steer human action away from intuitive impulses, most of the time it merely provides rationalizations for what the elephant intuitively did.

For instance, humans want to punish persons who violated important rules. The amount of punishment they want to inflict corresponds to a high degree with the emotions they felt when hearing about the crime.[14] However, when pressed to justify their punishing behaviour, people often mention the good effects that punishment has for the future, specifically prevention of new norm violations. Apparently, these justifications do not reflect the real causes of what drives people to prefer punishment. This does not mean that people are lying about their motives. They may be sincerely convinced of the good motives underlying their actions. The issue is that people are often unaware of what 'really' drives them; they believe their own rationalizations.[15]

This idea is also expressed in a famous article written by Haidt, 'The Emotional Dog and its Rational Tail'. Just as the tail of a dog reflects the dog's emotions, the reasons humans give for their behaviour reflect their emotions – not in the sense that the reasons reproduce the emotions; they provide rationalizations for what humans do on emotional – or better, intuitive – grounds. That is why the tail of the (human) dog was called rational: it provides rationalizations for behaviour that was caused by emotional intuition.

According to Haidt, the rider mostly provides rationalizations of what the elephant intuitively decided to do, and only sometimes it corrects the elephant. The rider exercises its corrective function mainly if a human agent tries to justify his behaviour to others and anticipates and reacts to critical comments. Law seems to have anticipated these scientific findings by requiring judges to justify their judgments to the public in general, thereby giving the rider an optimal opportunity to correct the elephant.

---

13 Haidt 2006, Chapter 1.
14 Baron and Ritov 1993, p. 9.
15 Wilson 2002.

10.6 Nature and Nurture in Morality

The above account of human decision-making may suggest that the decision-making process is dominated by system 1 (the elephant) and that this system is essentially irrational, intuitive and based on emotions. That suggestion would be wrong.

Yes, the decision-making process is intuitive. However, this does not mean that the process is irrational. The part of the mind that is responsible for most decisions has been developed over millennia of evolution and has adapted itself to the requirements of everyday life. Admittedly, this 'everyday life' was the life of animals in a period of time that stretched over millions of years, and it was not always the everyday life of human beings or even other primates. Nevertheless, system 1 must have had survival value, because otherwise it would not have existed.

There is even more. If a decision-making system is intuitive, this does not automatically mean that it is fully innate. It is possible that system 1 can learn from experience, and there is evidence that it actually does so. For example, the intuitive judgments of experienced lawyers are better than the intuitive judgments of beginning law students. Apparently, the experienced lawyers have learned something new, and this new knowledge does not only play a role in well-considered judgments (system 2 judgments), but also in a lawyer's sense of justice (system 1).

The same idea, that our system for intuitive judgments can learn, was defended with respect to moral intuitions by Marc Hauser.[16] All human beings – with a few exceptions for individuals suffering from anti-social disorders – have an innate system for morality that makes it possible to live together in small groups. This means that the basic structure of moral thinking is innate. However, the details, in the form of precise moral rules, are completed during moral education. For example, children raised in East Asia may start to see individuals as exponents of social groups. Children raised in Western Europe start to see individuals as the morally equal building blocks of society and consider societal organizations as means to improve the lives of individuals. They will also consider human rights, such as the freedom of expression, as the pinnacle of morality. Persons raised under Islam will typically assign a subordinate value to freedom of expression, certainly in relation to higher religious duties such as the prohibition against insulting the Prophet. As the results of this moral education are used in system 1, they produce moral intuitions, which can, if necessary, be justified by system 2.

---

16   Hauser 2006.

10.7 People Hate to Reconsider

The overall picture that arises from the previous sections, is of a decision-making process heavily reliant on intuition. Humans tend to offer reasons for their actions; these reasons typically justify decisions that were taken intuitively and not on the basis of the given reasons.[17] Intuition is the result of evolution, upbringing and experience. It will often be quite rational, but not necessarily so.

People also have a tool for reasonable decision-making (system 2), but this tool is more often used to rationalize intuitive decisions than to determine the decisions themselves. However, sometimes people use system 2 to correct the imprudent decisions made by system 1. This is, according to Haidt, particularly the case if they have to defend their intuitive judgments to others.

In general, people experience mental discomfort from, and try to avoid, inconsistencies in their belief sets. This phenomenon is known under the name of cognitive dissonance.[18] If a person's intuitive judgments are called into question by others, this may evoke cognitive dissonance and the associated mental discomfort. It should therefore not come as a surprise if people prefer not to reconsider their intuitive judgments.

Yet if people from different cultural backgrounds are brought together, it is likely that their intuitive judgments on particular situations will differ. Living together often necessitates some uniformity of action. For example, even though people from the Middle East and people from Western Europe intuitively disagree on whether the slaughter of sacrificial animals without anaesthesia should be allowed, they need to agree on a common policy.

Each person is sometimes faced with the necessity of reconsidering one's intuitive judgments, and this is not something that people like to do. A society in which people's intuitions are by and large similar produces less stress. If the need for reconsideration occurs frequently, people may describe this as 'not feeling at home in one's own country'. With this observation we are back at our original theme: as a result of the massive influx of people with a different cultural background, many intuitive judgments that used to be widely shared become a matter of reconsideration. In order to take the resulting discomfort away, people might theoretically become more open to alternative views. Psychologically speaking, it is more realistic to expect that they will try to remove the cause of the disagreements by blocking the influx of more intuitive dissenters. If Brexit, or – more in general –

---

17 Gigerenzer 2006, p. 17.
18 *See* Festinger 1957.

limiting the influence of the EU, can help in this connection, this would be welcomed. One possible explanation for Euroscepticism would be the desire to avoid cognitive dissonance.

10.8 Conclusion

In this chapter we have seen that most people in the EU see the membership of their home countries in the EU as something positive. This even holds for the inhabitants of the UK. Nevertheless, when there was a referendum on Brexit, a majority of the voters were in favour of the decision to leave the Union. More in general, although the EU benefits the inhabitants of most Member States, the phenomenon of Euroscepticism has gained a prominent role in modern discussions about the EU. How can this be explained?

We have considered two accounts, which most likely each explain, at least in part, the desire to leave the EU. One account has to do with solidarity. The UK and a number of other Member States are net payers to the EU, and if its inhabitants do not feel solidarity with the inhabitants of other EU Member States, this might explain their wish to leave the EU. On similar grounds, they may want to halt large-scale immigration, which may further explain Euroscepticism and the choice for Brexit.

The second account concerns the willingness to reconsider our intuitive judgments on what is right or wrong. If a country is 'flooded' by immigrants with a different cultural background, this makes the need for reconsidering intuitive judgments more frequent, with cognitive dissonance as a result. To remove the mental discomfort, people may experience the necessity of stopping this 'tsunami' of asylum seekers and economic refugees, even if this leads to leaving the EU.

Most likely, other accounts of why countries doubt their EU membership are possible. The two accounts discussed here have been selected because they show how people can decide to leave the EU on intuitive grounds, even if it is clear – also to them – that this is not rational. We can learn an important lesson from these psychological accounts of Euroscepticism: in order to keep the EU together it does not suffice to convince everybody that remaining is the more rational option. It is also necessary to make it the intuitive option.

Postscript

The discussion of Euroscepticism from the perspective of evolutionary psychology concluded the argument of this book. We have seen how the theme of European integration unites insights from different disciplines: (legal) history, political science, philosophy of science, economics, social ontology and evolutionary psychology. These disciplines, and many others, are connected with each other as parts of the bigger enterprise called 'science'.

It is a function of higher education to introduce students to this enterprise. It should show how the different disciplines supplement each other in an attempt to describe and explain the world around us, of which the EU in only one small part. Hopefully, this book has fulfilled its function as one possible introduction to science.

REFERENCES

Bache 2015
Bache, I. et al., *Politics in the European Union* (4th ed.), Oxford: Oxford University Press, 2015.

Balassa 1961
Balassa, B. *The Theory of Economic Integration*, London: Allew and Unwin, 1961.

Baldwin and Wyplosz 2015
Baldwin, R. and Wyplosz, C., *The Economics of European Integration*, McGraw-Hill 2015.

Baron and Ritov 1993
Baron, J. and Ritov, I., 'Intuitions about Penalties and Compensation in the Context of Tort Law', *Journal of Risk and Uncertainty* 7, 1993, pp. 17-33.

Bowles and Gintis 2011
Bowles, S. and Gintis, H., *A Cooperative Species. Human Reciprocity and Its Evolution*, Princeton: Princeton University Press, 2011.

Buonanno 2017
Buonanno, L., 'The European Migration Crisis', *in* D. Dinan *et al.* (Eds.), *The European Union in Crisis*, London: Palgrave, 2017, pp. 100-130.

Burke 1790
Burke, E., *Reflections on the Revolution in France*, many editions. https://archive.org/stream/in.ernet.dli.2015.45683/2015.45683.Reflections-On-The-Revolution-In-France#page/n3/mode/2up (last visited on 5 August 2019).

Davies 1996
Davies, N., *Europe. A History*, London: Penguin Random House, 1996.

Dawkins 2016
Dawkins, R., *The Selfish Gene* (4th ed.), Oxford: Oxford University Press, 2016.

Dinan 2004
Dinan, D., *Europe Recast. A History of European Union*, Houndmills: Palgrave Macmillan, 2004.

Dinan et al. 2017
Dinan, D. et al. (Eds.), *The European Union in Crisis*, London: Palgrave, 2017.

Elster 2007
Elster, J., *Explaining Social Behavior. More Nuts and Bolts for the Social Sciences*, Cambridge: Cambridge University Press, 2007.

Festinger 1957
Festinger, L., *A Theory of Cognitive Dissonance*, Palo Alto: Stanford University Press, 1957.

Forsyth 2003
Forsyth, M., 'The Political Theory of Federalism: The Relevance of Classical Approaches', *in* B.F. Nelsen & A. Stubb (Eds.), *The European Union. Readings on the Theory and Practice of European Integration* (3rd ed.), Houndmills: Palgrave Macmillan, 2003, pp. 195-214.

Gigerenzer 2006
Gigerenzer, G., 'Heuristics', *in* G. Gigerenzer & C. Engel (Eds.), *Heuristics and the Law*, Cambridge: MIT Press, 2006, pp. 17-44.

Goodhart 2017
Goodhart, D., *The Road to Somewhere*, London: Penguin, 2017.

Gutas 2016
Gutas, D., 'Ibn Sina [Avicenna]', *in* E.N. Zalta (Ed.), *The Stanford Encyclopedia of Philosophy* (Fall 2016 edition), Stanford: Stanford University, 2016. https://plato.stanford.edu/archives/fall2016/entries/ibn-sina/.

Haas 1958
Haas, E., *The Uniting of Europe*, Stanford: Stanford University Press, 1958.

Hage, Walterman and Akkermans 2017
Hage, J., Waltermann, A. and Akkermans, B. (Eds.), *Introduction to Law* (2nd ed.), Cham: Springer, 2017.

Hage 2017
Hage, J., 'Legal Reasoning', in J. Hage, A. Waltermann, & A. Akkermans (Eds.), *Introduction to Law* (2nd ed.), Cham: Springer, 2017, pp. 21-32.

Hage 2018
Hage, J., *Foundations and Building Blocks of Law*, Den Haag: Eleven International Publishing, 2018.

Haidt 2012
Haidt, J., *The Righteous Mind. Why Good People Are Divided by Politics and Religion*, London: Penguin, 2012.

Harari 2016
Harari, Y.N., *Homo Deus*, London: Penguin Random House, 2016.

Hart 1961
Hart, H.L.A., *The Concept of Law* (3rd edition in 2012), Oxford, Clarendon Press 1961.

Hauser 2006
Hauser, M.D., *Moral Minds. How Nature Designed Our Universal Sense of Right and Wrong*, New York: Harper Collins, 2006.

Hempel 1966
Hempel, C.G., *Philosophy of Natural Science*, Englewood Cliffs: Prentice Hall, 1966.

Heringa and Kiiver 2016
Heringa, A.W. and Kiiver, P., *Constitutions Compared. An Introduction to Comparative Constitutional Law* (4th ed.), Antwerp: Intersentia, 2016.

Heywood 2012
Heywood, A., *Political Ideologies. An Introduction* (5th ed.), Houndmills: Palgrave Macmillan, 2012.

Hobbes 1651
Hobbes, H., *Leviathan*, originally published in 1651, many editions.

Hodges 1977
Hodges, W., *Logic* (2nd revised edition in 2001), Harmondsworth: Penguin, 1977.

Hoffmann 1964
Hoffmann, S., 'The European Process at Atlantic Crosspurposes', *Journal of Common Market Studies* 3, 1964, pp 85-101.

Hoffmann 1966
Hoffmann, S., 'Obstinate or Obsolete? The Fate of the Nation-State and the Case of Western Europe', *Daedalus* 95, 1966, pp 862-915.

Hume 1978
Hume, D., *A Treatise of Human Nature* (original text 1739/40, Selby-Bigge edition), Oxford: University Press, 1978.

Ilievski 2015
Ilievski, N.L., The Concept of Political Integration: The Perspectives of Neofunctionalist Theory, *Journal of Liberty and International Affairs* 1(1), 2015, pp. 1-14, http://e-jlia.com/papers/34928593_vol1_num1_pap4.pdf (last visited on 25 August 2018).

Kahneman 2012
Kahneman, D., *Thinking, Fast and Slow*, London: Penguin, 2012.

Leeuw and Schmeets 2016
Leeuw, F.L. and Schmeets, H., *Empirical Legal Research*, Cheltenham: Edward Elgar, 2016.

Lenin 1917
Lenin, V.I., *Staat en revolutie*, Moscow: Progress, 1917.

Locke 1689
Locke, J., *Two Treatises of Government*, many editions.

Mankiw and Taylor 2017
Mankiw, N.G. and Taylor, M.P., *Economics*, Andover: Cengage Learning Emea, 2017.

Marx and Engels 1848
Marx, K. and Engels, F., *Manifest der kommunistischen Partei* (Communist Manifesto), many editions. http://ciml.250x.com/archive/marx_engels/me_languages.html (last visited on 5 August 2019).

Mitrany 1966
Mitrany, D., *Towards a Working Peace System*, Chicago: Quadrangle, 1966.

Mitrany 2003
Mitrany, D., 'A Working Peace System', *in* B.F. Nelsen & A. Stubb (Eds.), *The European Union. Readings on the Theory and Practice of European Integration* (3rd ed.), Houndmills: Palgrave Macmillan, 2003, pp. 99-120.

Montada 2018
Montada, J.P., 'Ibn Rushd's Natural Philosophy', *in* E.N. Zalta (Ed.), *The Stanford Encyclopedia of Philosophy* (Fall 2018 edition), Stanford: Stanford University, 2018. https://plato.stanford.edu/archives/fall2018/entries/ibn-rushd-natural/.

Nozick 1974
Nozick, A., *Anarchy, State and Utopia*, New York: Basic Books, 1974.

Nello 2012
Nello, S., *The European Union. Economics, Policies and History* (2nd ed.), Maidenhead: McGraw-Hill, 2012.

Nelsen and Stubb 2003
Nelsen, B.F. and Stubb, A., (Eds.), *The European Union. Readings on the Theory and Practice of European Integration* (3rd ed.), Houndmills: Palgrave Macmillan, 2003.

Nugent 2010
Nugent, N., *The Government and Politics of the European Union* (7th ed.), Houndmills: Palgrave Macmillan, 2010.

Palmer *et al.* 2002
Palmer, R.R., Colton, J. and Kramer, L., *A History of the Modern World* (9th ed.), New York: McGraw-Hill 2002.

Pistone 2003
Pistone, S., 'Altiero Spinelli and the Strategy for the United States of Europe', *in* B.F. Nelsen & A. Stubb (Eds.), *The European Union. Readings on the Theory and Practice of European Integration* (3rd ed.), Houndmills: Palgrave Macmillan, 2003, pp. 91-98.

Popper 1976
Popper, K.R., *Unended Quest; An Intellectual Autobiography*, London: Fontana, 1976.

Popper 2002
Popper, K.R., *The Logic of Scientific Discovery* (first edition 1959), London: Routledge, 2002.

Rawls 1971
Rawls, J., *A Theory of Justice*, Harvard: University Press, 1971.

Roberts 2015
Roberts, A., *Napoleon: A Life*, London: Penguin, 2015.

Ross 1957
Ross, A, 'Tû-tû', *Harvard Law Review* 70, 1957, p. 812.

Smith 1776
Smith, A., *The Wealth of Nations*, many editions, a.o. metalibri.wikidot.com/title:an-inquiry-into-the-nature-and-causes-of-the-wealth-of.

Wilson 2002
Wilson, T.D., *Strangers to Ourselves. Discovering the Adaptive Unconsciousness*, Cambridge, MA: The Belknap Press, 2002.

Wright 1994
Wright, R., *The Moral Animal*, New York: Random House, 1994.

Maastricht Law Series

The Maastricht Law Series is created in 2018 by Boom juridisch and Eleven International Publishing in association with the Maastricht University Faculty of Law. The Maastricht Law Series publishes books on comparative, European and International law. The series builds upon the tradition of excellence in research at the Maastricht Faculty of Law, its research centers and the Ius Commune Research School. The Maastricht Law Series is a peer reviewed book series that allows researchers an excellent opportunity to showcase their work.

Series editors
Dr. Bram Akkermans (editor-in-chief)
Prof. dr. Monica Claes
Prof. dr. Fons Coomans
Prof. dr. Mariolina Eliantonio
Prof. dr. Michael Faure
Dr. Bram van Hofstraeten
Prof. dr. Saskia Klosse
Dr. Denise Prevost
Prof. dr. David Roef
Dr. Marcel Schaper
Prof. dr. Jan M. Smits

Published in this series:
Volume 1: Reinhard Zimmermann, Does the Law of Succession Reflect Cultural Differences?, ISBN 978-94-6236-856-9
Volume 2: Anna Berlee, Access to personal data in public land registers, ISBN 978-94-6236-841-5
Volume 3: Marcus Meyer, The Position of Dutch Works Councils in Multinational Corporations, ISBN 978-94-6236-848-4
Volume 4: Jaap Hage, Foundations and Building Blocks of Law, ISBN 978-94-6236-860-6
Volume 5: Bastiaan van Zelst, The End of Justice(s)?, ISBN 978-94-6236-881-1
Volume 6: Lars van Vliet & Agustin Parise (eds.), Re- De- Co-dification? New Insights on the Codification of Private Law, ISBN 978-94-6236-900-9
Volume 7: Caroline Rupp, Rafael Ibarra Garza & Bram Akkermans, Property Law Perspectives VI, ISBN 978-94-6236-904-7
Volume 8: Aalt Willem Heringa, Europees Nederlands Staatsrecht, ISBN 978-94-6290-604-4
Volume 9: Symeon C. Symeonides, The "Private" in Private International Law, ISBN 978-94-6236-949-8
Volume 10: Jaap Hage, European Integration: A Theme, ISBN 978-94-6236-981-8

Volume 11: Jan M. Smits, Five Uneasy Pieces. Essays on Law and Evolution, ISBN 978-94-6236-982-5

Volume 12: Hannah Brodersen, Vincent Glerum, & André Klip, The European Arrest Warrant and In Absentia Judgements, ISBN 978-94-6236-985-6

Volume 13: Bram Akkermans & Gijs van Dijck, Sustainability and Private Law, ISBN 978-94-6236-986-3

Volume 14: Antonia Waltermann, David Roef, Jaap Hage & Marko Jelicic, Law, Science, Rationality, ISBN 978-94-6236-989-4